GENTRY CULTUR

MEDIEVAL ENGLAND

MANCHESTER
1824

Manchester University Press

MANCHESTER MEDIEVAL STUDIES

SERIES EDITOR Professor S. H. Rigby

SERIES ADVISORS Professor John Hatcher
Professor J. H. Moran Cruz

The study of medieval Europe is being transformed as old orthodoxies are challenged, new methods embraced and fresh fields of inquiry opened up. The adoption of inter-disciplinary perspectives and the challenge of economic, social and cultural theory are forcing medievalists to ask new questions and to see familiar topics in a fresh light.

The aim of this series is to combine the scholarship traditionally associated with medieval studies with an awareness of more recent issues and approaches in a form accessible to the non-specialist reader.

ALREADY PUBLISHED IN THE SERIES

The commercialisation of English society, 1000–1500
Richard H. Britnell

Reform and the papacy in the eleventh century
Kathleen G. Cushing

Picturing women in late medieval and Renaissance art
Christa Grössinger

The politics of carnival
Christopher Humphrey

Medieval law in context
Anthony Musson

Medieval maidens
Kim M. Phillips

Chaucer in context
S. H. Rigby

MANCHESTER MEDIEVAL STUDIES

GENTRY CULTURE
IN LATE
MEDIEVAL ENGLAND

edited by Raluca Radulescu
and Alison Truelove

Manchester University Press

Manchester and New York

distributed exclusively in the USA by Palgrave

Published by Manchester University Press
Oxford Road, Manchester M13 9NR, UK
and Room 400, 175 Fifth Avenue, New York, NY 10010, USA
www.manchesteruniversitypress.co.uk

Distributed exclusively in the USA
by Palgrave, 175 Fifth Avenue, New York, NY 10010, USA

Distributed exclusively in Canada
by UBC Press, University of British Columbia, 2029 West Mall,
Vancouver, BC, Canada v6T 1z2

British Library Cataloguing-in-Publication Data
A catalogue record for this book is available from the British Library

Library of Congress Cataloging-in-Publication Data applied for

ISBN 0 7190 6824 x *hardback*
EAN   978 0 7190 6824 9
ISBN 0 7190 6825 8 *paperback*
EAN   978 0 7190 6825 6

First published 2005

14 13 12 11 10 09 08 07 06 05   10 9 8 7 6 5 4 3 2 1

Typeset in Monotype Bulmer
by Koinonia, Manchester
Printed in Great Britain
by Bell & Bain, Glasgow

For Cristina Radulescu Bernard

and David Boughey

CONTENTS

CONTRIBUTORS

CHRISTINE CARPENTER is Reader in Medieval English History at the University of Cambridge and author of many studies on all aspects of the life of the English gentry.

PETER FLEMING is Principal Lecturer in Medieval History at the University of the West of England. He has published widely on political culture and urban communities and late medieval households and politics.

MAURICE KEEN is Emeritus Fellow of Balliol College, Oxford, and has written extensively on medieval chivalry and other aspects of medieval history.

PHILIPPA MADDERN is Associate Professor in Medieval History at the University of Western Australia at Perth and has published extensively on gentry culture.

NICHOLAS ORME is Professor of History at the University of Exeter. His books include studies of medieval childhood, education, religion, death and the history of sport.

RALUCA RADULESCU is Lecturer in Medieval Literature at the University of Wales, Bangor. She has published articles on Arthurian romance, fifteenth-century gentry culture and medieval historiography. Her monograph *The Gentry Context for Malory's* Morte Darthur was published by Boydell and Brewer in 2003.

TIM SHAW wrote his doctoral thesis on liturgical practice at Westminster Abbey in the fourteenth century. He has taught in the Music and English Departments at Royal Holloway, University of London, and now teaches English at Rugby School.

THOMAS TOLLEY is Senior Lecturer in History of Art at the University of Edinburgh. He is the author of *Painting the Cannon's Roar: Music, the Visual Arts and the Rise of an Attentive Public in the Age of Haydn*, c. *1750* to c. *1810* (2001), and is currently working on a history of spectatorship in late medieval France.

ALISON TRUELOVE is an independent researcher whose edition of the fifteenth-century English Stonor Letters is forthcoming as an Early English Text Society volume. As Research Associate at the University of Cambridge she worked recently on the new third volume to Norman Davis's edition of the Paston Letters.

DEBORAH YOUNGS is Lecturer in Medieval History at the University of Swansea and has published on the gentry, their education and literacy, and late medieval religious beliefs.

ACKNOWLEDGEMENTS

The editors would like to extend their sincere thanks to the contributors for working so enthusiastically to produce chapters for this volume. For their patience in dealing with our queries, and in awaiting publication of the book, we are immensely grateful. Staff at Manchester University Press have been very supportive at every stage of the project, and have shown exceptional attention to detail, patience and diplomacy throughout the editorial process. The anonymous readers of the book proposal and draft manuscript have provided us with valued suggestions for improvement, and we are grateful for these. Steve Rigby has been more than generous with his time and knowledge, going far beyond the call of duty in his role as series editor. His support and advice have been invaluable. We owe thanks to many colleagues who have helped us throughout the duration of this project, and would especially like to note our gratitude to Peter Coss, Peter Fleming, Colin Richmond, Nigel Saul and Carole Weinberg and for their encouragement and guidance.

RR and AT

My special thanks go to Steve Rigby for his unfailing confidence in this project ever since I first mentioned it to him five years ago, and Sarah Williams, whose gentry seminar at York in 1999 marked a new stage in my research into gentry culture, and whose involvement as co-editor during the early stages of this project helped to gain the participation of the first contributors. My sincere gratitude also goes to Alison for helping to bring my original idea to fruition. Sarah Alyn Stacey and Peter Field have imparted invaluable advice and personal support as colleagues and friends, and my sister Cristina Radulescu Bernard brought ever so much inspiration and encouragement throughout the project.

RR

My personal thanks are due to Raluca for inviting me to co-edit this volume with her. I have benefited, as ever, from the generous support of my family and friends, but I offer my deepest thanks to my husband, David Boughey. Despite his own demanding workload, he happily amused our young baby while I continued to write and edit; without his support my participation in this project would have been impossible. Benjamin has cheerfully tolerated my preoccupation with all things gentle, and continues to offer inspiration, motivation and distraction in his own delightful way.

AT

ABBREVIATIONS

BL	British Library
EETS	Early English Text Society
ES	Extra Series
MED	Middle English Dictionary
NA	National Archives, Kew
NS	New Series
OED	Oxford English Dictionary
OS	Original Series
SS	Supplementary Series

EDITORS' INTRODUCTION

After many years at the margins of historical investigation, the late medieval English gentry are now widely regarded as an important and worthy subject for academic research. A wealth of publications since the mid-1980s testifies to the appeal of this group to researchers within a range of disciplines, and new approaches are casting further light on the fundamental roles played by its members in late medieval society. Wider appreciation of the diversity of experience within the gentry is emerging from such research, acting as a warning against too readily regarding this sector of society as a uniform group. At the same time, with gentry-related studies becoming more prevalent, the quest to define the membership of the gentry, and to understand what characterised the gentle lifestyle, becomes both more urgent and more complex. Although writers from all disciplines persist in referring to the gentry and its culture as though both concepts were firmly established, even fixed, in the mind of the modern researcher, achieving satisfactory definitions is widely acknowledged as problematic. Historians thus continue to grapple with the problem of how to define the membership of the gentry, often turning to socio-economic factors for answers, whilst also acknowledging the value of looking beyond traditional defining characteristics such as wealth, pedigree and occupation.[1]

Increasingly, the examination of lifestyles and attitudes is seen as a key route to understanding past societies. We may assign individuals to the gentry by virtue of their socio-economic standing, but what else drew them together as a group? Indeed, did they even regard themselves as belonging to a distinct, privileged sector of society, and if so how was this status exhibited? This book seeks to address such issues. It aims to explore the culture of the wide range of people whom we might include within the late medieval gentry, taking in all of landed society below the peerage, from knights down to gentlemen, and including those aspirants to gentility who might under traditional socio-economic terms be excluded from the group. In regarding the gentry as an amorphous, ever-fluctuating group of individuals, we are able to approach the task of examining its culture less tied to the preconceptions about status, and the privileges it confers, which condition more traditional approaches.

1

The book begins by exploring the origins of, and influences on, the culture of the late medieval gentry, thus contributing to the ongoing debate on defining the membership of this group. It considers the gentry's emergence as a group distinct from the nobility, and looks at the various available routes to gentility. Through surveys of the gentry's military background, administrative and political roles, social behaviour, and education, it seeks to provide an overview of how the group's culture evolved, and how it was disseminated. Studies of the gentry's literacy, their reception, creation and circulation of literature, their religious activities, and their experiences of music and the visual arts more directly address the practice and expression of this culture, exploring the extent to which the gentry's activities were different from those of the wider population. Together, the chapters offer a broad view of late medieval gentry culture, which explores, reassesses and indeed sometimes even challenges the idea that members of the gentry cultivated their own distinctive cultural identity.

To appreciate fully the value of this cultural approach to gentry studies requires an understanding of the subject's historiography. How and when the gentry emerged as a distinct group has been the subject of much debate, and is complicated by the fact that the term 'gentry' was never itself used as a contemporary class designation, but is rather a modern construct that remains without firm definition.[2] That its constituent members were knights, esquires and gentlemen has long been recognised as an inadequate statement, not least because assigning qualifying characteristics to the last of these three has proved such a complex, if not impossible, task.[3] As T. B. Pugh noted in the early 1970s, 'in an age of social mobility the status of men who had advanced their fortunes might well defy precise classification'.[4] Moreover, the terminology used by medievalists is highly unstable, with some choosing to include the gentry within the nobility, and others regarding the two groups as distinct. In part this may be explained by the increasing stratification of the upper ranks of society during the fourteenth century, leading to the exclusion from the nobility of all those outside of the peerage.[5] By the middle of the fifteenth century, ownership of land and 'gentle' behaviour no longer automatically denoted or granted the highest social status, but they might still mark out an individual as privileged.

When medieval history was dominated by a constitutional approach, historians failed to give due attention to the gentry. Exceptionally, scholars such as James Gairdner, C. L. Kingsford and H. S. Bennett drew attention to the value of surviving gentry correspondence, but their enthusiasm was not universally shared.[6] In the mid-twentieth century K. B. McFarlane did much to encourage historical study of the gentry in its own right, resulting in a strong research output relating to many aspects of gentry life.[7] McFarlane's own study of William Worcester pioneered the biographical portrait approach to exploring gentry careers,[8] but it was at least another two decades before historians wholly embraced the gentry as a subject worthy of extended study. Colin Richmond's book-length study in 1981 of the Suffolk gentleman, John Hopton, reflected the growing interest in exploring late medieval society through detailed analyses of the lives of individuals, rather than focusing on institutions and wider political events.[9] Importantly, Richmond also challenged the view that the gentry were irrelevant to constitutional history, pointing out that members of the gentry were in fact 'at the heart of political life, whether of town, shire or kingdom', asserting that they needed 'to be seen as fully as they can be, as near multi-dimensionally as they themselves were'.[10]

Supporting the burgeoning interest in the gentry, conferences and colloquiums began to be held on various aspects of gentry life, sometimes leading to published proceedings. Michael Jones's edited volume on the European gentry, the result of a colloquium in 1984, containing D. A. L. Morgan's study of the English gentleman and Christine Carpenter's study of gentry estates, has been particularly influential.[11] Margaret Aston and Colin Richmond's volume on Lollardy and the gentry, the result of a conference held in 1995, provided a timely reassessment of McFarlane's 1972 publication on the subject.[12] Interdisciplinary seminars and research projects focusing on gentry identity and culture, including the significant contribution of literary and manuscript studies, also led to increased collaboration between the disciplines of literature and history.[13]

The evolution of gentry studies soon led to the study of gentry communities, resulting in a number of local studies that identified networks of sub-aristocratic landowners in various regions of the country.[14] Some of these studies took as their focus particular families and their associates, and offered especially intimate portraits of gentry life. Moreton's detailed study of the Townshends, Richmond's publications on the Paston family, and Carpenter's work on the Stonor and Armburgh families exemplify this approach.[15] However, the concept of communities has come under particular scrutiny by medieval historians, who have identified the confusion that can result from its use both as a term for individuals who lived in a specific geographic area, and for those brought together by a common activity, outlook or set of beliefs. It has also resulted in a tendency to study groups in relative isolation, without due regard for the permeability of the boundaries that surround the grouping, for the characteristics held in common with the wider population, or for the fact that individuals may belong to any number of different 'communities' concurrently.[16] Indeed, Carpenter has even gone so far as to argue for 'banning the word "community" from all academic writing', and highlights instead the value of pursuing 'structures of power, identity, and interdependence' and exploring identities. She notes the importance of studying 'how the gentry saw themselves, if possible how others saw them, bearing in mind that identities are multiple and changeable', and, moreover, asserts that the search for the gentry's 'attitudes and beliefs' is the 'most urgent task for historians of late medieval English politics'.[17] Similarly, in examining the culture and identity of the wider late medieval aristocracy, Kate Mertes has noted that 'the advantage of looking at social groups as cultures rather than as strictly political or economic entities is that it makes it possible to enter their mental world more fully, and to recognise the dynamic nature of the group in question'.[18]

Thus in focusing on the individual rather than on institutions, we can begin to understand motives, and approach a better view of how and why members of the gentry might have regarded themselves as having a group identity. Yet the identification of what prompted, dictated and influenced behaviour is a complex task, as has been noted by Michael Hicks, writing on identifying a political culture in fifteenth-century England:

> Self-conscious principles are no more important in determining conduct than the unconscious and even subconscious ideas that condition them or, indeed, combat them or insidiously undermine them. Standards and prejudices instilled in childhood may predispose or even predetermine one's political stance as an adult. Already there was a culture of childhood that may well have underpinned much that followed. We need also to allow for all those values and standards, criteria, assumptions and misconceptions, perceptions, attitudes and prejudices, conventions, customs and manners, myths, expectations and aspirations, sentiments and even instincts across the whole range of human experience from military prowess to potty-training.[19]

As well as examining the concept of a gentry culture in late medieval England, we need to investigate its origins, how it evolved, how it was learnt and how it was transmitted and perpetuated. In doing so we can come closer to understanding what, beyond socio-economic factors, brought this diverse range of individuals together, thus allowing us, retrospectively at least, to group them under the single term 'gentry'.

Chapters 1 and 2 of this book, by Philippa Maddern and Maurice Keen respectively, address directly the evolution of the gentry, and explore the complexities of finding an adequate definition of what it meant to be considered gentle. Attempts in the late twentieth and early twenty-first centuries to define the gentry unproblematically have accepted that its members possessed some degree of gentility, and were therefore all 'gentlemen' (or 'gentlewomen') even if some were also termed knights and esquires by virtue of other characteristics. Even those who regard the term 'gentry' as a near-synonym for 'landed society' readily acknowledge that characteristics other than lordship also distinguished them as a group.[20] Maddern explains in Chapter 1 the evolution of the gentleman as a peer-assessed phenomenon, and notes how the term 'gentleman/woman' encompassed a wide range of social ranks and types of behaviour. In tracing the term's evolution, including consideration of its increasing use in written documentation, she reaches the conclusion that the very vagueness of the concept of gentility was itself advantageous for those seeking to lay claim to it, and that status was in many cases as much a matter of reputation as of pedigree, wealth or political standing. Maddern also gives attention to the various opportunities available to the gentry for demonstrating their gentle status, and shows the considerable effort necessary to maintain that status.

In Chapter 2, Keen locates gentlemanly behaviour within the chivalric tradition, concentrating on exploring the routes to gentility through service. He emphasises how military activity gradually gave way to civilian service, with law and administration in particular being seen as appropriate professions for a gentleman. In identifying the importance of cultural exchanges among members of the gentry during their war experiences and political service, he shows how the process of acculturation led to chivalric values being adopted by the sub-knightly classes as, increasingly, they became involved in the same activities as their immediate social superiors. Both Keen and Maddern note the important development of honour as a non-martial concept, with loyalty to employers and friends becoming as important as that shown to military leaders. They also touch upon topics covered in more detail later in the book, such as the importance of heraldry to members of the gentry, and their literary tastes, including the significant role played by instructive literature and romances in guiding their behaviour. These chapters equally acknowledge that gentility was not defined by precise criteria but rather by a looser set of evolving codes of behaviour.

Peter Fleming's Chapter 3 builds on Keen and Maddern's explorations of the development of the gentry by concentrating on those administrative roles identified as increasingly important in the definition of the group. In particular, he surveys the structures of local administration and describes the political career-paths open to the gentry, showing that while many dedicated their public lives to upholding the law, they were not averse to bending or even breaking that law when their own interests were at stake. The fact that self-interest was a major motivation in the gentry's participation in local or national politics demonstrates concern not only for their economic welfare but also for their reputation, whether in the context of local affinities or more widely. This reinforces Maddern's view that the maintenance of a good reputation was vital when asserting or defending one's claim to gentle status. Although she focuses on the importance of peer-assessed qualities, inevitably recognition by one's superiors was also advantageous to the social-climber. Politics, whether local or central, provided a forum within which the gentry could interact with members of the nobility and so gain public recognition; Charles Ross has demonstrated that during the reign of Edward IV in particular the gentry's involvement at the royal court grew, resulting in a significant increase in the number of king's counsellors.[21] Two contributors to this book, Raluca Radulescu in Chapter 6 and Deborah Youngs in Chapter 7, place emphasis on the cultural exchanges brought about by the gentlemen who acquired a special place at the court, whilst also continuing to be involved in the cultural life of their local communities. Neither these exchanges nor the political role of the gentry more generally should be underestimated; government was a principal route to gentility for those not born into the gentry, but also led to interactions which resulted in reciprocal influences on culture between those from different backgrounds.

Nicholas Orme in Chapter 4 surveys the education received by gentle children, drawing on his substantial research into medieval childhood and schooling, thus continuing the exploration of the acquisition and transfer of gentility. He shows how, alongside academic learning, within the household, in schools, universities or the Inns of Court and Chancery, informal instruction in cultural and recreational skills helped to encourage a specific gentry culture. He draws particular attention to the gentry's love of hunting; although primarily a leisure activity, which enabled the gentry to interact socially, it also had the traditional role of helping to train young men in military skills. Accepting that by the fifteenth century experience of combat was rare among the gentry, he argues that hunting allowed them to continue to imagine themselves as warriors. Hence this recreational activity not only helped to unite the gentry in a common pursuit, but also contributed to its members' sense of their place in history, providing a means to situate themselves within traditions that emphasised their superior status within society. Orme's work demonstrates that even though the activities in which members of the late medieval gentry participated were often the same as those of the rest of society, their particular approach and attitudes to these activities were unique. He shows that even though their education provided them with a wide range of practical and intellectual skills, the learning and transmission of culture amongst the gentry was a lifelong process.

One of the most useful skills acquired by the gentry, and one that was increasingly central to the transfer of ideas and affirmation of status, was the ability to read and write. By the first half of the fifteenth century, English had become the primary language of the gentry, even though French (or Anglo-Norman) and Latin remained important to them in a range of recreational, devotional and commercial activities, the last of which also led them into contact with other European languages such as Flemish. An increased need and desire for the creation of documentation by individuals as well as institutions led to a huge growth in levels of literacy, yet, as Alison Truelove shows in Chapter 5, assessing the reading and writing skills of the gentry is not easy. She argues that the surviving gentry correspondence, in particular that of the Paston and Stonor families, is the most important resource available to us for judging writing abilities, and draws attention to the methodological complexities of interpreting epistolary evidence. The chapter reveals that while basic literacy seems to have been widespread among the gentry, literate abilities varied considerably, but according to need rather than from any availability of tuition or intellectual capacity.

As has been recognised for many years, personal letters are also a valuable resource for accessing gentry culture more generally. They provide direct evidence of activities and concerns, and of how literate and linguistic abilities allowed members of the gentry to use personal correspondence to affirm and reinforce their status. Alongside their primary practical function, letters were an important means of social interaction, helping to formulate a group identity. The evidence they provide of individual attitudes and beliefs is, however, limited by the practical realities of their composition and delivery: letters were only rarely private forms of communication, and their content was restricted by the knowledge that they could fall into the wrong hands. What is presented in surviving gentry correspondence is, perhaps, a projection of how the writers wished to be seen, and this makes it all the more valuable in the study of gentry culture and identity.

Another principal conduit for the transfer of ideas, both to and between members of the gentry, was literature. Raluca Radulescu in Chapter 6 shows how this helped to determine the gentry's group identity; her survey of courtesy books, chivalric romances and chronicles illustrates their influence in shaping gentry activities and interests. She shows that the models of manners proposed by 'books of nurture' and chivalric romances were reinforced through penitential literature, which emphasised the necessity to know and maintain one's place in society. Even if we acknowledge the gulf between the actual experiences of the gentry and the ideals presented in such texts, they provide a fascinating insight into how people learnt gentility, and how they were inspired to put it into practice. The gentry's interest in chronicles, even going so far as to insert their own (sometimes fabricated) family history into the narrative of the manuscript chronicles they read, reflects a desire both to understand the history of the nation and to emphasise their place within it.

Deborah Youngs in Chapter 7 furthers the discussion of the importance of literature in the lives of many members of the gentry by exploring how the circulation of these texts, whether in the form of manuscripts or printed books, created cultural networks. Like Radulescu, she notes how texts influenced the attitudes of the gentry, acting as a 'channel through which gentry culture could travel and hence they contributed to moulding a group consciousness'.[22] Youngs, however, places particular emphasis on how the physical objects were exchanged, or even specifically created for 'textual communities'. She notes that these exchanges reveal numerous networks of contact which often transcended not only localities but also status; the gentry's reading habits are shown to resemble both those of the nobility and those of the urban elite. Books were certainly prestige items, and in this respect the gentry emulated the nobility in their acquisition. As both Youngs and Radulescu note, book producers actively exploited the social aspirations of the gentry by marketing their texts as being popular with the nobility. That examples can be found of the direct exchange of manuscripts between gentry and nobility indicates the extent to which there was an overlap between the cultural interests of the two groups.

The coalescence of gentle and noble culture evident in such practices as manuscript exchange is mirrored at the lower end of the gentry by influences on gentle culture from below. It is important to recognise that gentry culture was not fixed, but rather evolved as the group accommodated an ever-wider range of individuals. Horrox's seminal study of the urban gentry, Morgan's survey of the evolution of the gentleman during the later Middle Ages, and Storey's study of gentleman-bureaucrats all place emphasis on the increasing fluidity of the lower boundary of the gentry.[23] Although landownership remained an important indicator of gentility, the professionals who increasingly sought gentle status depended upon other ways to affirm their right to the title of gentleman. As Keen in Chapter 2 and Fleming in Chapter 3 show in this book, office-holding and occupation could confer this status in the eyes of some, but in lacking the pedigree that automatically granted gentility, these professionals sought other ways of demonstrating their worthiness. For them, courtesy texts were invaluable in providing a guide to gentle manners, allowing them to emulate the behaviour of those they hoped might recognise them as equals. That these texts concentrated on knowing one's place in society, and the behaviour appropriate to that place, reinforces the importance of viewing the gentry not in isolation but in the context of the wider society of which they were a part. This is a vital aspect to locating and understanding gentry culture, since much of the motivation behind codifying gentle behaviour was to set the gentry apart from those below them on the social scale: the status of its members depended upon their being distinguishable from their perceived inferiors. Hence in defining what it meant to be gentle, it is as important to consider the gentry's interaction with other social ranks as it is to identify their internal identity and collective interests.

In this respect it is instructive to consider Coss's view of the gentry as a 'social formation', characterised amongst other things by its 'collective identity and collective interests which necessitate the existence of some forum, or interlocking forums, for their articulation'.[24] The forums within which the late medieval gentry participated were multiple; often shared with their non-gentle neighbours, they provided the opportunities not only to articulate their identity and interests, but also to formulate these as distinctive from those of the wider population. Politics and religion, discussed in this volume by Peter Fleming in Chapter 3 and Christine Carpenter in Chapter 8, are two of the most important arenas in which a group ethos and collective interests may have had the opportunity to develop, and to be perpetuated. Fleming shows that local government provided a forum within which the gentry could enhance and display their 'honour' and 'worship', the opportunities for which were enhanced by their interaction with both nobles and non-gentle individuals. Their social position, and hence their particular cultural identity, was reinforced and highlighted by being in close proximity with those outside of their group.

Similarly, many of the religious activities of the late medieval gentry were conducted within arenas shared with the rest of the population. In Chapter 8, Carpenter notes that, for the most part, their religion was orthodox. Moreover, it was distinctive in only small details, such as the scale of their charitable donations, their increasingly individualistic and private forms of worship, and their access to devotional literature. The parish church is shown to have been a stage for the demonstration of the gentry's elevated status; it was the object of their pious generosity, but it also provided the opportunity for displaying and augmenting family status. As Carpenter has noted elsewhere, 'the gentry's dealings with the church reflect their own sense of identity to a remarkable degree, in their conception both of the family and of social hierarchy'.[25] In this book she draws particular attention to how the doctrine of Purgatory was a stimulus for endowments to parish churches, which helped to absolve individuals of their worldly love for power and material goods, vices to which the gentry were especially susceptible. These endowments fell into two main categories, musical and artistic, which are considered separately in this book by Tim Shaw in Chapter 9 and Thomas Tolley in Chapter 10.

Shaw's chapter demonstrates that the gentry's contact with music was inextricably linked with their devotional activities. As major religious bene-factors, they are shown to have made a large contribution to the elaboration of musical provision within the parish church in particular. In making provision in their wills for the endowment of obits, funding the perform-ance of polyphonic song, and establishing chantries, members of the gentry contributed positively to the musical activities of the Church and, having performed 'good works', shortened the journey of their souls to Heaven. However, whether the fear of Purgatory was the sole motive for this reli-gious benefaction is questionable; alongside the very real possibility that a straightforward love for music to some extent prompted their actions, the generosity of the gentry in embellishing the liturgical music of their parish churches would have been recognised by their neighbours. In enriching the musical aspects of devotion within their parish church, or by requesting personal obits and masses for performance after their deaths, the gentry were able to make public statements about their status within the local community.

In Chapter 10, Tolley shows that although the Church had an ambiva-lent attitude toward artistic expression, much of the gentry's involvement with the visual arts was religious in focus. In commissioning elaborate tombs and memorial brasses, its members had an outlet for visual expres-sion of their status, which was legitimised by religious motives. Moreover, in contributing to the fabric of the parish church, they were able to enhance the religious experience of the wider congregation; once again, even if the motives for their benevolence were personal, the benefits were publicly appreciated, to the augmentation of their status. In addition,

Tolley notes that visual display was deemed acceptable if performed within what might be expected and allowed within one's social rank. This principle was central to many of the gentry's activities, vocalised again and again in surviving literature such as the courtesy books, and in the sumptuary legislation that sought to dictate the behaviour and appearance of individuals according to their status. Tolley shows how members of the gentry seized upon these rules of conduct in order to demonstrate their superior position within society, acquiring elaborate clothing and household objects that reinforced their status and identity.

By similar means the gentry used the visual arts to align themselves with the nobility. Their acquisition of coats of arms, which were then prominently displayed in the manuscripts they owned, or on the tombs and brasses they commissioned, involved them in artistic displays that differed only in scale when compared with their use by the nobility. Tolley observes that although the gentry's aspirations may have been curtailed by more limited resources, their tastes were much the same as those of the higher aristocracy. As Youngs notes in Chapter 7, the manuscripts and books owned by the gentry were more sparingly illustrated than those acquired by nobles, but their textual content was often identical.

Similar parallels may be found in the artistic, musical and literary tastes of the gentry and the urban elite. The urban environment provided many opportunities for cultural contact and exchange, and it seems that influences were reciprocal. Shaw explains that, where it existed, much of the formal musical education of the gentry would have been received within urban institutions: song schools and London's Inns of Court stood alongside the larger religious houses as the focus for musical instruction. It is also clear that, in being frequented by the gentry, urban institutions such as Westminster Abbey could influence the liturgical practices of local parish churches. Moreover, urban forms of entertainment, in particular civic ceremonies, which featured liturgical processions and the cycle and mystery plays, increasingly utilised song as an integral part of the display. These same activities provided opportunities for the display of material wealth, either of the Church, parading those items acquired by donation in processions to celebrate religious festivals, or of the individual, who was able to participate in these occasions while wearing the clothing and jewellery that was a public affirmation of his or her status. As Tolley notes in Chapter 10, the merchants' inherent sense of acquisitiveness led to the validation of consumption in its own right, so that mercantile values were instrumental in allowing the gentry to justify the materialism that was becoming more evident in their lives.

The idea that there might have been a specifically urban form of gentility, whereby civic administrative roles or mercantile activity granted gentle status within towns if not without, has been investigated in detail by both Rosemary Horrox and Pamela Nightingale.[26] Their work builds upon Sylvia Thrupp's comprehensive survey of the interaction between the mercantile world and that of the country gentleman,[27] and highlights the lack of clear cultural or social barriers between the gentry and merchants. The urban and rural worlds did not function as separate spheres of activity, and we should be careful to recognise the significant influence urban life may have had in the formulation of gentry culture in general. As noted above, the urban environment not only influenced the cultural attitudes of those country gentry who spent time there, but was also the locus of activities, most notably mercantile, which altered the very nature of what it meant to be gentle.[28] Thus Sir William Stonor's marriage to Elizabeth Ryche, the widow of a London merchant, and his subsequent commercial alliance with a wool-merchant, Thomas Betson, did not compromise his gentle status. Indeed, Elizabeth's letters indicate that she probably shared many of the same values as her gentry husband even before her betrothal to him.[29]

The role of women in defining what it meant to be gentle in the later Middle Ages must have been significant, yet the conventional discussion of the gentry as comprising knights, esquires and gentle*men* leaves little room for their consideration. As Maddern notes in Chapter 1, discussions of gentility much more readily accommodate women than the traditional debates centred on pedigree, service or landownership. Coss's recent study of the lady in medieval England acts as a significant corrective to the traditionally male-focused approach to the gentry; as he asserts, 'ladies played a major role in sustaining and transmitting gentility'.[30] His work, and that of many others, also testifies to the fact that they could help to formulate its character.[31] It is clear throughout this volume that the skills of gentry women as household managers and peacemakers, in particular, helped to maintain and augment the status of their families. Thus Tolley in Chapter 10 notes the significant role of widows in directing the making of their husbands' monuments, Truelove in Chapter 5 draws attention to women's skilled appropriation of the letter as a means of communication, and Youngs in Chapter 7 highlights gentry women's participatory role in literary networks. Women were undoubtedly instrumental in forging alliances and networks, which drew the gentry more closely together. Their informal friendship networks may have provided as many opportunities for the advancement and affirmation of their family's public status as the more formal arenas in which their male counterparts participated.[32]

Women's role in formulating a group identity is one aspect of late medieval gentry culture that deserves further research; as this book highlights, there are many others. The gentry's experiences of music and the visual arts are particularly neglected areas, and the scope for exploration of these topics is vast. Despite the wealth of research on the religion of the gentry, as attested by Carpenter in Chapter 8, there is much scope for further study of its members' devotional and spiritual lives. The same is true of their education: it remains the case that much of what we know about their formal instruction is extrapolated from our knowledge of how institutions operated, rather than being seen in direct evidence of individuals' experiences. There are many wider thematic issues that are touched upon in this book but await more thorough investigation, such as the gentry's involvement in both domestic and foreign trade and diplomacy, and the dynamics of family structures and their influence on social mobility.

As such, this book can only begin to outline the rich complexities of the cultural approach to the study of the late medieval gentry. Although the contributors draw upon a wide and varied range of source material, including wills, literature, court depositions, material evidence, statutes, legal records, petitions, tax returns, churchwardens' accounts, letters, inventories and household accounts, more evidence is continually coming to light.[33] As further gentry-related documentation is discovered and made available to the research community through publications such as those produced by the Camden Society and the Early English Text Society, the more complete our view of the activities and attitudes of the gentry becomes. Our methodologies are also becoming more rigorous and informed by the development of new theoretical approaches, many of which are shared across disciplines. The resulting interdisciplinarity has itself improved the quality of research, as, for example, historians' use of literary texts is better informed by more thorough understanding of authorial intent and audience reception. Similarly, more rigorous and transparent approaches to the use of historical manuscript evidence have encouraged researchers to understand more about document creation, leading to more accurate conclusions that reflect the potential bias inherent in the content of primary source material. With gentry studies so suited to interdisciplinary approaches, these advances are having a significant impact upon the quality and range of academic endeavour in this area; this volume is testament to the vitality of gentry-related research by specialists in late medieval history, literature, music and art.

The chapters that follow this introduction provide an overview of the activities that helped to shape the gentry's cultural identity, but are also drawn together by the common task of exploring whether lifestyle can be regarded as much an indicator of gentility as any measure of income, landholdings or pedigree. As such, this book calls for a reassessment of whether there was a distinctive gentry culture at the end of the Middle Ages. There are many indications that gentle and noble outlooks were very similar, the main differences emerging as ones of scale rather than substance. At the same time, the gentry's greater interaction with those below them in the social hierarchy, and the extent to which their interests coalesced with mercantile culture, suggest that these groups played an ever greater role in influencing the gentry's own culture. That there does not seem to have been resistance among the established gentry to the newcomers at the lower end of their rank suggests that gentle culture was especially open to reinvention and redefinition toward the end of the medieval period. This raises the question of whether the interests of the gentry's constituent members became so diverse that the concept of a specific and distinctive late medieval gentry culture might, in fact, be as much of an artificial construct as the term 'gentry' itself.

This book therefore makes a significant advance in the discussion of the culture of the gentry during this period. There is no doubt that almost all those with a claim to gentility held land, and regarded themselves as superior to those who did not. Yet the chapters, when read together, reveal that it is unwise to assume that this diverse group embraced a common culture rigorously uniform in all features. It is also evident that the ways in which members of the gentry were educated, worshipped, worked, communicated and participated in leisure activities were not always uniquely 'gentle'. Gentry culture was not a separate phenomenon; the gentry in all their diversity were, after all, an integral part of a wide and various society, and hence locating the ways in which late medieval gentry culture was distinct from that of the wider population is problematic. Yet a recurring observation throughout this book is that, whether they were knights or newly risen professionals, members of the gentry conducted their lives mindful of the need to project to others their perceived superiority. Display was of paramount importance to them in the affirmation of status, demonstrating that the maintenance of social rank was central to the gentle lifestyle.

Thus the culture of the gentry was pervaded by a sense of insecurity; these people knew that their position was subject to the vagaries of fortune, so they assiduously managed their own affairs in the hope to maintain, or indeed better, their status, and attempted at every opportunity to convince others of their worthiness. While the established gentry flaunted their perceived right to gentility in order to maintain their privileged position, the newly risen or aspiring members of the group sought in any way that they could to justify their claim to their elevated status. We must await further analysis of the gentry's attitudes and activities before definitively concluding whether lifestyle choices could play a role in admitting or excluding an individual to this elite sector of society. However, the evidence presented in this book shows how a shared mentality, prompted in part by increased social mobility, was present among the late medieval gentry. Despite wide variations in wealth, pedigree and occupation, it was in the interests of all those with a claim to gentility to perpetuate and defend the belief that they were worthy of the privileges they enjoyed. Alongside socio-economic measures of status, this cultural disposition helped to shape the identity of the gentry, and informed every aspect of its members' lives.

Notes

The authors are indebted to Stephen Rigby, Peter Fleming and the publisher's anonymous reader for their valued comments on earlier drafts of this introduction.

1 Two important recent contributions to the debate surrounding the definition of the gentry are Keen, *Origins of the English Gentleman* and Coss, *Origins of the English Gentry*. Other relevant work includes Morgan, 'Individual style', Acheson, *Gentry Community*, ch. 2, 'The gentry in the fifteenth century', pp. 29–44, and Carpenter, 'England: the nobility and the gentry', which surveys work in this area and includes extensive guidance for further reading.

2 Coss, 'Formation of the English gentry', p. 46.

3 Some historians have even questioned the inclusion of gentlemen within the fifteenth-century gentry: see, for example, Acheson, *Gentry Community*, p. 34, and Wright, *Derbyshire Gentry*, p. 6.

4 Pugh, 'Magnates, knights and gentry', p. 96.

5 McFarlane, *Nobility of Later Medieval England*, p. 275. Also see his essays in the same book, 'Stratification of the nobility and gentry', pp. 122–5 and 'Extinction and recruitment', pp. 142–67, and Given-Wilson, *English Nobility*, pp. 69–83. Mertes, 'Aristocracy' uses nobility as an inclusive term.

6 Bennett, *Pastons and their England*. A contemporary review of Kingsford's edition of the Stonor letters and papers dismissed it as a 'somewhat disappointing collection', drawing attention only to the three letters that 'touch upon other than local affairs', and ending with the comment that the rest are 'material for what is called social history', *English Historical Review*, 36 (1921), pp. 469–70.

7 See especially McFarlane, *England in the Fifteenth Century*, which reproduces a number of his articles, and *idem*, *Nobility of Later Medieval England*.

8 McFarlane, 'William Worcester'.

9 Richmond, *John Hopton*.

10   Richmond, 'After McFarlane', pp. 59–60.

11   Jones (ed.), *Gentry and Lesser Nobility*. Carpenter's contribution is very much a prelude to her *Locality and Polity*.

12   Aston and Richmond (eds), *Lollardy and the Gentry*; McFarlane, *Lancastrian Kings and Lollard Knights*.

13   A major urban gentry project is being conducted by Professor Felicity Riddy at the University of York, while another two manuscript projects, one based on the *Brut* chronicle (at Queen's University Belfast, conducted by Professor John J. Thompson), and the other on manuscripts in the Midlands (at the University of Birmingham, conducted by Professor Wendy Scase), are currently producing additional evidence of gentry ownership and readership of literary and historical texts.

14   For example, Saul, *Knights and Esquires*; Wright, *Derbyshire Gentry*; Carpenter, *Locality and Polity*; Moreton, *Townshends and their World*; Bennett, *Community, Class and Careerism*; Payling, *Political Society*; Pollard, *North-Eastern England*; Acheson, *Gentry Community*; Fleming, 'Charity, faith and the gentry of Kent'.

15   Moreton, *Townshends and their World*; Richmond, *Paston Family: The First Phase*, *Paston Family: Fastolf's Will* and *Paston Family: Endings*; Carpenter, 'Stonor circle'; Carpenter, 'Introduction' to *Kingsford's Stonor Letters*; Carpenter, 'Introduction' to *Armburgh Papers*.

16   See, for example, Rubin, 'Small groups'.

17   Carpenter, 'Gentry and community', pp. 340 and 379; *idem, Locality and Polity*, p. 3.

18   Mertes, 'Aristocracy', pp. 42–3.

19   Hicks, *English Political Culture*, p. 6.

20   See, for instance, Carpenter, *Locality and Polity*, pp. 1–9 and 615.

21   Ross, *Edward IV*, pp. 308–10.

22   Below, p. 120.

23   Horrox, 'Urban gentry', Morgan, 'Individual style', and Storey, 'Gentleman-bureaucrats'.

24   Coss, 'Formation of the English gentry', further explored in his *Origins of the English Gentry*.

25   Carpenter, 'Fifteenth-century gentry', p. 54.

26   Horrox, 'Urban gentry', and Nightingale, 'Knights and merchants'.

27   Thrupp, *Merchant Class*, esp. ch. 6 'Trade and gentility', pp. 234–87.

28   Caroline Barron's work on late medieval London is particularly useful in highlighting the urban activities of the country gentry. See in particular Barron, 'Centres of conspicuous consumption'.

29   Coss also draws attention to Elizabeth Stonor's gentility in his *Lady in Medieval England*, pp. 55–6. For further examples of widowed London gentlewomen, see Barron and Sutton (eds), *Medieval London Widows*.

30   Coss, *Lady in Medieval England*, p. 72. On gentry women's pivotal role in developing and maintaining local networks, see Ward, 'English noblewomen'.

31   On medieval gentry women and their activities in general, see further Archer, 'How ladies … who live on their manors'; Kirby, 'Women in the Plumpton correspondence'; Maddern, 'Honour among the Pastons'; Meale (ed.), *Women and*

Literature; Meale and Boffey, 'Gentlewomen's reading'; and Truelove, 'Commanding communications'.

32 It should be noted, however, that Maddern's research based on the Paston letters has led her to suggest that relationships between women were 'rarely spoken of as friendships': Maddern, 'Best trusted friends'.

33 The Armburgh papers were discovered only recently, for example: see *Armburgh Papers*, ed. Carpenter, pp. 1–2.

1

Gentility

Philippa Maddern

In 1421, Sir Edward Hastings had reached the nadir of his dispute over his right to bear the undifferenced arms of the Hastings earls of Pembroke. Imprisoned for refusing to pay the costs of the case against him, he petitioned furiously for release, portraying himself as 'liyng peyned in p[ri]son of [th]e marcheseye *liker a thef or a traitour than like a Gentil-man of berthe*'.[1] Clearly, he expected immediate understanding of the term 'gentilman', and sympathy for his claim that gentle status and imprison-ment were radically incompatible. Yet his easy assumption of unproblematic understanding is not shared by modern historians of late medieval English society, who have made many attempts at explicating the concept of gentility, whether embodied in the individual 'gentleman/woman', or in the wider – and arguably even more complex – collective term, 'gentry'.[2]

How can we understand terms which seem to depend on a variety of concepts of good birth, wealth, service (military and otherwise) and types of land tenure? How can historians accurately use terms of gentility, when they were employed inconsistently, if not downright arbitrarily, by contemporaries? Why, after approximately 250 years of seemingly desultory usage, did they suddenly spring into prominence and popularity in about the second decade of the fifteenth century?

One fundamental difficulty is that on close examination, 'gentleman/ woman' reveals itself to be a different kind of status term from others current in the Middle Ages. No other late medieval descriptor displayed such variance in its potential meanings. For instance, by the fifteenth century, barring some borderline cases, the male peerage can fairly be described as those who received summons to Parliament by right of their title. Similarly, to be a knight or esquire was to be identified as a member of a distinct armigerous club with very little wider application. At the opposite end of the social scale, unfree peasants could be distinguished either by their birth or by the tenure of the land they worked, and were subject to a range of specific legal disabilities.[3] In contrast, to be a 'gentleman' could mean either that one was claiming membership of the whole class of people, including knights and esquires, occupying the social space between the peerage and the free peasantry, or, more narrowly, that one was from the lower range of this group, ranking above a mere yeoman or franklin, but not aspiring to the title of knight or esquire. Thus, the writer of a 1427 letter warning the king's council of escalating disputes between Sir John Howard and Sir Thomas Kerdeston referred to the protagonists' supporters as 'as weel ... lordis of astate as ... othyr gentilmen as knyghtis and squyers'.[4] Similarly, a 1452 petition drafted on behalf of John Paston, and whose signatories included knights and esquires such as Sir John Heveningham, Nicholas Appulyerd, John Pagrave, Robert Mortimer and William Rokewode, cited 'we and othire jentilmen of the shire of Norffolk'.[5] On the other hand, legal descriptions of status were more precisely differentiated; in a 1434 Kings Bench suit, for instance, John Brethenham, the defendant, was clearly demarcated 'gentleman' as against his 'esquire' plaintiff, Christopher Straunge.[6]

A second major distinction between the term 'gentleman/woman' and other status descriptors is that most other status words had a single, fairly precise criterion attached to them. Thus, a knight originally signified a man who gave military service in return for a fief, and whose income was consequently expected to provide what we would now call the infrastructure costs of such service. Not all late medieval knights could afford armed service, and by the fourteenth century, many were as likely to fulfil civil, as military, duties; but the original meaning of the term survived in such practices as classifying upper-class landholdings as 'knight's fees', setting a notional minimum limit of £40 annual income from land as the income for a knight, and requiring esquires who had such an income to take up knighthood or pay a fine in lieu of the service they did not render.[7] The most common Latin version of the term 'esquire' clearly signified its origins: an esquire was an 'armiger', one who bore either real or heraldic arms, though by the late fourteenth century rich esquires had moved into county administrative positions.[8]

At the other end of the social scale, a 'bond man/woman', 'villein' or 'serf' was defined by legal standing, witnessed in such aspects as his or her duty to pay labour services to a manorial lord, and his or her general disability to sue freely for justice in the king's courts. The legal distinction between bond and free in turn helped to characterise a range of free men, who might be further distinguished by occupation or service. A 'husband-man' was a free man, further identified by his particular occupation (working with his hands as an agriculturalist). Thus a contemporary opponent of the Pastons claimed that their ancestor, Clement Paston, had been a 'good pleyn husbond, and lyvyd upon hys lond ... The seyd Clement yede att on Plowe both wynt[er] and som[m]er, and he rodd to mylle on the bar hosbak wyth hys corn und[er] hym'.[9] A 'franklin' literally meant a freeholder, and 'yeoman', originally a service term translating the Latin 'valettus' for 'one who attended his lord', had by the end of the fifteenth century widened to denote a respectable free tenant: an agriculturalist who might lease, rather than own, land, but who was of higher status than a mere husbandman.[10]

In contrast to these prescriptive criteria, the term 'gentleman/woman' seems to have lacked any precise definition relating to legal status, land ownership, occupation, arms-bearing or service. The history of the term, far from cohering around any single set of meanings, is filled with varying and diffuse definitions. Early definitions centred vaguely on 'what is characteristic of a gentleman', naming qualities such as excellence, nobility, graciousness or courtesy, whose components shimmer with a variety of cultural assumptions.[11] In Latin, 'generositas' seems to have signified nobility by birth in the early thirteenth century, but by 1295 it also signified gentility bestowed by royal title. The phrase 'gentile man' is first recorded in English in *c.* 1150, associated less with birth or wealth than (tauto-logically) with 'wis lore and genteleri'.[12]

There is evidence to suggest that some attempt was made in the fifteenth century to use level and source of wealth to distinguish a gentleman from other ranks. In 1474, for instance, Edward IV ordered all 'gentilmen' and other Coventry residents 'being of the lyvelode of x li. by yere and aboue' to attend him on his visit to the city.[13] In practice such categories were, however, discouragingly hazy. Christine Carpenter's meticulous examination of the income of Warwickshire taxpayers in 1436 indeed shows that all Warwickshire knights had a higher annual income than any Warwickshire 'gentleman', and that the average income of gentlemen (£13) accorded well with the notional £10 minimum. But a closer look at Carpenter's figures dispels initial optimism about the match of income levels and social status. The incomes of the gentlemen over-lapped markedly both the lower and middle range of esquires' incomes, and encompassed the *whole* range of incomes of the non-gentle taxable popu-lation. Some gentlemens' incomes were as low as £5 per year, others as high as £30–40.[14]

The only factor that clearly influenced almost all late medieval status terms, including 'gentleman/woman', was the contemporary belief, in defiance of some well-known cases of social mobility, in the strict heritability of status.[15] Sir John Fortescue wrote firmly that 'a serf can beget in matrimony none but a serf';[16] while clerks recording deponents in the Morley-Lovell dispute of 1386 used the terms 'gentil home' and 'de gentil sanc' interchangeably, as if blood alone established gentility.[17] When the Pastons obtained their patent of gentle status in *c.* 1466 they justified it by the claim that they were 'linealy descended of right noble and worshipfull blood'.[18] But the problem with such a view, as even contemporaries tacitly acknowledged, was that it imposed a microscopic veneer of certainty over a seething mass of contradiction. In the absence of DNA tests, or even reliable records of births and marriages, bloodlines were easier to forge than to prove.[19] The Pastons, despite their large talk of Norman knightly ancestry, were known to be not a century removed from the blood of their peasant forebears, a fact of which their neighbours did not fail to remind them.[20] John Russell, instructing fifteenth-century ushers on orders of precedence, was forced to include guidelines for those occasions when his readers might encounter incompatibilities of bloodline and wealth.[21] Fifteenth-century fiction restated such dilemmas. William Caxton's audiences, for instance, read Malory's 'Tale of Sir Gareth of Orkney', whose hero, though indisputably of noble birth, came incognito to King Arthur's court, asking for only food and drink. Despite Arthur's and Lancelot's uncomfortable forebodings that the mysterious stranger was 'com of men of worshyp', he became an unrecognised kitchen-hand.[22]

In these circumstances, bloodline could hardly function as a reliable marker of gentility, either in its special or more generalised sense. We are forced to the conclusion that unlike other late medieval status descriptors, the term 'gentleman/woman' was always a portmanteau one, whose meaning stretched to encompass various levels of specificity, many criteria of social standing, and different kinds of social behaviours. For example, gentility by service easily modulated to encompass certain classes of men who offered professional services to the king, magnates and upper gentry. As Carpenter remarks, by the late fifteenth century '"gentleman", not esquire, was … universally understood to be the proper title for lawyers and minor administrators'.[23] In turn, the class of professionals who might be called 'gentle' was almost infinitely elastic. In 1467 the churchwardens of East Dereham, Norfolk, accounting for church upkeep, evidently decided that anyone with non-agricultural expertise could qualify as a gentleman, since they 'payid [6/8] to the Ientylma[n] for his labor' in repairing the organ.[24] Furthermore, whole ranges of personality, lifestyle and behaviour relating to the various criteria of service, bloodline or natural excellence might be implied in the term 'gentleman/woman'. For instance, early fifteenth-century jurors in an inquisition at Litcham, Norfolk referred to a landowner's 'grete jentre' in granting common rights to a local prior, using the word 'gentry' to imply (apparently) qualities such as generosity and magnanimity.[25]

Perhaps not surprisingly in view of the vagueness of the category, exact identification of any individual as a gentleman/woman remained haphazard throughout the fifteenth century. Several different styles could apply to the same person at varying times and in different contexts. Thus, only six years after figuring as a 'gentleman' in his dispute with Christopher Straunge, John Brethenham was demoted to 'franklin' in another case of trespass; while Geoffrey Walle, of Billockby, Norfolk, within the space of the five years 1432–37 was described variously as 'husbandman', 'yeoman', 'franklin' and 'gentleman'.[26] On the higher edge of the county status-group, Simeon Fyncham, a comfortably circumstanced and undoubtedly armigerous West Norfolk manorial lord, vacillated between styling himself 'gentleman' and 'esquire'.[27] In the urban sector, late medieval merchants, even though their income might derive less from land than from trade, were thought to be equal, or superior, to the gentry in status, while even the civil servants of the mayors of great cities might be accorded honorary gentle status for the terms of their appointment. In these circumstances, Rosemary Horrox argues that the style 'gentleman' held little attraction for wealthy urbanites, though they might aspire to gain the title 'esquire'.[28] John Grey, Robert Wilford and John Webber were wealthy Exeter burgesses; but in 1384, they were also styled 'esquires' of Edward de Courtenay, 4th earl of Devon.[29] Thomas Wetherby (fl. 1413, d. 1445) of Norwich combined a prosperous mercantile career with a manorial lifestyle, and was recognised both as 'esquire' ('armiger') and as 'citizen and alderman' of Norwich.[30]

The breadth of meanings that came to be associated with gentility may itself have encouraged extended usage of the terms, making them, for example, peculiarly applicable to women as well as men. Status terminology which was strictly linked to bloodline, service (especially military service) or landholding applied most easily to males, through whom lineages were commonly calculated, who more commonly held title to land, and who performed all the military and almost all the civilian service of their society. But words associated with gentility, which did not depend solely on tenurial, professional or sanguineal references, were perhaps more easily adapted to feminine forms. We hear of no yeowomen, frank-linesses, or *armigera* in late medieval England, but 'generosa' is attested from the twelfth century, and 'gentilwoman' occurs in King's Bench records as early as 1429, in letters from *c.* 1437 onwards, and, authorita-tively, in the *Promptorium Parvulorum c.* 1440 ('Gentilwoman. *Generosa*').[31]

What, then, was the value of so shifting a set of terms to the holders and users? And why, despite a scatter of examples before 1300, and a gradually rising number of instances from 1300–1415, were the words 'gentleman/woman' so quickly popularised in the fifteenth century, appearing with increasing frequency in central legal records from 1415 onwards, in local court records from at least 1424, in deed evidence from *c.* 1425 onwards, and as a self-description in wills from at least 1439?[32] Did the appearance of a new class (perhaps of rising yeomen enriched by the economic opportunities of the post-plague countryside) produce the need for a blanket term to describe them? Or is the growth in usage more apparent than real, merely the effect of an increasingly intrusive and bureaucratic royal government demanding more precise status definitions in a greater volume of paperwork?

Some historians favour the explanation that a tendency in the fourteenth century for ranks below the peerage to be progressively specified with greater minuteness was given statutory force by the Statute of Additions, and hence produced more use of gentry terms.[33] But the argument that the 1413 Statute of Additions was the prime mover in the adoption of the terms 'gentleman/woman' faces several difficulties. Firstly, the Statute did not specify which terms should be used to define *'estat ou degree ou …mistere'*.[34] Why then should it produce a sudden flurry of instances of the word 'gentleman' as opposed to other comparable descriptors (such as franklin, which appears much more rarely in the records)?[35] Secondly, the Statute of Additions required only that *defendants* in cases where the process might lead to outlawry should be identified by status. Yet, in fact, by the 1420s a sizeable minority of plaintiffs were registering their status, but in almost all cases, *only if* that status was either gentle or clerical.[36] Hence the mere fact of a plaintiff having a recorded style witnessed to his upper-class standing. But since the Statute of Additions did not require plaintiffs' status to be given, the impetus most likely came from plaintiffs themselves, who apparently recognised some social value in having their status noted in a court of record. Why did they require such recognition, and what value did they derive from it?

That it was the term 'gentleman' which particularly benefited from the statutory impulse suggests that the word was already in general use or demand, as documentary evidence confirms; 'Gentilman' occurs as a surname throughout the fourteenth century, and possibly as early as 1222.[37] It may be that litigants were influenced by another factor that has been adduced as the cause of a greater use of gentry terminology: the rise of a new class in English society, that of the prosperous free peasant who accumulated lands held by various forms of freehold and leasehold, who sometimes farmed, if he did not own, manorial land, and whose wealth and lifestyle demanded a new status term.[38] How valid is this argument? No one doubts that conditions after the Black Death favoured the formation of a more prosperous upper stratum of the peasantry, some of whom began to lease, or even acquire, whole manors on which to pursue agricultural capitalism, though clearly a peasant family's power to accumulate land varied with a number of factors including geographical location and family life-cycle.[39] E. B. Fryde cites the case of the Giffards of Bibury, Gloucestershire, who moved from being reeves of the manor in 1387 to farmers of it in 1396.[40]

But two problems remain with the assumption that these newly-rich peasants successfully demanded the title 'gentleman'. There is the difficulty, firstly, in finding enough of them, and secondly, in discovering examples of any who were recognised as acquiring gentle status. Jim Bolton has calculated on the basis of tax returns that at most this rising class can have comprised no more than 1.5 to 2 per cent of the fifteenth-century population.[41] Furthermore, it seems that relatively few men achieved the title 'gentleman' through agricultural success alone; 'yeoman' seems to have become their standard descriptor. Those rare families who did achieve gentility by such means did not do so quickly or easily. Carpenter found only one Warwickshire case of a yeoman farming family who entered the gentle class (the Spensers), and even they 'were not recognised as gentlemen until long after they had acquired manorial lordship'.[42] Rising men may have found it easier to gain gentility through professional service plus manorial holdings, rather than through agriculture alone; but since service had been a route to social advancement since at least the twelfth century, the existence of such a phenomenon does not explain why, in this era alone, it should have produced a new use of the term 'gentleman'.[43]

Nevertheless, the possibly increasing prosperity of free peasants may have had two differing effects on the use of status terminology. Firstly, it is in this period that the term 'yeoman' began to acquire implications not merely of lower-ranking military service, but of respectable landed prosperity. A 1452 petition, for instance, urged the king to take action against one Roger Cherche, who, it was claimed, had unjustly 'enbilled diuers gentilmen and many thryfty and substanciall yomen, and thryfty husbondes and men of gode name and fame'.[44] Secondly, and probably consequently, it is likely that, as Carpenter shrewdly reflects, the lower echelons of the gentry were increasingly anxious from the fourteenth century onward to distinguish themselves from peasants whose 'obedience and subordination' could no longer be taken for granted, and whose appearance and wealth may sometimes have seemed all too easy to confuse with those of people of greater lineage and a longer status history.[45]

Definitive evidence for this socio-cultural development is not easy to find. Yet a range of late medieval literature – statutes, prescriptive writings and satire – all imply that whatever the real difficulties of rising from peasant status, the late medieval reading public thought they saw groups of lower-class individuals trying to ape the manners and reputation of their betters, and were divided only as to whether one should join or censure such a movement. Thus, on the *contra* side, writers such as Trevisa (translating Ranulf Higden) excoriated would-be social climbers who,

> despiseth hir owne, and preiseth other menis, and vnneth beeth apaide with hir owne estate ... therfore hit is that a yeman arraieth hym as a squyer, a squyer as a knyght, a knight as a duke and a duke as a kyng ... [Yet] they that wole take eueriche degree beeth of non degre, for in berynge the beeth menstralles and heraudes, in talkynge grete spekeres, in etynge and in drynkynge glotouns, in gaderynge of catel hoksters and tauerners, in aray tormentoures ... [46]

Similarly, the audience of the N-town plays was clearly expected to recognise the targets of a satirical speech by the Devil, purporting to teach eager followers how to reinvent themselves as gentlemen on the shaky basis of pride and credit-bought finery:

> Off fyne cordewan a goodly peyr of long pokyd schon
> hosyn enclosyd of the most costyous cloth of Crenseyn
> Thus a boy to a ientylman to make comp[er]ycon ...
> A shert of feyn holond but car[e] not for the payment ...
> Thow poverte be chef lete p[ri]de ther be p[re]sent.[47]

Even a 'beggerys dowter', the Devil urged, could 'cownterfete a jentyl woman dysgeysyd as she can'. In another anonymous late fifteenth-century work, the lyricist had come to recognise a distinct upward step between yeomanry and gentry, but cynically advised that money was the main engine of transfer between the two:

> If thou be a yeman, a gentleman wold be
> Into sum lordes cort than put thou thee:
> Lok thou have spending, larg and plente,
> And always the peny redy to tak to.[48]

More seriously, late medieval sumptuary legislation was specifically designed to discourage dress behaviour that might blur social distinctions.[49]

On the other hand, a flourishing genre of late medieval instructive poetry and conduct literature explicitly aimed to teach aspiring gentlemen/women how to achieve a rise in status. John Russell's and Hugh Rhodes' advice on gentility functioned on at least three levels. Ostensibly, their work operated only to provide guidance for young gentlemen undertaking the 'nurture' appropriate to their birth. In fact, of course, their writings implicitly operated equally well to inform and reassure socially-mobile readers fearful lest their manners should betray their lowly origins, and to clarify for the 'gentry' the criteria through which the distinctions of gentle and non-gentle were reconstructed and reinforced, and by which gentlemen/women could be known from ambitious peasants and town workers.[50]

But does the hypothesis that status-anxiety drove the development of new usages of old status terms actually help to explain the increasing popularity specifically of the words 'gentleman' and 'gentlewoman' in the fifteenth century? I think it does. In a climate of perceived intense social competition, the breadth, vagueness and flexibility of such terms, and of the even more slippery 'gentry', however infuriating to historians, rendered them particularly valuable to contemporaries. To those fighting to maintain a place at the margins of gentle society, too precise a definition of gentility might be a disadvantage, automatically debarring candidates who lacked some vital quantifiable element from even claiming gentle status. Not all claimants to gentility could muster a credible bloodline, evidence of long-standing royal service, or sufficient landed income. But almost all could lay claim to some aspect of the broad range of gentle qualities and behaviours. Furthermore, honour and status ('worship', in the common fifteenth-century term) were themselves not measurable absolutes, but, as Mervyn James brilliantly argued, matters of reputation, only to be established and judged by the 'community of honour itself'.[51]

In other words, one became gentle by a consensus of recognition among one's supposed peers (other reputable gentlemen and esquires). As John Paston I succinctly put it in relaying news of a possible marriage prospect for his sister, what mattered was that the man was '*countyd* a jantylmanly man and a wurchepful'.[52] To claim the title 'gentleman', then, was to assert, implicitly, that one was already a member of that group of high-bred equals who alone could recognise true gentility. Hence, both to recognise and to be recognised enhanced one's status. In Malory, Lancelot's immediate apprehension of Gareth's gentle birth is evidence not only of Gareth's, but of his own 'jantylnesse and curtesy'; whereas Kay's over-legalistic assessment ('he is a vylayne borne … for an he had be com of jantyllmen, he wolde have axed horse and armour') ineradicably marks him as an 'unjantyll knyght'.[53] The self-referential nature of the knowledge involved in this mutual recognition ('he is gentil, by cause he doth / As longeth to a gentilman')[54] itself maintained the exclusiveness of the club, implying that gentle perceptions were simply not teachable to those outside the charmed circle. In this discourse, either one recognised (apparently instinctively) what 'longeth to a gentilman', or one showed oneself not to be a gentleman/woman. Ironically, of course, these essentialist constructions themselves gave rise to the handbooks of behaviour, to provide checklists of otherwise imponderable standards of manners; yet the existence of teaching-aids to gentle manners undercut any notion that gentility was instinctive or inborn. But throughout the whole process, the fact that the term 'gentleman/woman' could be made to include such a wide range of the social hierarchy, and so many criteria of social distinction, meant that they could be easily adopted by those anxious to raise their status and/or distinguish themselves from the upper peasantry. Unlike 'franklin' which might imply only that one held freehold land, or 'yeoman', the other increasingly popular term of the late-fourteenth to fifteenth century, whose status connotations had never been more than moderate, 'gentleman/woman' offered a term that brought its bearers within the same circle of gentility as great knights and esquires, without demanding that the holder necessarily sustain all the expenses, or acquire all the trappings, of knighthood or squiredom.

This theory of the particular usefulness of gentry terms to the post-plague upper classes also helps to explain the phenomenon noted by Carpenter that the word 'gentleman' appeared earlier in texts deriving from local communities than in documents produced by the central government (excluding legal documents).[55] To members of the upper classes of county communities, minute status distinctions articulated within a system of honour-recognition could be vital for both men and women, determining whose word and reputation were held to be sound, who should hold administrative power, who would control the execution of law, and whose patronage should be sought by whom. To Westminster, on the other hand, so long as eminent men were found to staff the offices of county government and lesser men paid their taxes, the exact differentiation of status between them was of little consequence.

How then, could an individual prove that he or she was gentle? Not, it seems, simply by amassing objectively-verifiable status markers such as wealth, office, manorial lands or written genealogies, though all these things might, in different ways, be useful to sustain a claim to gentility. Peter Coss has recently argued that the gentry were formed around a set of six social processes, including identity as a type of lesser nobility, a basis of landownership which nevertheless accommodated professional and urban members, territoriality, public authority in a system with little paid bureaucracy, collective social control of a territorial populace, and 'collective identity ... and interests'.[56] This formulation is subtle and useful, not least because it suggests that gentry-formation was an ongoing process. To be a member of the gentry was to be constantly undertaking a performance: behaving like a gentleman/woman in the eyes of the world, and particularly for the benefit of the 'gentry' society whose recognition alone could establish who was gentle and who was not. Thus, to own a manor might be a necessary condition of upper-class status; but one had also to support one's claims to ownership and status by an appropriate display of manorial lordship. '[Y]e be a gentilwoman, and it is worshep for yow to confort yowr tenantis; wherfor I wold ye myth ryd to Heylisdon and Drayton ... and speke with hem' wrote John Paston I to his wife Margaret, in 1465, when his manors of Drayton and Hellesdon were under threat from the Duke of Suffolk.[57] Similarly, not only the possession of a good livelihood, but its prudent maintenance and expenditure was, according to the Pastons, a vital component in maintaining a 'worshipful' reputation; 'but if ye take odere heed to your exspences ye shall do yourself and your frendes gret diswurchep' wrote Margaret Paston to her son John in 1470, complaining that county rumour ran that 'I haue departed so largely wyth you that I may nowthere help you my-self ner non of my frendes, which is no wurchep and causeth men to set the lesse be vs'.[58]

Clearly the component behaviours of these performances encompassed the widest variety of circumstances; gentlemen and gentlewomen could be on show in every aspect of their lives, at every hour of the day, from birth to death. In the late medieval period, gentility may be seen less as an inherited quality than as a syndrome that might or might not encompass matters such as lineage, title, service to the great, arms-bearing, wealth and manorial lordship, along with more widely achievable characteristics of behaviour and general lifestyle. Late-medieval writers themselves admitted as much. Chaucer, in his translation of the *Romance of the Rose*, painstakingly problematised the connection between birth and gentility. In a passage where Love censures low-born 'vilany', Chaucer departs from his source to add:

> That this is not myn entendement,
> To clepe no wight in noo ages
> Oonly gentill for his lynages.
> But whoso is vertuous,
> And in his port nought outrageous,
> Whanne sich oon thou seest thee biforn,
> Though he be not gentill born,
> Thou maist well seyn, this is in soth,
> That he is gentil by cause he doth
> As longeth to a gentilman.[59]

Another source from *c.* 1500 noted frankly that where criteria for gentility were concerned, two out of four ain't bad: 'Trauthe, pettee, fredome and hardynesse … Off thisse virtues iiij who lakkyth iij / He aught never gentylmane called to be.'[60]

Dress and material circumstances were certainly two common makers of reputation and markers of gentility. The N-town Devil's sarcastic speech mocks such pretensions, but they were nevertheless taken seriously; in 1453 Margaret Paston borrowed an item of jewellery (a 'devys') from her richer neighbour, Elizabeth Clere, to wear when Queen Margaret of Anjou came to Norfolk because 'I durst not for shame go wyth my bedys among so many fresch jantylwomman'.[61] The Pastons, bent on making their way into the upper classes, apparently deliberately set out to acquire the visible accoutrements of status: manors, servile tenants, stately houses.[62] But behaviour, aptitudes and education could be just as, if not more, vital. In Malory's tale, Gareth displayed his gentility by his otherwise inexplicable interest in, and aptitude for, knightly duels and his unwavering forbearance with disdainful damsels.[63] The idea that table manners could make a gentleman appears in a late fifteenth-century etiquette booklet, whose readers were advised to practise the etiquette of dining so that 'men will say thereafter / That a gentleman was here.[64] According to Trevisa's translation of Higden, 'gentil men children [*filii nobilium*] beeth I-taught to speke Frensche from the tyme that they beeth I-rokked in here cradel … and vplondisshe men [*rurales homines*] wil likne hym self to gentil men and fondeth with greet besynesse for to speke Frensce, for to be I-tolde of'.[65]

They may have been right; certainly the somewhat parvenu Pastons took pains to polish their French.[66] For adults, undertaking the right sorts of leisure activities was clearly imperative. Hunting, for instance, was a highly socially stratified and status-ridden activity. According to Malory, only gentlemen were supposed to know the esoteric 'tearmes that jantyl-men have and use' in the course of the chase; hence a knowledge of hunting alone could enable 'all men of worshyp [to] discover a jantylman frome a yoman and a yoman frome a vylane'.[67] Serious consequences could fall to those caught indulging in pursuits regarded as above their rank: a 1390 statute imposed a year's imprisonment on any 'artificer or labourer' or lay person with less than 40 shillings annual income from land or rents who owned greyhounds ('*leverer*'), or used other implements to 'take or destroy deer, hare, rabbits, or other gentles' game' ('*prendre ou destruire savagine levees ne couilles nautre desduit des gentils*').[68] More sedentary sports could also be honourable or otherwise, depending on circum-stance. Margaret Paston wrote, probably in 1459, to her husband John reporting that she had carefully checked with two of her more prestigious countrywomen (Lady Morley and Lady Stapleton) 'qwat sportys were husyd' in 'placys of wvrschip' on the first Christmas following a death in the family. They informed her that while no 'lowde dysportys', such as 'dysgysynggys nere harpyng' were appropriate, quieter pastimes such as 'pleyng at the tabyllys and schesse and cardys' were allowable.[69]

Even material goods and services could be taken either to be possessed of gentle characteristics, or to comprise the particular perquisites of gentle-men. Two fifteenth-century wills (dated 1415 and 1445) specified among their legacies 'gentilmennys shetis',[70] and paradise, according to the author of the N-town plays, abounded in 'gentyl rys'.[71] By the early sixteenth century, whole lifestyles were marked off for gentlemen. In 1509 the prior of St Laurence Mountjoye, demising his house to the prior of Walsingham in return for perpetual board, stipulated that he should be provided with 'mete and drinke and a servant to wait uppon hym as a gentilman haught to have'.[72]

Virtues such as truthfulness, courage and courtesy were also taken to be concomitants of gentility. Thus, in 1428, Robert Eland accused William Clopton in the Court of Chivalry of saying that he (Eland) had sealed forged documents 'encontre honeste & gentilesse d'armes'. William Paston in 1426–7 accused Walter Aslak of slandering him 'othyr wyse than othyr gentilnesse or trowthe wolde'.[73] Accusations of lying could produce, literally, a response of physical assault from insulted gentry.[74] In these cases, there seems to have been some element of ritual in the process: one of the best ways to insult a member of the gentry was to impugn his or her truthfulness in public, and the recipient was perhaps bound to defend his or her honour and gentility by either a physical or legal challenge.

The enormous range of performative behaviour and cultural participation by which the gentry defined themselves, under what seems to have been the increasingly intense scrutiny of their peers and subordinates, itself demands a book such as the present one to explicate; this chapter has only hinted at the range of 'gentle' preoccupations. One forum in particular for the lifelong performances of the gentry – the law – still requires major research attention, though space prohibits more than a passing mention here. Court sittings were public affairs, where the status and power of the participants were openly displayed and tested before county and national communities.[75] Particular legal roles – such as sitting as Justice of the Peace at Quarter Sessions – displayed honourable status to the county community. Even to be a mainpernor or surety for bail (one of the lesser legal roles) was evidently thought to be the province of 'gentlemen' in the narrower sense of the term.[76] Conversely, as Sir Edward Hastings well knew, to be a prisoner rather than a plaintiff, judge or even mainpernor, was to appear anything but gentle.

Whomever we might choose to include within a definition of 'the gentry' – all those who styled themselves 'gentle', or only those just below the nobility in status – it is clear that a much wider group of individuals could aspire to gentility.[77] Fifteenth-century gentility was constructed not on unchangeable status, based on indisputable social criteria, once gained and never lost. Instead, claimants to gentility were involved in a world of fluid social meanings, where their social status was continually being tested and negotiated by peers and neighbours in their community of honour. Within this community, to be a gentleman/woman was to be forever acting out a role: eating the right foods, playing the right sports, making the right kinds of bargains, relating in the right ways to one's tenants, building the right kinds of houses, and at death endowing the right monuments. Before a perpetual audience of superiors, peers and inferiors, they acted their parts in a world which, to them, was truly always a stage.

Notes

1 Norfolk Record Office (hereinafter NRO) Lestrange NA 52a fol. 10 (italics mine). Cf. *Complete Peerage*, II, pp. 358–9, under 'Hastings'.
2 See Morgan, 'Individual style'; Saul, *Knights and Esquires*, pp. 6–29; Carpenter, *Locality and Polity*, chs 3–4; Coss, 'Formation of the English gentry'.

3   Hyams, *King, Lords and Peasants*.

4   BL Cotton Cal D iii fol. 159 (modern numbering fol. 213).

5   *Paston Letters*, ed. Davis, I, pp. 64–5.

6   NA KB 27 694 m 1d.

7   Carpenter, *Locality and Polity*, pp. 39–42. Saul, 'Social status', esp. pp. 16–17.

8   *Ibid.*

9   *Paston Letters*, ed. Davis, I, pp. xli–xlii.

10 Pollard, 'Yeomanry of Robin Hood', esp. 52–5.

11 *Dictionary of Medieval Latin*, under 'generose', 'generositas', and 'generosus'.

12 *MED*, 'gentilman' (n.).

13 *Coventry Leet Book*, II, p. 413 (quoted in Morgan, 'Individual style', p. 16).

14 Carpenter, *Locality and Polity*, pp. 57–9; esp. Figure 4: Distribution of incomes in Warwickshire, 1436.

15 Cf. three references to 'gentleman born' or 'gentlemen of birth' in *MED* citations under 'gentleman' (1a), in *c.* 1400, *c.* 1410 and 1444.

16 Fortescue, 'In praise of the laws of England', in his *On the Laws and Governance of England*, p. 60.

17 NA C 47/6/1; e.g. William de Mauston, 'gentil home', Philip de Warenner 'de gentil sanc', Henry de Hoo, 'de gentil sanc' and Giles Albert 'gentil home'.

18 *Paston Letters*, ed. Davis, II, pp. 549 and 551–2.

19 Both the Pastons and the Townshends of Rainham, Norfolk, produced impressive, but fake, genealogies: *Paston Letters*, ed. Davis, I, pp. xl–xli; Moreton, *Townshends and their World*, p. 5.

20 Richmond, *Paston Family: The First Phase*, pp. 3–20.

21 John Russell's 'Boke of Nurture', in *Babees Book*, pp. 189–90.

22 Malory, *Works*, pp. 293–5.

23 Carpenter, *Locality and Polity*, pp. 89–90.

24 NRO PHI 461/8 Box 577 x 8.

25 NRO KIM 1/9/16, italics mine; my thanks to Paul Routledge, who drew my attention to this document. See *MED* 'gentri(e)' (n.), 2a.

26 For John Brethenham, NA KB 27 718 97r (Michaelmas 1440); for Geoffrey Walle, NA CP 40 684 m 402 d (1432), gentleman, defendant in plea of debt against Sir Henry Inglose; *ibid.* m 70d (1432) yeoman defendant in plea of debt against Nicholas Wichyngham, esquire; KB 27 694 m 55r (Michaelmas, 1434), husbandman, defendant in plea of trespass v. Sir Henry Inglose; KB 27 700 m 43r (Easter 1436), franklin, defendant in plea of trespass v. Thomas Sausere of Billockby; and KB 27 705 m 41r (Trinity 1437), franklin defendant in plea of trespass against Thomas Sausere.

27 Cf. NRO Hare 5982 Box 227 x 3; the last will of Simeon Fyncham 'gentilman' (1452) against NRO Hare 3895 Box 209 x 1 (1442) and Hare 1775 Box 192 x 5 (1450), all titling him 'esquire'.

28 Horrox, 'Urban gentry', pp. 32–3.

29 Kowaleski, 'Commercial dominance', pp. 195–6.

30 He is named 'esquire' in some lawsuits and in the Inquisition Post Mortem (NA CP40 726 mm 334r and 348r, Trinity term 1442, C139/121 no. 16, IPM of 20

October 1445), but as citizen and 'alderman of Norwich' in NA CP40 703 m 252d (Michaelmas 1436) and as esquire, citizen and alderman of Norwich in NA CP 40 726 m 334d, (Trinity 1442).

31 *Dictionary of Medieval Latin*, under 'genus'; NA KB 27 673 Rm 1r (Trinity term 1429), gives Elizabeth Lathe 'gentilwoman' of London; NRO Lestraunge MSS, P20 no. 7 (letter from Robert Osbern to 'Maister Calthorpe' referring to his marriage to 'the gentilwoman, your sistir' which took place in 1436); Anglicus, *Promptorium Parvulorum*, I, p. 190.

32 See, e.g., NA KB 27 615 m 22r, 34r and 62d (Hilary 1415), John Breton of Tamworth, Warwickshire, 'Gentilman' (twice) and John Turges of Petworth, Sussex 'Gentylman'; NRO DCN 45/12/34 (5 June 1428) William Norwych of Norwich 'gentylman'; NRO Case 16a, Mayors Court Book, security given to Nicolas Metyngham 'Gentilman' (12 November 1424); NA KB 9 938 m 83 (presentment from Hundred court, 1427, of John Belsham of Hadleigh, Suffolk, 'jantylman'; *MED* 'gentilman' (n.), 1b (1439 will of Thomas Lyndley of Yorkshire).

33 Saul, *Knights and Esquires*, pp. 6–29; Morgan, 'Individual style', p. 16; Carpenter, *Locality and Polity*, pp. 45 and 69.

34 *Statutes of the Realm*, II, p. 171 (1 Henry V c. 5).

35 In East Anglian cases in King's Bench, 1422–42, for example, 195 litigants were styled 'gentleman/woman', but only 33 were categorised 'franklin'; numbers derived from Maddern, *Violence and Social Order*, p. 40 (Table 2.5).

36 Of 839 East Anglian plaintiffs in King's Bench 1422–42 who recorded an occupation or style, 495 (59 per cent) were of gentry status or above, and less than 5 per cent were of non-gentle status (the remainder were almost entirely clerics or women); figures derived from Maddern, *Violence and Social Order*, p. 40.

37 *MED*, 'Gentleman' 1 b.

38 Cf. Morgan, 'Individual style', p. 21: 'the gentleman is there in landed society, developing a presence in the field of private enterprise as a 'farmer of leased out demesnes'.

39 Dyer, 'Changes in the size of peasant holdings', esp. pp. 282–3, 287–8 and 292–3; Campbell, 'Population pressure'; Fryde, *Peasants and Landlords*, esp. chs 5 and 8.

40 Fryde, *Peasants and Landlords*, pp. 79–80.

41 Bolton, 'World upside down', p. 53.

42 Carpenter, *Locality and Polity*, pp. 135–7; *ibid.*, a quote from p. 76.

43 Turner's *Men Raised from the Dust* surveys a slightly more prestigious group (men of the lower to middling knightly classes who achieved baronial status through royal service), but notes a general tendency from the time of Henry I onward for civil servants to rise to greatness from obscure origins.

44 *Paston Letters*, ed. Davis, I, p. 63.

45 Carpenter, *Locality and Polity*, pp. 44–5.

46 *Polychronicon Ranulphi Higden*, II, p. 169. Note that 'gentleman' has not yet appeared in this hierarchy.

47 *N-Town Plays*, fols 136r and 137d.

48 *Medieval English Lyrics*, ed. Davies, pp. 224–5 (no. 126).

49 *Statutes of the Realm*, I, pp. 379–80 (37 Edward III c. 6).

50 *Babees Book, passim.*

51 James, 'English politics', esp. pp. 22–7, quote from p. 22.

52 *Paston Letters*, ed. Davis, I, p. 155 (italics mine).

53 Malory, *Works*, pp. 295–8.

54 See note 59, below.

55 Carpenter, *Locality and Polity*, pp. 46–7.

56 Coss, 'Formation of the English gentry', p. 50.

57 *Paston Letters*, ed. Davis, I, p. 133.

58 *Paston Letters*, ed. Davis, I, p. 350; see Maddern, 'Honour among the Pastons' for a fuller analysis of the very varied forums of honour in fifteenth-century county society.

59 *Riverside Chaucer*, p. 710 (lines 2188–97). My thanks to Associate-Professor Andrew Lynch for directing me towards this reference.

60 *MED* 'Gentilman' (n.), 2.

61 *Paston Letters*, ed. Davis, I, p. 250.

62 Richmond, *Paston Family: The First Phase*, esp. chs 1–2.

63 Malory, *Works*, pp. 296–313.

64 *Babees Book*, p. 22.

65 *Polychronicon Ranulphi Higden*, pp. 158–60; the anonymous fifteenth-century translator has it that 'the childer of nowble men' speak French, and are imitated by 'churles … willenge to be like to theyme'.

66 *Paston Letters*, ed. Davis, I, pp. 150–3 (William Paston II's notes on French grammar) and p. 328 (John Paston II's 'boke of Freynsh price xv d.').

67 Malory, *Works*, p. 375 (the tale of Tristram).

68 *Statutes of the Realm*, II, p. 65.

69 *Paston Letters*, ed. Davis, I, p. 257. The death in question was Sir John Fastolf's, to whom the Pastons were not closely related, but from whom they were trying to claim an inheritance.

70 *MED*, 'gentilman' (n.), 1b.

71 *N-Town Plays*, fol. 12r.

72 *Descriptive Catalogue of Ancient Deeds*, III, p. 258, No. A 6056. My thanks to Dr Benjamin Thompson who brought this reference to my attention.

73 BL Harley MS 1178 fol. 44r; *Paston Letters*, ed. Davis, I, p. 11.

74 See, for example, the case of John Belsham, who tried to kill a man who called him a liar: NA JUST 3 220/2 m 165.

75 Maddern, *Violence and Social Order*, pp. 65–7.

76 In a random sample of 121 mainpernors in King's Bench cases in 1422–42, only six (5 per cent) were esquires, while seventy-eight (64.5 per cent) were held to be gentlemen (at least for the purposes of the occasion) and the remaining thirty-seven (30.5 per cent) comprised groups such as yeomen, husbandmen, merchants, artisans or clerics.

77 See Chapter 2 by Maurice Keen in the present volume, pp. 35–49, for further explication of the term 'gentry'.

2

Chivalry

Maurice Keen

O ne of the meanings of chivalry is a collective of knights (whence 'cavalry'): gentry stands as a collective for gentlemen. The word gentleman, in its social sense, is nowadays likely to evoke mentally one of two prototypes, both for most of us culled principally from the literature of the nineteenth and early twentieth centuries. One is the 'officer and gentleman' (until the eve of the Second World War, trainee officers at Sandhurst continued officially to be called 'gentleman cadets'). The other is the country gentleman (who very likely may have spent time in his youth as an officer and gentleman): the squire, living off his rents, busy about county business, probably a keen shot and a figure in the hunting field. Both prototypes have roots that can be traced back into the Middle Ages.

When one starts setting about to trace back those roots, a point of difference between the two models becomes quickly apparent, and one which looks as if it may be of significance. The image of the country gentleman, as sketched above, is essentially English, and so are the features that identify his medieval ancestor in regional landowning society, involvement as a man of property in the business of the distinctively English community of the county and the activities of the local magistracy. The quest for the medieval origins of the other image, of the officer and gentleman, leads back into the chivalric world where the knight was recognised as the type of Christian warrior aristocrat, a context that by contrast is not national but international. In a period of French cultural dominance, it was in French handbooks of knighthood and in romances in French that the ideals of medieval European chivalry found their most powerful expression. From the time of the Norman Conquest until well into the fourteenth century, Anglo-Norman French was the first language of the upper echelons of English aristocratic society: chivalric values with a strong northern French tinge were in consequence very much part of their cultural heritage.

Very comparable points of contrast, which can again be related to the two prototype images of the gentleman, are nicely reflected in two of the pen portraits traced by Chaucer in the General Prologue to his *Canterbury Tales*: those of his Knight and of his Franklin.[1] As a way into the subject of this present chapter, it is worth taking a closer look at the pictures he has drawn of them. The Knight first: he was a 'worthy' man, a veteran of the wars also and of the crusade which was the common enterprise of European chivalry; precious of honour, a 'parfit gentle knight'. Reading between Chaucer's lines (and *pace* Terry Jones),[2] it seems apparent that he was an aristocrat, a man of birth and heritage. Here is a clear lineal ancestor for the officer and gentleman. He had two companions with him. One was his son, the Squire, a young man, sharply and fashionably dressed, a good horseman and jouster who had already seen war service, courteous and skilled in the courtly arts, in dancing and singing and making verses of love – a 'parfit gentle knight' in the making (lines 79–100). The other was his yeoman, an archer, wise in woodcraft, a forester: the kind of man who, one guesses, could be equally useful to his master in his company at the wars and in the hunting field on his estate at home (lines 101–17).

The Franklin is a very different figure. The salient point that the General Prologue makes about him is his love of good living, that he was 'Epicurus' owene sone' (line 336). He was a fine judge of wine, and game in season was always at his board, for he was a great host; 'it snewed in his hous of mete and drynke' (line 345). But other details about him need to be noted too. His background is the countryside world of the English county. He was a landed man, with a keen eye for a good purchase: no wonder that he joined the pilgrim band in company with the man of law, that great 'purchasour' of land (line 318). He himself had served as a sheriff, and he was prominent as a justice of the peace: he had represented his shire in parliament 'ofte tyme'. In these respects he begins to look like the lineal ancestor of the country gentleman prototype. It does not look as if Chaucer intended him to be a man of gentle ancestry – that is not what the description 'franklin' implies[3] – but he was plainly seen as a man of authority nevertheless, a householder of substance and a squire in our sense of the word if not in fourteenth-century title.

There is a strong contrast in the tone of Chaucer's two pen-portraits. The Knight is presented as an almost ideal figure, embodying the virtues apposite to his chivalrous degree and calling: whereas in the portrait of the Franklin, Chaucer's gift for satire has been given free rein. But if one turns

from literary satire to prosopographical record, it becomes clear that the
two would not really have stood so very sharply apart in the society of the
age of Richard II. The outline of the career of Sir Richard Waldegrave,
born *c*. 1338 and later a king's knight to Richard II, will offer an illustration
of this point.[4] He came of a genteel landed family with estates in Northamptonshire and Lincolnshire, and his marriage to the widow of a Suffolk
knight brought him wealth in that county, which he enlarged by purchase.
He was a veteran of the French wars, and had been on crusade to the East:
like Chaucer's knight, he was at 'Satalye' and at 'Alisaundre ... when it was
wonne' – that is, when King Peter of Cyprus briefly took Alexandria in
1365. He was also notable as a jouster. Altogether, his martial career was a
distinguished one. There was another side to his story, however. As a
Suffolk landowner, he was on the commission of the peace for the county
from 1382 to 1397, and served on numerous local commissions. He also
represented the shire in parliament no fewer than twelve times, and in 1382
he was Speaker of the Commons. One side of his career would have
brought him into the company of men like Chaucer's Knight, the other into
the company of men like Chaucer's Franklin. One could put this in
another way. Chaucer has set his picture of the Knight, deliberately, in the
context of international chivalry; his picture of the Franklin is set in the
context of regional society and local government. As Waldegrave's career,
and indeed Chaucer's own too, both illustrate, these were in their day
overlapping worlds, not separate ones.

Chaucer himself, indeed, hints at a point on these same lines, in the
words spoken by the Franklin to the Squire between their two tales.[5] The
Franklin is portrayed as clearly impressed by the Squire's telling of his tale,
by his wit and eloquence, and by the tale's courtly and romantic matter. He
too, he explained, had a son, but he was a wastrel; if only he were more like
the Squire, and would mingle more with young men like him, that he
might 'lerne gentillesse aright' (line 694). The Franklin would rather that,
he declared, than that 'twenty pound worth lond' should fall into his lap.
What the Franklin aspired to for his son, that is to say, was the 'gentillesse'
that he perceived in the son of one born in a higher degree, for something
of his courtly manner and virtue, and his chivalrous sense of honour. The
rising man did not propound for his son a standard of his own (though that
reference to twenty pounds' worth of land indicates clearly enough what
sort of a standard was his own): he wished to see him look and live like a
knight's son, not like a bumpkin with too much money.

One of the problems that commentators on Chaucer regularly encounter with the Franklin is that his wealth, and the status of the local offices

that he had discharged, seem out of line with his title of degree. Historically, a 'franklin' seems most commonly to be intended to denote a substantial freeholder, someone closer to a yeoman than to a squire, and not the kind of man to make a JP or a sheriff. Nigel Saul has suggested a way out of this dilemma: that Chaucer probably had in mind when he pictured his Franklin one of that breed of solid freeholders who, in the aftermath of the Black Death, were advancing themselves in wealth and station through the shrewd lease and purchase of vacant holdings and parcels of demesne, so building themselves into substantial farmers and employers of labour, and working up into the local squirearchy.[6] Certainly it looks as if we should picture Chaucer's Franklin as a rising man, and that looks significant in the context of the matter in hand, the gentry and chivalry.

The fourteenth century saw what may be labelled a 'rise' of the sub-knightly gentry. Partly in consequence of the administrative pressures of the wars, and partly in consequence of the perceived decline in local order of the first three decades of the century, we find landed men of sub-knightly status, and of decidedly heterogeneous social origins, coming to play a steadily expanding role in local justice and administration. They began to serve on local commissions, in such offices as commissioners of array and collectors of subsidies, and later on the peace commissions: offices that in the past had been principally the preserve of the county knights. The development coincides with the visibly growing influence of the Commons in Parliament, and of the knights and substantial gentry who represented the shire communities there. Peter Coss, in his authoritative essays on the formation of the English gentry,[7] has pointed to other significant signs of a new dignity associated with the sub-knightly landowning estate, such as the recognition of the esquires as, like the knights, armigerous, and their extending use of armorial seals to authenticate deeds.

There are some problems of vocabulary here, it must be admitted. The word 'gentry' was not much in use, as a class designation, before the Tudor age, unlike the word 'gentleman' of which it became a collective: and that title embraced a very wide spectrum. A duke was as much a gentleman as a landed squire, and more so. 'Gentle' embraced in its implication all the aristocracy of blood, high and low. The kind of men who were gaining new prominence on the commissions of the peace and in local administration would, in the fourteenth century, have been described as esquires rather than as gentlemen; esquire was the addition that identified the sub-knightly genteel in such texts as the Statute of Apparel of 1363 and the graded poll tax grant of 1379.[8] The significant point, however, is that they were now accepted as among the *gentils*, and that thereby the range and number of persons and families accepted as such was greatly extended. By and large, it is hard not to accept that Coss's main thesis is absolutely right, that the fourteenth century was a vital period in the formation of the estate that historians have come to call the gentry, and that by the middle years of the century its identity and social significance can be discussed in terms of an established element in the social and political order.

It is feasible, in the context of the developments outlined above, to speak of a 'rise of the gentry' in the fourteenth century, but the word 'rise' needs to be used with some caution. There are no signs of the sub-knightly as a group fretting at barriers set in the way of their social and economic advancement by an older dominant elite and seeking to force their way forward (as some historians have argued was the case with the new gentry of the Elizabethan and early Stuart period). The force behind their 'rise' seems rather to have been their recognition by the old elite – the Crown, the lords and the greater knights – of the significance of the gentry's role and standing as comparable and complementary to their own, and a consequent willingness to admit them, in due measure, to a share in their privileges, and social esteem, and in the exercise of offices of authority, as junior partners as it were. The sub-knightly landowning gentry of the fourteenth century were not a new class: there had always been people like them about. What was new was their recognition as being of the gentility, a recognition visibly expressed in the extension to esquires – who were not knights and might not aspire to be such – of the right to coats of arms, the traditional chivalrous ensigns of lineage and of a family history of honourable service. Later, in the fifteenth century, this right was extended to those at the margin of esquire status, who came to be described as gentlemen, *tout court*, with no further addition of degree.[9]

Thus the gentry did not in a strict sense 'rise' as a class; it would be better to say that they 'arrived'. Individuals, and individual families, did, however, rise into the now extended spectrum of degrees of gentility, and it becomes pertinent to ask why and how they did so? What fitted them for admission into the hierarchy of gentlefolk? Saul may be right in picturing Chaucer's Franklin, in the poet's imagining, as one on the rise through good husbandry and making the most of the opportunities that the post-plague years offered. That, however, does not look as if it were the most common way forward into gentility. Mercantile success, perhaps combined with a genteel marriage, looks to have carried a good many more upward into gentility than skilful agriculture and acquisition did (usually in the second generation).[10]

The commonest road of all, though, was through service, which might be of many kinds: legal, administrative, in local office or a magnate household. In the fourteenth century it might above all have been military service, which was particularly prized by the king and the magnates, as well as the greater knights, and was a kind of service in which more men from the lesser landowning estate were likely to become involved, at one time or another in their lives, than any other.[11] The fact remains also that it was a form of service notably and explicitly recognised as an upward path. Sir Thomas Gray wrote in his *Scalacronica* of 'those young fellows who had hitherto been of no account', who at the wars had made themselves 'exceedingly rich, many of them beginning as archers, and then becoming knights, sometimes captains'.[12] Nicholas Upton, writing nearly a century later, had much the same to say: 'in these days we see openly how many poor men, labouring in the French wars, are become noble [i.e. genteel], one by prudence, another by valour, a third by endurance'; of whom many, he adds significantly, 'on their own authority have assumed coats of arms to be borne by themselves and their heirs'.[13] That no one tried to stop them is unsurprising: the valour, skill and endurance of the kind of men whom Gray and Upton wrote about was a key factor in the English triumphs in the French wars of the fourteenth and fifteenth centuries. There was good reason for prizing their service and for recognising its chivalrous, genteel quality.

Gray and Upton were clearly quite right in their perception of martial service as a common upward path into gentility. The examples are legion, and no doubt there are plenty more that are not known, or not yet researched. Sir Robert Knollys, the great English captain in Brittany, almost certainly began his career as an archer; Sir Hugh Browe, another captain, was the son of a yeoman; Thomas Maisterson of Cheshire, son of a Nantwich townsman, caught the eye of John of Gaunt on the Najera campaign and rose steadily thereafter in his service.[14] Sir Robert Salle, who was killed by the insurgents of 1381 on Mousehold Heath outside Norwich, had made himself rich on the ransoms of French prisoners, but he had started from small beginnings: 'we know who you are', Lister's rebel peasants told him, 'you are not a gentleman, but the son of a poor mason, just such as ourselves'.[15] Successful war service had carried Salle up to knighthood, and to be of 'great weight in this country' as a landowner. For it was in land and estates that the prudent among those who enriched themselves by war service principally invested their profits, as did the Cheshire soldiers Robert Knollys, John Norbury, John Merbury and David Craddock, whose careers Michael Bennett has illuminatingly researched;

and as did later and more famously Sir John Fastolf of Norfolk (though he started from rather more substantial beginnings than these others).[16] The contract of companionship in arms, struck between the two esquires John Winter and Nicholas Molyneux at the end of Henry V's reign, stipulated explicitly that their winnings of war should be pooled, and sent home to be invested in 'the purchase of manors'.[17] As they, and many others, clearly saw, the chivalrous business of war, Chaucer's Knight's calling, was also a way to establishing a secure niche for a successful soldier and his family in the local, landed world in which Chaucer's Franklin flourished.

The importance of gains of war in facilitating upward social mobility, first systematically studied by K. B. McFarlane, has been much discussed.[18] As Simon Walker and Bennett (among others) have forcefully argued, the personal contacts made by men at arms on war service could be at least as significant, and probably were more so.[19] In the context of chivalry, contact looks to have been important in another way too. For the fortunate individual, war service could be a road to wealth and social advancement: for the sub-knightly landed estate that contributed so substantially to hosts raised for war it was also, culturally, an educative experience, and collectively as well as individually. In the contracted martial companies of the fourteenth century, esquires of relatively humble and obscure local landed families rubbed shoulders as men at arms with knights and the sons and kin of old established knightly lines. As men at arms (as opposed to archers) they were expected to arm and mount themselves similarly with their social superiors, and to fight with the same weapons, mounted or on foot. The prime real distinction was in rates of pay, 2s. a day for a knight and 1s. for an esquire, and that left the latter still on the same footing as the son of a knight who had not yet taken up knighthood. As the companions and partners with the chivalrous knighthood in the chivalrous business of war, the culture and values of chivalry rubbed off naturally on the newcomers to recognised gentility, and was absorbed by them as theirs as well as the knights'.

Some of the visible indicators of this process of acculturation have already been mentioned, such as the recognition of the right of the esquire to coat armour: there are plenty more. 'Esquire', the word that came first to distinguish apart a segment among the crowd of sub-knightly freemen from others as being genteel, and so gave them a place in the stratified aristocratic hierarchy, was drawn from the martial vocabulary of chivalry. In the depositions of witnesses in cases brought before the fourteenth-century Court of Chivalry, there are constant references to what has been heard from 'the talk of old knights and esquires', the two being repeatedly grouped together.[20] The extracts from such talk, which the court's records note as commanding mutual interest, include shared memories of the wars, of high deeds done in them, of past tournaments, of local family history and of lines reputed to go back to companions of William the Conqueror, matter essentially chivalrous and genteel. There was clearly much talk too of heraldic arms, to which, as has been pointed out, the right of the esquire as well as of the knight had come to be recognised and established. At much the same time as this, we find esquires coming to be admitted to jousts and to tourneying, participation in which had formerly been reserved to the knighthood. When Richard II, by patent, received John Kingston into the 'estate of gentleman', and 'made him an esquire', granting him arms of *argent* charged with a *chapeau azure*, it was explicitly in order that he might take up the challenge to joust of a French *knight*.[21] When, in the fifteenth century, the Crown finally began, through the heralds, to take a regulatory interest in the right to arms, which marked out from others the sub-knightly genteel as well as knights, it was with the national significance of their chivalrous, military service in mind. The heralds in their marches were to inquire into and have knowledge of the 'cognisances' of 'all estates noble and gentle' and to know the names 'of those who ought to bear coats of arms in the service of the king our sovereign lord'.[22] The military experience of the fourteenth century had cemented a mental equation of chivalry and *gentillesse*, which now included the esquires, and had anchored it firmly in the mind-set both of the gentry themselves and of their superior patrons.

Amid the exigencies of the major wars which beset England from the end of the thirteenth to the middle of the fifteenth century, it is not surprising that developments should have worked out this way. Nor is it surprising that the process of acculturation of the gentry to chivalry should have had an impact far wider than the circle (itself not a narrow one) of those among the sub-knightly who had actually seen war service. English military triumphs and reverses were the chief focus of interest in news filtering home from abroad; the war was the focus of the prayers that were ordered in churches for the king and his hosts overseas: it was the justification for the taxes that his people were being asked, rather regularly, to pay. It was a venture in which the leaders of both national and local society were visibly personally involved. More than any other factor, except perhaps parliamentary service in which comparatively very few were involved, it nourished among the gentry themselves, as well as with the Crown, a sense of their identity as an estate with a part to play in national as well as local affairs. It was a role, moreover, that was gratifyingly assimilated to the traditional elite role of their superiors, the lords and the greater knights.

Gentlemen of the fourteenth century could find guides to the manners and values associated with that traditional role through their reading as well as from martial contact and experience. They belonged to an estate now substantially literate (in English if not in Latin). Romances in English (many of them based on earlier Anglo-Norman poems) made accessible to the fourteenth-century gentry literary models of knighthood in the French courtly and chivalrous tradition. Such pieces as *Ipomydon*, *Arthur and Merlin*, *Floris and Blancheflour* and *Havelok*, and the masterpieces of the alliterative revival, nourished their awoken interest in chivalry, and served as instructors in *gentillesse*, in what was expected of those among the orders of the genteel.[23] The later (fifteenth-century) romance of *The Squire of Low Degree* offers a hint of how this sort of material could work on the gentry imagination.[24] It is the story of a poor squire at the court of Hungary who, by his fidelity and his deeds of chivalry in Tuscany, Lombardy and the eastern Mediterranean (the same region where Chaucer's Knight distinguished himself fighting against the infidel), ultimately proved himself worthy of a coat of arms, of knighthood, and of the hand of the king's daughter, whom as a squire he had worshipped from afar.

War, the demands of war, and a vernacular literature that romanticised the well-born warrior all played their part in shaping both the cultural vocabulary and the social self-perception of the gentry in the formative period of their emergence as an identifiable estate. Wars, however, do not go on forever. Between 1390 and 1415 there was a long lull in active Anglo-French hostilities, general truces being regularly renewed. When in Henry V's reign fighting began again in earnest, gentlemen who went to serve abroad tended to spend longer periods overseas than their fourteenth-century forebears, and their ties with their native English regional societies were consequently loosened. Finally, after the military collapse in France, in Normandy in 1450 and in Gascony in 1453, overseas military service ceased to be a major option for the ambitious and socially aspiring Englishman.

The significance of this changing pattern of experience is apparent if we turn back to the issue of upward social mobility, and the kinds of service that could carry men forward into gentility, among which war service was so prominent in the age of Edward III and the Black Prince. In the first half of the fifteenth century we can still trace plenty of stories of individuals who were doing well for themselves, some of them notably well, through martial service. Far more striking as roads to social advancement in this age, however, were civilian services, especially those associated with the

43

law. The great family and individual success stories of the fifteenth century are most often those of the judges and sergeants, the Fortescues, Pastons, Fairfaxes and Kebells, rather than of martial men. William Worcester in the 1450s saw already the way things were going, and lamented it:

> now of late daies ... many one that ben descendid of noble bloode and borne to armis, as knightis sonnes, esquiers, and other of gentill bloode, set hem silfe to singuler practise ... as to lerne the practique of law or custom of lande, or of civil matier, and so wastyn theire tyme in suche nedelesse besinesse as to occupie courtis halding, to kepe and bere out a proud countenaunce at sessions and shiris halding ... And who can be a reuler and put hym forthe in such matiers, he is, as the world goithe now, among all astatis more set of than he that hathe despendid xxx or xl yers of his daies in gret jubardies in your conquestis and werris.[25]

Worcester was clear-sighted: among magnates and with the Crown, the services of men with a knowledge of the law, and of such civil matter as accountancy and estate management, were coming to be ever more highly prized, and the skills such men possessed were becoming the surest roads to advancement.

Iconographic evidence, such as that of the armed figure drawings of Nevilles, Montagus and Monthermers in *Wrythe's Garter Book*, or of Richard Beauchamp's feats at joust and in the heat of battle in the *Warwick Pageants*, testify to the enduring hold, in the later fifteenth century, of traditional chivalrous culture among the higher aristocracy.[26] The question that must now be asked therefore is this: do the developments that Worcester so nicely pin-pointed suggest a different story for the gentry? Are there signs of the forging of a specifically 'gentry' set of cultural values, distinguishable from those of the higher aristocracy and of traditional chivalry, and related to a life-pattern typically closer to that of Chaucer's Franklin than to that of his Knight?

There are certainly pointers in this direction. Sir John Fortescue clearly and explicitly deemed the law a fitting profession for a gentleman.[27] Rosemary Horrox has drawn attention to the variety of the kinds of civilian service that were deemed honourable in the eyes of fifteenth-century gentlemen.[28] Robin Storey has pointed to the appearance on the scene of a new figure, the gentleman bureaucrat.[29] Philippa Maddern, on the basis of close reading of the *Paston Letters*, has detected signs of the development among the provincial gentry of a distinctive and non-martial concept of honour, focusing on faithful service, loyalty to one's word and one's friends, on 'livelihood' and the ability to pay one's way, and on reputation – on being well spoken of among one's social equals in one's own country.[30] There is nothing strictly at odds with chivalry here, but there is nothing strictly chivalrous either. The circumstances to which these values that she finds in the letters relate are not those of martial chivalry, but of local genteel coexistence.

Whether one accepts this sort of evidence as indicative of an identifiable gentry culture drawing away from the chivalrous mould, which had been such a powerful influence in the formative fourteenth-century period, may depend on how one is using the word culture. If one uses it in a broad, anthropological sense, in terms of patterns of behaviour and style underpinning a distinguishable manner of living, then the answer is probably yes. If one is using it in a narrower way, and concentrating on the mental rather than the social aspects of living, and on ideas and ideology, then the answer is much less clear, and may be no. As that shrewd businessman William Caxton, Sir Thomas Malory's publisher, perceived, the gentry's interest in chivalry, in King Arthur's knights, and the courtly example that they gave, was as sharp as ever in his time: and they wanted to hear of them on mettlesome steeds and in full armour, performing prodigies in battle and on the tournament field.[31] Caxton was also the publisher of translations into English of Christine de Pisan's *Book of Fayttes of Armes and of Chyvalrye* and of Ramon Lull's *Book of the Ordre of Chyvalry*. Other printings of his included English versions of the *Romance of Troy*, of *Godefroy of Bologne*, of the *Four Sons of Aymon* and of *Blanchardyn and Eglantine*. Chivalrous romance was, essentially, the only brand of secular, creative and image projecting literature that the gentry knew, and they clearly liked it: and they liked the heroes to be knights, chivalrous men. Their taste in history (which they distinguished from romance less sharply than we would do) was similar: when Lord Berners brought out his translation of Froissart in the early sixteenth century it was an immediate success.[32] Chivalrous material, again, was just the kind of matter that readily caught the eye of genteel compilers of commonplace books. The Paston family's traditions were legal, but Sir John Paston's *Grete Boke* is a marvellous repertory of descriptions of jousts and challenges, ordinances for a host in the field, accounts of the manner of making knights and suchlike chivalrous matter.[33]

The gentry's interest in the martial insignia of heraldry was notably avid. William Paston, Sir John's uncle, put together his own book of arms, of shields illustrating the descents in blood that had come into the family since its first ancestor (apocryphal of course) had crossed from Normandy in the eleventh century.[34] Here, gentry pride in pedigree and coat armour, and the quest for ancestors who had come with the Conqueror, or had been on crusade with King Richard, or had distinguished themselves in the French wars, mirrored the attitudes of the higher aristocracy – though in the gentry case the ancestors and their martial deeds were much more likely to be fictional. There was a good deal of plain snobbery here, no doubt: what Lawrence Stone has called the cultivation of genealogy 'by the older gentry to reassure themselves of their innate superiority … by the new gentry in an effort to clothe their social nakednesse'.[35] In the world of heraldry, however, it was impossible to get away entirely from the chivalrous mythology in which the whole subject was steeped. Heraldic treatises and collections (often excerpted into commonplace collections) were careful to explain how arms first came into use among the heroes of the Trojan war as a means of distinguishing one from another in the battlefield;[36] how that remained their basic purpose; and how a gentleman's coat armour showed that he was a man at arms, since a man is not called gentle on account of his riches or his wisdom but solely on account of his warlike prowess in arms.[37]

Gentlemen's effigies, on their tombs and brasses, demonstrate how well the lessons to be drawn from this kind of teaching went home. Regardless of whether they had ever been involved in martial business, gentlemen liked to be shown in armour on their tombs or brasses, and to have escutcheons of their arms displayed beside them. Once again here, in sepulchral fashions, the taste of the gentry mirrored (on a less lavish scale) that of the higher aristocracy. Long after the ending of the Anglo-French wars, as Christine Carpenter has nicely put it, 'landowners as a body, whether knighted or not, continued to see themselves as the repository of the knightly virtues … military prowess, even if no longer indicated by knightly rank, remained the spiritual *raison d'être* of the landed class.'[38]

Carpenter wrote this passage as a reservation on her main thesis, that territoriality – landowning and manorial lordship – together with office holding were principal defining and formative influences in the self-identification of the late medieval gentry. Coss, focusing on the earlier, fourteenth-century period is of much the same view.[39] Territoriality and office holding are very close, since a stake in the land was a *sine qua non* for advancement to such offices as sheriff or justice of the peace. Around these sorts of preoccupations and qualifications one can clearly argue for the development of a gentry culture that is distinguishable from that of the higher aristocracy. In the narrower mental and ideological sense of the word culture, it seems harder to draw a distinction, because the culture of the gentry in that sense was so largely derivative, certainly – and perhaps particularly – in the matter of chivalry. Absorbed into the estate of gentility by recognition, given the hand up, as it were, rather than thrusting themselves forward, the sub-knightly among the gentry absorbed with their new-found social dignity the traditional culture and values of the old chivalrous landowning elite. The hold which that traditional culture established in the gentry mentality proved very powerful, as their literacy tastes, their funerary fashions, their pride in pedigree and in hereditary coat armour all attest. Long after the great foreign wars that had helped to raise them into the gentility had ceased, they continued to reckon themselves part of 'the chivalry', the word Edmund Dudley was still using in Henry VII's reign to distinguish the genteel and dominant collectively from the 'commonalty'.[40] As A. B. Ferguson has nicely put it, 'accepted values [tend] to change more slowly than the society that ultimately conditions them'.[41]

Acculturation must be the keynote in any assessment of the place of chivalry in the culture of the gentry in the late Middle Ages. If Chaucer's Franklin had founded a gentry lineage, as all that we are told of him suggests he was well placed to do, then it seems likely that the wish he expressed in his *Wordes* to the Squire would have been fulfilled. Through association with social peers of longer and more martial ancestry, the chivalrous *gentillesse* of the squire would have rubbed off, if not yet fully on the Franklin's wastrel son, then pretty certainly on his grandson in the next generation. By his time or his son's, the family might very probably have 'discovered' an ancestor from before the Franklin's time, who had been at Falkirk, say, or at Crécy, or even perhaps with Chaucer's Knight at the siege of Algeciras. A descendant of Chaucer's Franklin would probably have sent his son to be educated in the Inns of Court, rather than in a noble household to be brought up to the use of arms, as William Worcester would have wished; but in the traditional threefold ordering of society, those who pray, those who fight and those who labour, he would have instinctively placed himself and his offspring in the second, the chivalrous estate. When in Henry VIII's reign Archbishop Cranmer put it to his colleagues on a commission that 'it was through the benefit of lernyng and other civil knowledge [that] for the moste parte all gentils ascend to their estate', they did not agree; 'for the most part' they retorted 'the nobilitie came up by feat of arms and martial acts'.[42] The conscious sense that chivalry was 'the spiritual *raison d'être* of the landed class' was one that died very hard; it retained its central place in the mental culture of the gentry to the end of the Middle Ages, and well beyond.

Notes

1 'General Prologue' to *The Canterbury Tales*, in *Riverside Chaucer*, pp. 24, 28–9 (lines 43–78 and 331–60).

2 Jones, *Chaucer's Knight*: I cannot accept this interpretation of the description of the Knight.

3 Saul, 'Status of Chaucer's Franklin', an article to which I am greatly indebted. Saul's identification of the status of a franklin seems historically surer than that of H. Specht, who argues for a more elevated status in his *Chaucer's Franklin*.

4 Roskell *et al.* (eds), *House of Commons 1386–1421*, IV, pp. 735–9.

5 *Riverside Chaucer*, p. 177 (lines 673–94).

6 Saul, 'Status of Chaucer's Franklin', pp. 22–3.

7 Coss, 'Formation of the English gentry' and 'Esquires and the origins'.

8 Stat. 37 Ed. III, cc. 8–15; *Rotuli Parliamentorum*, III, pp. 57–8.

9 See further Keen, *Origins of the English Gentleman*, chs 5 and 7, and Sitwell, 'English gentleman'.

10 See Thrupp, *Merchant Class*, pp. 279–87.

11 On the numerical scale of the involvement of esquires and gentlemen in military service generally in the fourteenth century, see Ayton, 'Knights, esquires and military service', p. 83.

12 Gray, *Scalacronica*, p. 134.

13 Upton, *De Studio Militari*, pp. 257–8.

14 Bennett, *Community, Class and Careerism*, pp. 173, 182.

15 Froissart, *Oeuvres*, p. 408.

16 Bennett, *Community, Class and Careerism*, pp. 187–9; McFarlane, 'Investment of Sir John Fastolf's profits'.

17 McFarlane, 'Business partnership'.

18 McFarlane, *Nobility of Later Medieval England*, pp. 19–40: see also his two articles cited above, notes 16 and 17.

19 Walker, *Lancastrian Affinity*, pp. 19–40; Bennett, *Community, Class and Careerism*, pp. 184–91.

20 Keen, *Origins of the English Gentleman*, pp. 50–1, 64.

21 Wagner, *Heralds and Heraldry*, pp. 66, 123.

22 I quote from the 'Ordinances of Thomas Duke of Clarence, for the government of the Office of Arms', printed by Wagner, *Heralds and Heraldry*, pp. 136–8.

23 What is said here owes a substantial debt to Peter Coss's illuminating article, 'Aspects of cultural diffusion'.

24 The text is printed in *Middle English Verse Romances*, ed. Sands, pp. 249–78.

25 *Boke of Noblesse*, p. 77. The *Boke* is dedicated to Edward IV, but was almost certainly drafted by Worcester for Henry VI; see McFarlane, 'William Worcester', p. 210.

26 The figures of Monthermers, Montagus and Nevilles are reproduced in Wagner *et al.* (eds), *Medieval Pageant*, plates 56–75; the drawings of Richard Beauchamp are in Dillon and Hope (eds), *Pageant of the Birth*.

27 Fortescue, *De Laudibus Legum Anglie*, pp. 116–19.

28　Horrox, 'Service'.

29　Storey, 'Gentleman bureaucrats'.

30　Maddern, 'Honour among the Pastons'.

31　See further Ferguson, *Indian Summer*, pp. 34–58.

32　*Ibid.*, pp. 69–72.

33　See Lester, *Sir John Paston's* Grete Boke, pp. 9–12.

34　Norfolk Record Office, Rye MS 38.

35　Stone, *Crisis of the Aristocracy*, p. 23.

36　See e.g. the *Tretys of Armes* printed by Keiser, '*Tretys of Armes*: a revision'.

37　Quoted from Strangway's Book, BL Harley MS 2259, fol. 135vo.

38　Carpenter, *Locality and Polity*, p. 49.

39　Carpenter, *Locality and Polity*, ch. 3; Coss, 'Formation of the English gentry'.

40　Dudley, *Tree of Commonwealth*, p. 44.

41　Ferguson, *Indian Summer*, p. xiii.

42　Cranmer, *Miscellaneous Writings*, p. 398.

3

Politics

Peter Fleming

From Chaucer's representations of the Knight and the Squire in the General Prologue one might deduce that domestic politics and administration formed no part of the gentry's existence. The Knight spends his time, when not on pilgrimage, fighting for Christendom in far-flung places; his son has also seen military service abroad, but pursues 'courtly love' with at least equal gusto.[1] To the historian of later medieval England, these descriptions might evoke another image, that of Geoffrey Chaucer, esquire, giving a knowing wink to his gentle audience: 'this may be how we wish to see ourselves, but we know only too well that this is not how things really are'. The other pilgrim with at least pretensions to gentility is the Franklin. Most likely a man of this status in the later fourteenth century would have occupied a position between the free but ungentle yeomanry and the esquires; a generation or two later, he would have been described as a gentleman, the lowest rank of the gentry. While most memorable for his showers of 'fissh and flessh', of 'mete and drynke', we also read that 'An housholdere, and that a greet, was he', 'At sessiouns ther was he lord and sire; / Ful ofte tyme he was knyght of the shire', and that 'A shirreve hadde he been'.[2] While the chivalrous were away serving Venus and Mars, were the shires left to the likes of this well-padded epicure?

In the middle of the fifteenth century, William Worcester complained that Mars had lost out to the delights, not of Venus or Epicurus, but of litigation and local government. Knights nowadays, he wrote, spend too little time in harness: they would rather fight opponents in the law courts than on the battlefield, and they are immersed in the administration of their estates and their counties.[3] Some years later, the ideal nobleman in *Gentleness and Nobility* presents a genealogy that balances chivalry and civil administration:

> Myn auncestours also have ever be
> Lordys, knyghtes, and in grete auctoryte,
> Capteyns in the warr and governers,
> And also in tyme of pease gret rulers[4]

Could the later medieval gentry be characterised as 'governers' and 'gret rulers'? How and why were they involved in government and politics, local and national? Before these questions can be answered, we need to know something about the structures of local administration. While the magnates strutted across the national stage, the interests of all but the greatest of the gentry were confined to the localities. For them, it was the county that provided the arena for their public lives.[5]

The king's chief officers in the counties were the sheriffs. Their duties were extensive: they normally presided over the county court; they supported the royal justices when they held court in the shire; they were keepers of the county gaol and were expected to serve royal writs. They oversaw elections to parliament and the appointment of lesser officials. They could be ordered to raise troops, and the posse, a group of men from the county to aid in the arrest of suspected wrongdoers. Sheriffs were appointed by the Crown. Since 1371 they were supposed to have lands in the county for which they acted yielding at least £20 per annum, and to be resident in the shire. Their period of office was limited to one year.[6] Sheriffs had little official remuneration for their work, but there were other compensations. For example, the composition of juries could be vital to the outcome of a case, and the sheriffs' role in empanelling jurors meant that litigants often found their co-operation worth buying.[7] The Franklin would have made a most unusual 'shirreve'. The shrievalty was customarily the preserve of knights and esquires; those few lesser men who held this office were probably there through magnate influence.[8]

That the Franklin had been 'lord and sire' at the 'sessiouns' means that he was also a justice of the peace. This office emerged in the mid-fourteenth century. By the beginning of the following century, JPs had rights of arrest and trial, and jurisdiction over a wide range of crimes, misdemeanours and economic regulation. The justices held sessions four times a year. The transfer of the sheriff's judicial powers to the JPs in 1461 set the seal on the latter's gradual ascendancy. After 1414 JPs were supposed to be resident in their shire, and in 1439/40 a property qualification was introduced of £20 per year landed income, but the former condition at least was sometimes disregarded. The typical fifteenth-century bench of JPs was composed of magnates and prelates, usually with some connection with the county, a few judges from the central courts, but usually outnumbering these were local gentry. While the social composition of the bench could vary according to place and time, the emphasis among the gentry members was very much on the knights and esquires. Attendance at quarter sessions could be infrequent; it was usually those of lesser social significance, particularly lawyers and gentlemen with a legal background, who most regularly attended. For the greater gentry the status and influence they derived from being a JP was normally of more importance than participation at the sessions.[9]

Despite frequent requests from the commons in parliament for control of the JPs to be vested in the county gentry, appointments continued to be made by the king, who maintained his influence over the county benches through dependable judges, magnates or senior gentry. While the composition of the bench could be politically sensitive at times of national crisis, purges of JPs or the insertion of royal placemen were rare, which suggests either that Crown interference in the face of local resistance was impractical or, perhaps more likely, that most of the gentry were willing to acquiesce with whoever was in power.[10]

The Franklin had also been 'knight of the shire', or MP. Parliament was not part of the county administration, but parliamentary representation was an important part of the gentry's role. For the county, parliament was where the opinion of the local leaders could be heard. For the Crown, parliament was where its wishes could be publicised, taxation agreed and statutes enacted. Parliament was thus a two-way valve; it was also the possession of the king, for him to summon and dismiss as he wished. Representatives of the counties – knights of the shires – and of the leading towns – burgesses – were regularly elected to parliament after 1325, forming the parliamentary 'commons'. While the king doubtless found these representatives a useful channel of communication, the primary motive in allowing their participation was financial. The demands of war meant that a comprehensive system of taxation was essential, and this could only work with the assent of the local elites.[11]

Most counties returned two MPs, elected in the county court with the sheriff as the returning officer. From 1429/30 the franchise was restricted to free holders with a yearly income of at least 40s., which meant that many below gentry status had at least a theoretical say in elections. Who was allowed to take part in elections before this date is unclear. In most cases the county's representation was decided by the local elite before election-day, so that the process in county court was one of affirmation rather than selection. This was not necessarily seen as corrupt, and a contested election would have been regarded as indicating the breakdown of local consensus.[12]

As a knight of the shire, Chaucer's Franklin would again have found himself in exalted company. While most knights of the shire were not actually knights, the medieval commons nonetheless became an increasingly exclusive club. This trend was acknowledged and reinforced by legislation of 1445, which imposed a property qualification of £40 per annum on candidates (the level of income theoretically required of a knight), and barred anyone of non-gentle status from standing.[13]

There was beginning to appear a 'career path' that the successful local office-holder could expect to follow. In the early fifteenth century few Nottinghamshire MPs had experience of high county office when they were first elected, but most became JPs or sheriffs soon after their first parliament, or even during it.[14] Perhaps these novice MPs were able to attract the Crown's attention, to be remembered when appointments were made; or maybe they used their positions to lobby for preferment. High county office was increasingly the preserve of the greater gentry, a trend reinforced by the introduction of property qualifications. Men of greater substance were thought more likely to act independently of the magnates: the humbler sort would be assumed to be their creatures.[15] Like the Franklin, one who hoped for high county office would need to be 'An housholdere, and that a greet'. Such offices became the preserve of a tightening circle of substantial landowners. Whether as MPs, JPs or sheriffs, the same names tend to appear. The administration of fourteenth-century Gloucestershire, for example, was in the hands of never more than eighteen men at any given time. In fifteenth-century Leicestershire, only seven families dominated county administration.[16] Within the gentry an inner circle emerged of men who were the 'workhorses' of their county: but workhorses who could find ample rewards for their labours, and who jealously guarded their burdens.

County office was not always sought simply for the legitimate rewards it could bring. Complaints against corrupt officials were common. We need not believe all of them: in any age, bureaucrats, judges and tax collectors rarely become popular heroes. However, there are plenty of instances where the balance of probability weighs against a notorious county official. One example must serve for many. The accusations made against John de Oxenford in 1341 were that as sheriff he had confiscated corn and cattle to supply the king's armies in Scotland, but had sold them on for his own profit, and that he had taken bribes, and extorted money, threatening his victims with a spell in the county gaol if they did not pay up. He also abused his position as sheriff by returning himself four times as MP. The county of which this notorious man was sheriff was Nottinghamshire, and it has been suggested that John de Oxenford was the real-life inspiration for Robin Hood's infamous adversary.[17]

The yeomen and lesser gentry who formed the most likely audience for the Robin Hood ballads would doubtless have savoured another outlaw tale, *The Tale of Gamelyn*, composed in the later fourteenth century.[18] Gamelyn is the youngest son of a knight, cheated out of his inheritance by his eldest brother John. Gamelyn is prevented from securing his rights by the sheriff – who is in cahoots with evil brother John – and pursued by the posse, takes to the woods, where he becomes the leader of a band of outlaws. Meanwhile, John becomes sheriff, and Gamelyn is outlawed. Gamelyn appears before a corrupt judge and a jury bribed by John, who wishes to see his brother hang. But Gamelyn has brought his outlaws with him, and they surround the courthouse. He assaults the judge and then organises a kangaroo court – with his fellow outlaws as jurymen – to try his brother, the judge and the original jurors. They are found guilty and all of them hang. The conclusion to this tale of mayhem is, to modern sensibilities, remarkable: Gamelyn is pardoned by the king, and he and his followers are appointed to high office in the county. Even more remarkable is that broad parallels can be found in the records for all but one of these outrages: the massacre of an entire jury seems to be the one exception, although intimidation of juries was common.[19] Law and office were both prone to abuse, and the gentry were often the worst culprits. The same people could appear either side of the bar, present on one occasion as accused, on the other as judge. Contemporaries recognised this, but we should not assume that they shared our attitudes. The 'persuasion' of local officers through favours, and the influencing of jurors, known as 'maintenance', were sometimes regarded with insouciance. Resort to law was rarely expected to produce definitive solutions, but was one among several tactics. These could include violence, but often as a last resort, and usually accompanied by attempts to negotiate.[20]

To return to Chaucer's Knight, Squire and Franklin: making war, making love and making a good dinner were clearly not how most of the gentry spent most of their time. These pursuits were important nonetheless: the cultural dimension of the first – chivalry – is explored elsewhere in this volume; the second, seen in unromantic terms as the pursuit of heiresses, was for some a necessary preoccupation; the last, manifested as *largesse*, was a key characteristic of nobility, to be demonstrated to the fullest extent possible. To prowess, courtesy and largess – all, in their different ways, predicated on landed wealth – must be added service. As the author of *Gentleness and Nobility* acknowledged, and as Worcester bemoaned, administrative service was another defining characteristic of the gentry.

Service, to lord and king, could take a gentleman much further afield than his own county. Service in the king's wars, either on campaign or as part of a castle garrison, gave many of the gentry experience of England's Celtic neighbours and, of course, France. Those following lords with ambitions to win fame and fortune elsewhere in Europe, such as John of Gaunt or Henry Bolingbroke, might have found themselves in places every bit as exotic as those through which Chaucer's Knight blazed his trail, as might those who took part in diplomatic missions. Throughout the later Middle Ages, the king of England was also lord of some continental possessions, even if after 1453 these constituted nothing more than Calais and its immediate environs. Before England's military collapse, there were ample opportunities for military and administrative service, as well as landholding, in Gascony and, following Henry V's conquests, Normandy. To take two examples among many, the Kentish knight Sir John Scott was marshal of Calais under William, Lord Hastings in the 1470s, and Sir John Paston, of the famous Norfolk family, was in Scott's retinue. In 1477 another Kentishman, John Pympe esquire, sent a poem to his friend Paston, in which he expressed his fear that:

> Fresh amorouse sihtys of cuntreys ferre and straunge
> Have all fordoone your old affeccioun

From the other side of the Channel, even Calais, it seems, appeared to offer exotic pleasures.[21]

Office-holding provided the framework within which the greater gentry led their public lives. We need to penetrate beyond these surface features to understand what was really going on in the shires. Administration provides the muscle and bone; politics provide the life-blood.

The politics of later medieval England have acquired an unsavoury reputation: this was an age of king-killers, after all. This was also the age most strongly associated with 'bastard feudalism', defined by Professor Hicks as 'the set of relationships with their social inferiors that provided the English aristocracy with the manpower they required.'[22] Manpower could take the form of fighting men, but it could also include household servants, counsellors, lawyers, friends and well-wishers. To those Victorians who invented and first popularised the phrase, 'bastard feudalism' summed up a world of short-lived loyalties based on calculations of immediate self-interest, of shifting alliances and of bloodthirsty barons backed by huge private armies. Modern historians take a different view. For one thing, it has not been demonstrated that relationships based on indentures and retaining were inherently more unstable or likely to breed violence than what had gone before. Earlier estimates of the size and ubiquity of private armies were based largely on extrapolations from the thoroughly exceptional retinues of John of Gaunt, duke of Lancaster, in the late fourteenth century, and William, Lord Hastings in the later fifteenth. Virtually no other magnate could afford to retain on this scale.[23]

Lordship lay at the core of this society, but it was not confined to secular magnates. The Church held vast estates, and the major religious houses needed servants, estate officials, lawyers and well-wishers, creating their own 'affinities' within which the gentry found employment. While prelates were not usually as active in national politics as lay magnates, they could still be important locally.[24]

While counties such as Warwickshire, Devon, Gloucestershire, Norfolk or Lancashire were dominated by one or more magnate families, others, including Kent, Derbyshire, Leicestershire and Nottinghamshire, appear to have been run largely by networks of their greater gentry.[25] Historians tend to make neat distinctions between vertical and horizontal communities, the former being gentry networks that cohered as magnate affinities, and the latter those that existed between gentry families in areas free of magnate domination. This is slightly misleading, since the two cannot always be clearly distinguished in practice, and horizontal relationships were still intensely hierarchical. In counties where there was no locally dominant magnate, the leading gentry families exercised their own lordship, acting as patrons to their clienteles of lesser gentry, as channels of communication between locality and centre, and as chief agents of the Crown.[26] The management of such counties was a process of negotiation, not only with the Crown, but also with those lords – lay and ecclesiastical – who had interests in the region. Every county had some land or office held by a magnate, each a potential bridgehead for the extension of an ambitious lord's power. Magnate interests in a given county fluctuated in accord with family alliances, royal favour and the abilities and character of individual lords. However, the magnates' first priority was reasonably efficient estate administration, and while the local gentry supplied estate officials and legal counsel, such services did not necessarily imply close political connections; nor were they inevitably used to influence county affairs. In many cases, the greater gentry were perfectly capable of maintaining their autonomy.[27] Generally speaking, a lord's domination of a county depended on a substantial and secure territorial base and a local tradition of service to his family. Even the greatest magnates faced problems if they tried to assert themselves in areas with which they had little previous connection. John of Gaunt, duke of Lancaster, was regarded as an interloper by the gentry of Sussex, who resisted his attempts to impose his rule.[28]

Sometimes the king was the leader of a gentry affinity. Richard II, as earl of Chester, created a powerful affinity among the Cheshire gentry. The Cheshire connection showed conspicuous loyalty to Richard. A number of Cheshire gentry made brilliant careers in Richard's service, including Sir John Stanley, whose descendants entered the peerage and who himself became king: albeit of the Isle of Man. Sir John was granted the lordship of Man by Henry IV, and the culmination of his career came under the Lancastrians. That he was not permanently discomforted by the usurpation of 1399 illustrates that the leading gentry were usually too useful to be jettisoned by a new dynasty, even if they had been closely associated with the previous regime. Only the most die-hard, maladroit or unlucky suffered ruination.[29]

The king could extend his influence within a county through his household and immediate family. Kent is a case in point. In the 1420s and 1430s Humphrey, duke of Gloucester, Henry VI's brother, exerted considerable influence over the county as warden of the Cinque Ports. In 1447, after his disgrace and death, this position was taken by the Sussex knight James Fiennes, freshly ennobled as Lord Saye and Sele, and a leading member of the court faction. Saye and Sele, according to later allegations, suborned Kentish sheriffs, JPs and other officials to create a virtual mafia within the county. Sir John Scott and Sir John Fogge dominated Kentish politics during their time as, respectively, controller and treasurer of Edward IV's household. Each of these local leaders had his own gentry networks.[30] After 1399, kings used the duchy of Lancaster to place dependable members of the gentry in positions of local authority. The use of Duchy offices was crucial in the extension of the influence of William, Lord Hastings into the Midlands acting, in effect, as Edward IV's regional governor.[31]

The greater gentry were the key to control of the shires. Through them and their networks kings and magnates could extend their power far beyond their own circle of retainers. These leading gentry demanded tangible benefits in return. They wanted material rewards: fees, grants of office, lands and their share of the perquisites of local governance. They required protection and support in their own affairs. The lord was expected to keep order and resolve conflicts within his affinity. The affinity might also provide a matrix for marriage alliances.[32]

Probably more important, however, was stability. Landowners wanted their counties to be managed effectively, allowing them to do business unmolested. The interests of neither magnates nor their affinities were served by acting habitually as 'robber barons'. There was thus no essential contradiction between the political aims of the Crown, the magnates or the gentry. The lord was seen as fulfilling many of the same basic functions as the king: he provided justice, balanced the competing claims of interest groups and defended the community from threats internal and external; in addition, he was the conduit through which the gentry's opinions and desires could be represented to the Crown.[33]

That was the ideal. Things did not always run so smoothly. There were constant complaints, in parliament, in the law courts and in literature, about the abuses committed by gentry retainers and the corruption of local government and justice by lords' affinities, although gentry acting on their own behalf were also frequent malefactors.[34] A certain level of law-breaking and rule-bending was a constant, borne with weary resignation.[35] The situation could deteriorate rapidly, however, when lordship was contested. Lordship was not constant: family relationships were in constant flux, alliances came and went, individuals fell into and out of royal favour, people died and came of age. Most lords faced actual or potential competitors in their spheres of interest. This may have produced something like a market for lordship. Lords risked losing their market share of local influence if they did not satisfy their followers.[36] This competition increased the potential for instability. Examples abound. The extinction of the Beauchamp male line in 1446 drew the Nevilles into a dispute with the Beauchamp heiresses in Warwickshire.[37] This was nothing like a 'range war', but the story was different in fifteenth-century Devon. Here, the earls of Devon were challenged by the up-and-coming Lord Bonville, plunging the county into private warfare.[38] The murder of the duke of Suffolk in 1450 left the dukes of Norfolk and earls of Oxford squabbling to fill the power vacuum left in East Anglia. This made life very difficult for the Pastons, a parvenu gentry family with an eye to the main chance but too few friends among the powerful.[39] Fifteenth-century Gloucestershire was disturbed by the struggles between the claimants of the male and female lines to the Berkeley inheritance, resulting in the death of Viscount Lisle during a clash with Lord Berkeley at Nibley Green.[40] None of these was as nationally important as the Neville-Percy dispute in the North East, which was a major catalyst of the Wars of the Roses.[41] In each of these conflicts, it was the gentry who provided the contending magnates with their local 'officer class', who managed – or corrupted – the processes of local justice, and who might fight on their behalf.

The gentry were sometimes prepared to kill and die in their lords' quarrels, which brings us to the issue of political motivation. Was it principles, or only hope of material reward, that motivated them? Patronage has been seen as a lynchpin of medieval political society, but some historians believe that insufficient weight is given to principle; while political ideas are also touched upon in Chapter 6 of this volume, the following concentrates on the immediate motivations for gentry behaviour.[42]

The bond between lord and man was essentially personal. Some gentry families had a long tradition of service to a magnate dynasty.[43] Those embroiled in disputes usually knew their opponents well, and in many cases were their close kinsmen. A sense of personal betrayal must sometimes have added an additional note of bitterness to these conflicts.

The restoration of the heir to his rightful inheritance is one of the themes of *Gamelyn*, and of much chivalric romance. All of the magnate conflicts mentioned above concerned right to property and title; so too did the Wars of the Roses, in that the Crown and the realm were regarded as property. In a society based on land and inheritance, challenges to rightful possession threatened order and security. Not to resist those challenges, even where the immediate material gains were negligible, was to betray one's ancestors and descendants, for this was a lineage society for whom property-holders were stewards for future generations. The gentry were part of a continuum of self-interest embracing all levels of landed society. Property rights had divine sanction: the divinity that increasingly hedged about the king stretched to the humblest proprietor. The correct disposition of property, rights and title was part of natural and divine law. Good governance lay in justice, or in the guaranteeing of every subject's right to what should be his or hers. Here the gentry and nobility saw their role as crucial: through them right and justice could be enforced. Those gentry who rose for Henry Bolingbroke in 1399 may have been motivated partly by what they perceived as Richard II's illegitimate attacks on private property and Bolingbroke's assertion that he was coming only to claim his rightful inheritance. Dynastic principle has been asserted as an important factor in medieval politics, and some of those who supported Richard, duke of York and his son, the future Edward IV, in 1460 and 1461 may have done so because they believed them to be the rightful claimants to the throne. In October 1483, the southern gentry who rebelled against Richard III may have been outraged by his usurpation and suspected treatment of the princes. However, the dynastic issue never carried the day against successful, secure kings, and in all of these cases it would be naive to dismiss self-interest as perhaps the overriding motivation. In the mid-fifteenth century the Mountford family of Warwickshire was split by a property dispute. One side sought help from the Lancastrians, the other from the Yorkists, determining their allegiances in the Wars of the Roses. In its broad outlines this story was repeated many times.[44]

The career of Sir Thomas Malory of Newbold Revel, Warwickshire, whom Professor Field has convincingly claimed as the author of the *Morte Darthur,* illustrates what appears to be a central paradox in the gentry's political behaviour. This Sir Thomas was a political prisoner for over a decade and, allegedly, a turncoat, attempted murderer (his intended victim being no less than the duke of Buckingham), rapist, extortioner and sacrilegious thief.[45] More akin to Gamelyn than Chaucer's 'verray parfit gentil knight', he is difficult to reconcile with the chivalric principles of the *Morte.* On the other hand, this Sir Thomas fits all too easily the more pessimistic readings of 'bastard feudal' society, with its lawlessness, lack of principle and easy resort to violence.

The greater gentry were indeed 'governors' and even, within their limited spheres, 'gret rulers'. England was relatively well governed, and its elites had considerable respect for the law; many dedicated much of their public lives to its operation. However, many of those same toilers for the public weal were willing to bend and break the law and, on occasion, to bribe and peculate, threaten and use violence, and bargain their loyalties. Doubtless, the more jaundiced views of later medieval society have been swayed by the self-serving testimony of the law courts – another paradox, perhaps – but even discounting the extremes still leaves a considerable residue of lawless and unscrupulous behaviour, which is hard to argue away. Principles might seem rare things in politics. The extent to which this makes the later Middle Ages substantially different from any other period must be left up to the individual to decide.

Notes

1 'General Prologue' to *The Canterbury Tales,* in *Riverside Chaucer,* pp. 24–5 (lines 43–100).

2 Saul, 'Social status'; 'General Prologue' to *The Canterbury Tales,* in *Riverside Chaucer,* pp. 28–9 (lines 331–60).

3 The text is cited by Maurice Keen in Chapter 2 of the present volume, pp. 44.

4 Partridge and Wilson (eds), *Gentleness and Nobility,* lines 36–9.

5 There is not space to deal with the many liberties where administrative arrangements differed from the norm: Carpenter, *Wars of the Roses,* pp. 54–7; Pollard, *North-Eastern England,* pp. 144–53; Clayton, *Administration of the County;*

Walker, *Lancastrian Affinity*, pp. 141–81.

6 Jewell, *English Local Administration*, p. 182 ff; Brown, *Governance of Late Medieval England*, pp. 109–10, 142–3. Saul, *Knights and Esquires*, pp. 106–17; Pollard, *North-Eastern England*, pp. 154, 159–60.

7 Virgoe, 'Crown, magnates and local government', p. 77; Saul, *Knights and Esquires*, pp. 147–51.

8 Saul, 'Social status of Chaucer's Franklin', pp. 18–23; Virgoe, 'Crown, magnates and local government', p. 75; Payling, *Political Society*, pp. 111, 113; Acheson, *Gentry Community*, pp. 107–12; Saul, *Knights and Esquires*, pp. 117–19.

9 Lander, *English Justices*; Jewell, *English Local Administration*, pp. 145–7; Saul, *Knights and Esquires*, pp. 128–35; Pollard, *North-Eastern England*, pp. 162–6.

10 Lander, *English Justices*, pp. 108–44, 162–4; Walker, 'Yorkshire justices'; Biggs, 'Henry IV and his JPs'.

11 Brown, *Governance of Late Medieval England*, pp. 156–201; Davies and Denton (eds), *English Parliament*.

12 Virgoe, 'Aspects of the county community', pp. 8–11; Payling, 'Widening franchise'; McFarlane, 'Parliament and "bastard feudalism"', in his *England in the Fifteenth Century*, pp. 1–21; *Paston Letters*, ed. Davis, I, pp. 577–80 (no. 354), and II, pp. 47–9 (no. 460) and p. 54 (no. 464).

13 Saul, *Knights and Esquires*, pp. 120–2; Payling, *Political Society*, pp. 110–12.

14 Payling, *Political Society*, pp. 114–16.

15 Saul, *Knights and Esquires*, pp. 152–67; Moreton, *Townshends and their World*, pp. 56–8.

16 Saul, *Knights and Esquires*, pp. 160–2; Acheson, *Gentry Community*, pp. 132–3.

17 Maddicott, 'Birth and setting'.

18 Knight and Ohlgren (eds), *Robin Hood*, pp. 184–226.

19 Kaeuper, 'Historian's reading of *The Tale of Gamelyn*'; Shannon, 'Mediæval law'; Scattergood, '*The Tale of Gamelyn*'; Keen, *Outlaws of Medieval England*, pp. 78–94.

20 Hicks, *English Political Culture*, pp. 121–6. Rowney, 'Arbitration in gentry disputes'; Payling, 'Law and arbitration'; Maddern, *Violence and Social Order*; *Paston Letters*, ed. Gairdner, II, pp. 195–200 (no. 162).

21 *Paston Letters*, ed. Davis, II, pp. 410, 414, 417. Ayton, 'War and the English gentry'; Allmand, *Lancastrian Normandy*; Massey, 'Land settlement in Lancastrian Normandy', and Vale, *English Gascony*, are among the many works with relevant material on the experiences of the English gentry in France during the Hundred Years War. Such experiences were not always positive: see, for example, Walker, 'Profit and loss in the Hundred Years War'.

22 Hicks, *Bastard Feudalism*, p. 1, and *passim* for much of what follows. See also, McFarlane, 'Bastard feudalism', in his *England in the Fifteenth Century*, pp. 23–43.

23 Walker, *Lancastrian Affinity*, pp. 252, 255; Saul, *Knights and Esquires*, pp. 98–101; Pollard, *North-Eastern England*, pp. 121–40.

24 DuBoulay, *Lordship of Canterbury*; Swanson, *Church and Society*, pp. 122–39; Saul, *Knights and Esquires*, pp. 86–7.

25 Carpenter, *Locality and Polity*; Cherry, 'Courtenay earls of Devon', and 'Struggle for power'; Saul, *Knights and Esquires*; Virgoe, 'Crown, magnates and local

government'; Walker, *Lancastrian Affinity*; Wright, *Derbyshire Gentry*; Acheson, *Gentry Community*; Payling, *Political Society*; and Fleming, 'Character and private concerns', pp. 90–4. For general discussions: Watts, *Henry VI*, pp. 91–101; Hicks, *English Political Culture*, ch. 9.

26 Wright, *Derbyshire Gentry*, pp. 60–145.

27 Acheson, *Gentry Community*, pp. 95–7; Walker, *Lancastrian Affinity*, pp. 252–3.

28 Walker, *Lancastrian Affinity*, pp. 127–39, 161–2.

29 Bennett, *Community, Class and Careerism*, pp. 37–40, 168–71, 203–35.

30 Griffiths, *Reign of King Henry VI*, pp. 630–4; Harvey, *Jack Cade's Rebellion*, pp. 36–43.

31 Castor, 'Duchy of Lancaster'; Wright, *Derbyshire Gentry*, ch. 6; Castor, *The King, the Crown*.

32 Walker, *Lancastrian Affinity*, pp. 145–8; Rawcliffe, 'Great lord as peacekeeper'; Saul, *Knights and Esquires*, pp. 87–94.

33 Watts, *Henry VI*, pp. 91–101.

34 Scattergood, *Politics and Poetry*, pp. 311–18. Gaunt's inability to control his retainers weakened his power base in several areas: Walker, *Lancastrian Affinity*, pp. 157–8, 163, 166–7, 173–4, 179–81, 219–21, 226–8.

35 Wright, *Derbyshire Gentry*, ch. 9.

36 Walker, *Lancastrian Affinity*, pp. 167–9, 173–4, 212–13; Moreton, *Townshends and their World*, pp. 54–6.

37 Carpenter, *Locality and Polity*, pp. 399–486; Hicks, *Warwick the Kingmaker*, pp. 51–2; Walker, *Lancastrian Affinity*, pp. 174–8, 228–32; Pollard, *North-Eastern England*, pp. 141–3.

38 Cherry, 'Courtenay earls of Devon' and 'Struggle for power'.

39 Richmond, *Paston Family: Fastolf's Will*.

40 Fleming and Wood, *Gloucestershire's Forgotten Battle*.

41 Pollard, *North-Eastern England*, pp. 245–55.

42 Richmond, 'After McFarlane'; Powell, 'After "After McFarlane"'; Carpenter, 'Political and constitutional history'; Watts, 'Ideas, principles and politics'; see also Chapter 6 'Literature' in the present volume.

43 Saul, *Knights and Esquires*, p. 95. For the following, see Hicks, *English Political Culture*.

44 Saul, *Richard II*, chs 16–17; Bennett, *Richard II*, pp. 155–6; Griffiths, 'The sense of dynasty in the reign of Henry VI', and 'The hazards of civil war: the Mountford family and the Wars of the Roses', in Griffiths, *King and Country*, pp. 277–304 and 365–82; Ross, *Edward IV*, ch. 2; Horrox, *Richard III*, pp. 175–6.

45 Field, *Life and Times*.

4

Education and recreation

Nicholas Orme

Ideas of education

The romance of *Sir Gawain and the Green Knight* tells how its hero
stays at a castle in a wild upland landscape on Christmas Eve and is
recognised as a leading member of King Arthur's court. The discovery
gives his hosts much pleasure and they say, to paraphrase their words,
'Now we shall enjoy seeing skills of manners and faultless expressions of
noble talk. Now we may learn, without asking, what succeeds in speech,
since we have received this fine master of good breeding'.[1] Gawain was
famous for knowing how to behave and for his skill in doing so.

This episode is one of many in medieval literature that introduces an
idea of education, and shows that people understood what it meant to be
well educated. The words 'noble', from which 'nobleman' and 'nobility'
are derived, and 'gentle', from which we get 'gentleman' and 'gentry',
originally meant the same thing. They were used interchangeably up to
about 1400 to describe anyone from the king down to a country squire, and
both meant that their owners had a special quality over that of ordinary
people. After 1400 the words acquired more specialised meanings
whereby 'nobility' denoted the richer and more important aristocracy –
the peerage families – while 'gentry' meant the more numerous but lesser
aristocracy. But the implication of the words did not change. The nobility
and gentry ought to be well behaved: '*noblesse oblige*' – nobility gives one
obligations. And since high rank and blue blood could not be trusted to
produce good behaviour automatically, they needed to be reinforced by
teaching and training.

People living in the fifteenth century did not use the same words as we
do for the process of education. The Romans had a word *educatio* meaning
'education', but it was not common in medieval Latin and was equally rare

63

in French and English. Indeed, only one example of its use in English is recorded from the fifteenth century.[2] The verb 'to school' and the noun 'schooling' are occasionally found, but they meant 'going to school', and the verb 'to train' in an educational sense does not occur until the Tudor period.[3] Instead, two different verbs were used: 'to foster' and 'to nurture', and from them words were developed to express the process of care and teaching: 'fostering' and 'nurture'. These words could mean 'upbringing' in the sense of feeding and rearing, or education in the sense of teaching or learning something.[4] There were also words for good manners. One was Old English, 'thew', which meant both strength and behaviour, and you could 'thew' people, meaning to train them.[5] Another was French, 'courtesy', with its associated word 'courteous', which came from 'court' and implied that people who belonged to the court of a king or a nobleman would be well mannered. A third word that sometimes appears is 'urbanity' from the classical Latin word *urbs*, meaning a town, reflecting the fact that, in the classical world, civilisation was based in such places. Most of the words to express the process of education tended to signify what we would call 'upbringing' – the whole process of growing up, as opposed to our word 'education', which implies a more formal and structured process, centred on schooling. This reflected a society in which people grew up at home and learnt things informally to a greater extent than we do.

Did education matter? If you had asked people this in the fifteenth century, they would have given a similar answer to that of people today: it is needed by the individual and by society. Medieval people saw life as a series of stages, 'the ages of man', best known to us today from Shakespeare's summary of them in *As You Like It*.[6] Each stage had its characteristics: infancy was dominated by feeding, childhood by play. Neither of these was enough for adult life, and you needed to implant knowledge and virtue while children were growing up, otherwise they would become inadequate adults. Both knowledge and virtue were necessary because medieval people saw education not simply as a learning process but one of self-discipline. The tendency of children merely to play ought to be countered with good religious habits like prayer, temperance and obedience, and good social skills such as being well mannered and articulate. Society needed well-trained people, and the leaders of society – clergy, nobility and gentry – required this training especially.

The way we are brought up owes much to tradition and imitation. Parents care for their children as they themselves were cared for, or as they see other parents doing. This must have happened in the Middle Ages, but there were also writings about education, and these were likely to influence the English gentry who read them. Romances were important in this respect. They featured heroes and heroines who were usually young adults, and the stories about them often began by explaining how they grew up, or by describing their accomplishments. There are good examples of this in Chaucer's *Canterbury Tales*, written in the 1380s and 1390s and much read by the gentry of the fifteenth century. At the beginning of the story, Chaucer introduces the 20-year-old Squire, son of the Knight, as a well-educated young gentleman:

> Syngynge he was, or floytynge, al the day...
> Wel koude he sitte on hors and faire ryde.
> He koude songes make and wel endite,
> Juste and eek daunce, and weel purtreye and write...
> Curteis he was, lowely, and servysable,
> And carf biforn his fader at the table.[7]

The Squire has virtues: courtesy, humility and willingness to serve. He also possesses a range of skills: physical, artistic, polite and literary. Physically he can ride and joust – use weapons on horseback. Artistically he can sing, 'endite' or compose songs, play the flute, and dance. Politely he has good manners (courtesy) and knows how to carve meat: young people were expected to wait on their elders at meals. Finally he can write, which means that he can read.

Chaucer also describes well brought-up women in his writings. Here we might take the example of Virginia, the 14-year-old child of a knight and the tragic heroine of his 'Physician's Tale'. He starts by describing her beauty; then he goes on to list her qualities:

> As wel in goost as body chast was she,
> For which she floured in virginitee
> With alle humylitee and abstinence,
> With alle attemperaunce and pacience,
> With mesure eek of beryng and array.
> Discreet she was in answeryng always...
> Shamefast she was in maydens shamefastnesse,
> Constant in herte, and evere in bisynesse
> To dryve hire out of ydel slogardye.
> Bacus hadde of hir mouth right no maistrie.[8]

Here the approach is different from that of the Squire. We are not told what Virginia did to keep herself busy, and her description does not include activities and skills. It is more passive, concentrating on her virtues of humility, temperance and 'shamefastness' meaning modesty. Even her wisdom, we are told, was sparingly expressed because she did not wish to seem wiser than she was. The picture of Virginia undoubtedly sums up how some people regarded the perfect young gentlewoman. But it is misleading. In practice, such women would have had various skills – reading, sewing, singing, dancing and even hunting – which writers like Chaucer chose to ignore in favour of virtues.

The medieval gentry also read about education in didactic literature, meaning literature whose purpose was to instruct. A large category of writings, nowadays known as 'mirrors for princes', described how kings and nobles should be educated and what they should learn about. One of the most popular was the *Secretum Secretorum* or 'Secret of Secrets', which claimed to be the advice of the Greek philosopher Aristotle to his pupil Alexander the Great on how to be a king. It discusses kingship, care of the body, justice, how to choose ministers and servants, war, astrology and the lore of precious stones and herbs. Not only royalty read it; its many versions and manuscripts show that it was popular among the nobility and gentry. For them it would have been a reference book, but possibly more: a book that might make you as wise as a king. When we wonder about the boldness of the aristocracy in challenging their rulers, especially in the fifteenth century, we need to remember that the texts with which they were educated did not differ from those of kings and princes.[9]

Mirrors for princes were primarily produced for boys and men. There were fewer such texts for girls, but one that people read in fifteenth-century England was *The Book of the Knight of the Tower*, written by and named after a French knight, Geoffrey de la Tour Landry, who composed it for his daughters in the early 1370s. It consists of a number of stories showing how and how not to behave, which range in a rather disorderly way through the virtues that women ought to possess – meekness, chastity and devoutness, and the vices they should avoid – pride, vanity, lechery and extravagance. There is also a chapter about literacy, which recommends that women should be able to read, though they are not bound to learn to write. The stories that illustrate the work are vivid, amusing and sometimes sexually explicit. It was translated into English twice during the fifteenth century, printed by William Caxton in 1483 and was still known in the 1530s.[10]

Two more serious books on education also circulated among the fifteenth-century gentry. Two hundred years earlier, Bartholomew Glanville, an English friar, had produced the most popular encyclopaedia of the later Middle Ages, *De Proprietatibus Rerum*, 'On the Properties of Things'.

Its many topics included an account of birth, babyhood, childhood, parents and nurses. The work was translated first into French and then into English (in 1398), and achieved some popularity in England. Eight manuscripts of the English version are known, and in 1495 the work was printed, remaining well known throughout the sixteenth century.[11] The education of children was covered by a famous Latin work, *De Regimine Principum*, 'On the Government of Princes', written by another friar, Giles of Rome, for the son of the king of France in the 1270s or early 1280s. This dealt with the bringing up of infants and the training of boys from seven into adolescence in religion, literacy, athletics and military skills, and included a short section on girls. It circulated among the nobility and gentry in Latin or in French, and there was even an English translation, made soon after 1400, although that has survived in only one manuscript.[12]

Certainly, then, there were ideas about education in Lancastrian and Yorkist England. The badly- or well-educated young man or woman was a common figure in story literature, and there were numerous books supplying information for young people and preaching the virtues that they ought to acquire. We must not assume, of course, that the books were accurate or that people put their teachings into practice. This is particularly the case with the treatment of girls in literature. Some writers, like Chaucer, tend to praise beauty and virtue while ignoring skills. Others sketch impossibly learned women like Felise, the heroine of the romance of *Guy of Warwick*, who was taught astronomy, arithmetic and geometry by learned clergymen, or King Arthur's wicked half-sister, Morgan le Fay, who was skilled in astronomy and necromancy.[13] The education of real women in gentry families was more varied and less extreme.

Homes and households

The home is the place where all education begins, and this was so for the English gentry in the fifteenth century. They grew up in households consisting of parents, nurses and servants, all of whom might play a part in raising and educating the children. There was no such thing as a standard childhood. The gentry ranged in wealth and importance from knights who were scarcely inferior to the peerage nobility down to country lords of manors and senior officers in great households. The greater had large resources of possessions and servants; the lesser might live in relatively straitened circumstances. A boy or girl might have brothers and sisters of similar ages, or grow up as an only child.[14]

Religion was an important element of gentle childhoods. Almost all babies were baptised on the day of their birth, and their godparents undertook to ensure that they learnt the three basic prayers of the Church: the Lord's Prayer (Paternoster), Hail Mary (Ave Maria) and Apostles' Creed (Credo) in Latin. Works like *The Book of the Knight of the Tower* and shorter 'courtesy books' written for children during the fifteenth century recommend to children and young people, when rising from bed, that they cross themselves and say prayers.[15] Those who could read were urged to say the 'hours of our Lady', the short daily Latin services in honour of the Virgin Mary, contained in the 'book of hours'. Most houses of the gentry had a chapel by the fifteenth century where members of the family might go to pray and venerate images or (if there were clergy available) to watch the celebration of mass. Meals too were religious occasions. Children of gentry rank were expected to say Latin graces before meals, and sometimes to read aloud while their elders ate.[16] Friars cultivated the rich and important, and were likely to visit for meals and conversation, as were parish clergy. Outside the home children might go on visits with their parents to religious houses and to shrines.

But not all growing up took place at home. Most of the gentry held their lands from a superior lord by feudal tenure, and if a father in this category died leaving an heir under the age of majority, the lord had right of wardship. He replaced the father as the person in charge of the heir, the heir's land and the heir's marriage, until the heir reached full age: fourteen for a girl, twenty-one for a boy. If the heir was a young child, it might be left in its mother's care, but if it was older, it was likely to go to live with the lord as a ward. Parents who remained alive might also send their children away from home. Busy adults, who travelled frequently, might leave them with relatives or in a religious house, although this was probably more common among the nobility than the gentry. But less busy gentry parents also looked to place their offspring elsewhere as they approached the age of puberty: usually in someone else's household. This was a custom that went back to ancient times. The Anglo-Saxon epic *Beowulf* tells how its hero left his father's house at the age of seven to live with his grandfather, the king of the Geats, who brought him up and gave him wealth to support him.[17]

What was the motive for sending children away? A Venetian visitor to England in about the year 1500 famously remarked that it was due to 'want of affection', and said that parents 'do it because they like to enjoy all their comforts themselves, and that they are better served by strangers than they would be by their own children'.[18] There are some problems with this evidence. The visitor seems to have been thinking primarily of apprenticeship, which involved only some of the gentry, and he imagined that children left home younger than was normally the case. He admitted too that parents believed that sending their children away enabled them to learn better 'how to live'.[19] That was certainly how the English justified the system. Sir John Fortescue, the great political and legal writer who discussed wardship in the 1460s, praised it for taking boys from smaller households to larger ones, run by lords of higher rank who were better at teaching manners and military skills.[20] Moralists argued that parents were too indulgent, and that children grew up better under the discipline of other people.[21] One could add that, by leaving home, they enlarged their horizons and gained new patrons who might be able to help promote their marriages or (in the case of boys) their careers.

The most important household in the kingdom, and the most prestigious place to be educated, was that of the king. This included a permanent group of youths in training, known as the 'henchmen', first mentioned in the 1340s and numbering eight by 1445: six for the king and two for the queen.[22] They were sons of peers or knights, and might or might not be wards. Examples from the gentry include Thomas Howard, henchman to Edward IV, whose father was later made duke of Norfolk, and Robert Knolles and Peter Carew, henchmen to Henry VIII. A description of the royal household, written in about 1471–72, tells us that they were supervised by a master of the henchmen, who was a squire of the royal household and therefore himself of gentle rank. He is said to have taught them a range of skills which probably formed the ideal curriculum of young noblemen and gentlemen in the fifteenth century:

> to learn them to ride cleanly and surely, to draw them also to jousts, to learn them wear their harness [i.e. armour], to have all courtesy in words, deeds, and degrees …, to teach them sundry languages and other learnings virtuous, to harping, to pipe, sing, dance, and with other honest and temperate behaving and patience …, to have his respects unto their demeaning, how mannerly they eat and drink, and to their communication [i.e. conversation].[23]

These accomplishments remind us of Chaucer's Squire. There was also a grammar master in the royal household, skilled in grammatical rules and poetry, to whom the henchmen could go to improve their Latin.[24]

Other great households paralleled that of the king. Archbishops and bishops kept retinues of clergy and lay servants, and had long taken in boys and young men, either in wardship or for education. Cardinal Morton employed a schoolmaster in his London household in the 1490s, where

69

Thomas More grew up, and Cardinal Wolsey's retinue in the 1520s contained nine or ten young lords with an instructor to teach them. The great lay magnates also modelled their practices on those of the king. George duke of Clarence, the brother of Edward IV, had five henchmen in his household in 1468 with a squire 'to be master of them and to see their rule'. Henry Percy, earl of Northumberland, maintained a schoolmaster, three henchmen and two other young gentlemen in 1512, while Edward Stafford, duke of Buckingham, had a master, henchmen and some wards in 1521. Some lords may have specialised in training young men. When Sir Thomas Lovell of Enfield, Middlesex, knight of the garter, died in 1524, two henchmen rode in the carriage that bore his body to burial, and funeral clothes were bought for nine young gentlemen, their yeoman 'keeper' and their writing master – all evidence of a finishing school in the knight's household.[25]

Great lay households were predominantly male. Gentry with daughters to educate had to find one that included a wife or widow with a small number of ladies in waiting, where room might be found for a girl or two as well. The boarding out of girls, and the difficulties of finding appropriate places, is illustrated in the letters of the famous Paston family of Norfolk. Margaret, the wife of John Paston I, was approached in the early 1460s to take in a girl called Agnes Loveday. The request came from Margaret's cousin, Sir John Heveningham, who said that he had tried to place Agnes elsewhere without success and offered Margaret money in return. When Margaret's own daughter Margery fell in love with the family bailiff in 1469, Margaret made efforts to separate them. Writing to her eldest son John II, she asked if Margery might go to stay with the countess of Oxford or Lady Bedford 'or in summe othere wurchepfull place where as ye thynk best, and I wull help to here fyndyng [*maintenance*], for we be eyther of vs wery of othere'. Another of Margery's daughters, Anne, was already living away from home at this time, probably with Sir William and Lady Calthorp, but in 1470 Sir William asked for her to be removed, as he intended to reduce the size of his household.[26]

Gentry who could not place sons or daughters in a household had another option: a monastery or nunnery. Monasteries were suitable for older boys, who would board with the abbot or prior in his lodging on the edge of the monastic precinct. This was manned by a household of lay servants, and resembled that of a bishop. Thomas Bromele, abbot of Hyde at Winchester, had eight gentle boys with him 'for reason of study' in about 1450, eating at his personal table and provided with grooms to wait on them. Smaller boys were sometimes sent to nunneries. Sir John Stanley of

Honford in Cheshire, for example, when making his will in 1527 and needing to provide for the education of a 3-year-old son, arranged for him to stay in the keeping of the abbess of Barking, Essex, until he was twelve and then move to that of the abbot of Westminster. Thomas Cromwell's son Gregory was brought up by nuns at about the same time, probably at Little Marlow in Buckinghamshire. Nunneries were also popular for boarding girls of gentle rank up to the age of puberty, when they could be sent to a lay household. Nuns tended to be of gentle birth and lifestyle, and their routine was not vastly different from that of a gentlewoman: regular worship, meals, reading and sewing.[27]

The association of nuns with teaching finds echoes in the two main places in which they are mentioned by Chaucer. One is his portrait of the Prioress with her good manners, knowledge of French (albeit of a homely English kind), and anxiety to model her behaviour on that of the king's court.[28] The other occurs in the 'Reeve's Tale', in which a rich parish clergyman places his illegitimate daughter in a nunnery, where she learns *nortelrie*, Chaucer's deliberately distorted form of 'nurture'.[29] Both these references seem to hide an ironic view of nuns and their pupils. This may have been unfair: a priest who made his will in early Tudor Norwich went out of his way to compliment the nun who 'was the first creature that taught me to know the letters in my book'. Nunnery education was certainly popular with noble and gentle parents. Sopwell Priory in Hertfordshire, for example, accommodated the daughter of Lady Anne Norbury in 1446, and Cornworthy Priory, Devon, took in Jane and Elizabeth Knight, daughters of a neighbouring gentleman, who put them there so that the nuns might 'teach them to school' and then failed to pay for their costs. In 1536 St Mary's Abbey, Winchester, accommodated twenty-six girls from the knightly and gentry families of Hampshire.[30]

Schools, universities and the Inns of Court

Any literate lay person could teach a child the alphabet, how to pronounce Latin prayers and how to pronounce and understand English. This knowledge was enough for gentle girls whose literary needs were primarily centred on Latin prayer books and English recreational reading, and their literary education was usually confined to the households they lived in. Boys, on the other hand, had to be trained to manage property, take part in public life or follow professional careers, and for these purposes Latin was necessary – the 'internet' that gave access to knowledge. Latin was a difficult language to teach, however, and beyond the capabilities of most parents or servants. Most of the gentry could not afford to keep a private tutor for this purpose, as some of the nobility did, and they were obliged to send their sons to learn Latin elsewhere, sometimes to a great household but more commonly to a grammar school, 'grammar' meaning the study and teaching of Latin.[31]

Grammar schools were common in England by the fifteenth century. Some, in the larger towns, were institutions with public status, patrons responsible for their government, and an enrolment of several dozen pupils. Others were small private schools, less formally run by clergy or lay schoolmasters. Gentlemen with schools close by might send their sons to them on a daily basis; Sir Henry Willoughby of Middleton in Warwickshire appears to have sent his son Hugh, the future Arctic explorer, to the neighbouring school at Sutton Coldfield in 1522.[32] This was often impossible, however, for families based in the countryside, whose boys would have to travel a long way to study and to board in or near the school they attended. Some pupils lived with their schoolmaster, like Edmund Stonor of the well-known family of gentry in Oxfordshire, who did so in Oxford in about 1380.[33] Others were placed in private lodgings of an appropriate kind for their status. When Sir William Carew, of Mohun's Ottery in east Devon, wished his son Peter to study at Exeter High School in about 1520, he lodged him with Thomas Hunt, a prosperous Exeter alderman.[34] During the late fourteenth and fifteenth centuries the ancestors of modern boarding schools began to appear: Winchester College (founded 1382) and Eton College (1440). These foundations accommodated boys in the school buildings and attracted many boys of gentry rank, but they were not typical schools of the period.

Grammar schools catered for boys from about seven to eighteen, although sending a boy away from home was probably delayed until the age of ten or so. The course of study lasted for several years, depending on intelligence, the amount of Latin that needed to be learnt, and disruptions caused by outbreaks of plague. By the fifteenth century Latin was taught through the medium of English, and there were elementary textbooks of grammar in English, notably those produced by the Oxford schoolmaster John Leland (d. 1428). Boys began by learning Latin vocabulary, the inflexions of the words (known as 'accidence'), and how to put words together to make clauses and sentences ('syntax'). Having mastered elementary Latin, they went on to study more advanced grammars that were themselves in Latin, and developed their skills in Latin composition. This involved composing and writing short prose passages (called 'latins'), formal letters and pieces of verse. Boys (unlike girls) became practised in handwriting skills.

Schools aimed to deliver other abilities. Emphasis was placed on the speaking of Latin, and senior pupils were sometimes forbidden to talk English in school. Boys were questioned by the master, a process known as 'apposing', and held debates about the rules of grammar and composition, thereby learning the methods of logical argument. They were introduced to Latin literature through late-classical and medieval poetry of a moral and religious nature. This included the *Distichs of Cato*, a collection of wise observations in couplets; *The Eclogue of Theodulus*, a debate about the relative merits of classical mythology and Christian history; the *Proverbs* of Alain de Lille; *Cartula*, on the vanity of the world; *Peniteas cito*, on penance; the Latin hymns and sequences of the Church services; *Stans Puer ad Mensam*, on table manners; and *Facetus*, on good behaviour. In the 1480s some English schools began to study humanist Latin – meaning classical Latin and its literature – but this took time to become universal and the medieval works just mentioned continued to be taught until the 1510s.[35]

The grammar-school curriculum was a unifying force because it was similar throughout England, and indeed across western Europe. It gave the gentry something in common, both among themselves and with the clergy. Latin had practical benefits in enabling its pupils to read and understand prayer books, services, charters and legal documents. There is little sign, however, that the fifteenth-century gentry were highly Latinate, any more than most modern children who learn French or German grow up to be fluent in these languages. One encounters a few exceptions. Peter Idley, lord of the manor of Drayton in Oxfordshire and a minor household official of Henry VI, composed a series of moral *Instructions* for his son in about the 1450s, partly translated from works in Latin. Sir John Fortescue, who came from a gentry family in north Devon, wrote his Latin work on the English legal system, *De Laudibus Legum Anglie*, during the 1460s. But such men were unusual. On the whole fifteenth-century gentlemen seem to have preferred to read and write in English or French rather than Latin, a view that changed only under the influence of humanist Latin at the very end of the century.[36]

From the thirteenth century many boys of gentry rank went to study in the university towns of Oxford and Cambridge. This was not always to follow a university degree-course. Both towns, particularly Oxford, contained a number of grammar schoolmasters, and boys were often sent to them to be taught rather than to other schools. The universities were originally intended for future clergy, and the gentry who studied there did so to enter the Church. Occasionally this aim was not fulfilled because they failed to develop a religious vocation or succeeded to the family inheritance through the deaths of their elder brothers. We know of some members of the peerage to whom this happened, and the same must have been true among the gentry.[37] During the fifteenth century, however, we see increasing traces of a new development. Sons of the gentry were taking up university studies not in order to become clergy but to pick up useful knowledge for lay careers. This practice is aptly illustrated in the Paston family, who left an unusual number of records about themselves but whose interest in education is likely to have been shared by others.

The founder of the Paston family was William I, a royal justice and Norfolk landowner. He identified Cambridge as a useful place to educate his children by the early 1440s, sending his eldest son, John I, to study there and subsequently (it seems) John's three younger brothers. None of them followed much of the undergraduate degree course. They stayed for only a year or two, learnt grammar, logic or civil (Roman) law, and then went to London to study English common law. By the end of the century, this kind of plan was becoming popular. In Yorkshire, for example, Ninian Markenfield was bequeathed money to go to Oxford for three years in 1497, Marmaduke Constable to attend Cambridge for a similar period in 1501, and Thomas Wentworth to spend a single year at Cambridge in 1505, in each case a prelude to legal studies in London. At this point the gentry seem to have been merely dipping their toes in the water of university education, as far as their non-clerical sons were concerned. Youths were not yet being sent to university for long periods, as happened in the later sixteenth and seventeenth centuries. Instead they came for fairly short periods to improve their knowledge of Latin and to get some training in logic – a good preparation for legal studies.[38]

London had been a centre of legal education since at least the thirteenth century. By the early 1400s the barristers who practised in the courts had formed residential communities, known as inns. There were ten or so lesser 'Inns of Chancery', and four major 'Inns of Court': Gray's Inn, Lincoln's Inn and the Inner and Middle Temple. A modern estimate suggests that the inns collectively housed 700–800 men in the fifteenth century, of whom 200–300 were students and the remainder practising lawyers.[39] The students were required to learn and behave themselves. Rules were laid down against dicing, card-playing and the bringing in of women at night. Lectures were given by senior members, probably in return for fees, and moots were held in which students pleaded mock cases before their seniors. At Lincoln's Inn in 1436 it was ordained that there should be two 'learning vacations', a month in Lent and a month at harvest time, during which both senior and junior members of the inn should remain in residence, evidently so that they could take part in educational tasks. By 1539 there was a well-developed system of teaching. During the four law terms of the year, when the courts were in session, a moot was held at each inn every evening. During the learning vacations, still in Lent and in August, a morning lecture was followed by discussions and debates among the barristers, with a moot in the evening. A student who had stayed at an inn for three years, studying the law and engaging in the moots, was eligible to be chosen an 'utter barrister' of his inn and to plead in the courts.

The inns did not cater only for those who wished to become profess-ional lawyers. Sir John Fortescue, who wrote a glowing account of legal education in *De Laudibus Legum Anglie*, tells us that 'knights, barons, and other magnates and noblemen of the realm' place their sons at the inns, 'although they do not desire them to be trained in the science of the laws, nor to live by its practices, but only by their inherited possessions'.[40] Law was seen as a useful study for landed noblemen and gentlemen. Agnes Paston, widow of William I, recalled that her husband 'said many times that whoever should dwell at Paston should have need to con [i.e. know how to] defend himself', meaning at law.[41] Much of the Pastons' property was disputed, and because they were not a very wealthy family, they could not simply leave their legal business to professional lawyers. A gentleman could save himself future trouble and money by acquiring a basic know-ledge of the law in London, while making social contacts and improving his cultural skills. Fortescue claimed that the students at the inns learnt 'all the manners that nobles learn. There [the students] learn to sing and to exercise themselves in every kind of harmony. They also practise dancing and all the games proper to noblemen, just as those in the king's household are accustomed to practise them.'[42] As a result the inns were more attrac-tive places for young men than the universities, which is no doubt why we hear so much more about the lay gentry there in the fifteenth century than we do at Cambridge and Oxford.

Culture and recreations

It is not only schooling that trains us for adult life. Play and recreations help to form our interests and attitudes, and this was true of the gentry. There is little documentary evidence about the play of individual children, but we know the kinds of toys and games that were popular in the later Middle Ages and it is reasonable to assume that they were current in gentlemen's families. Boys' toys included mass-produced metal soldiers and tops for whipping. For girls there were dolls and miniature cooking utensils – a difference that helped reinforce the convention that men should be active and warlike while women were caring and domestic. Games, on the other hand, were probably often common to girls and boys. Some were sedentary pursuits with small objects such as cherry stones (played like marbles); others were lively activities such as running, chasing, stone-throwing and archery. Gentry children probably played in much the same way as ordinary children, but with more expensive toys and games, conveying a sense of wealth and privilege. It seems unlikely that they played with their social inferiors on equal terms. Such play would have undermined the social hierarchy, so either gentle children played together or, if they played with lesser children, did so in ways that kept their status unharmed.[43]

The children of the gentry also learnt cultural skills, such as singing, playing musical instruments, dancing and listening to (if not reading) literature.[44] Indoor games continued to be popular even through adolescence. Fifteenth-century sources frequently mention dice, 'tables' (backgammon) and 'quek' (a game played on a chequer board, perhaps like draughts). Playing cards also came into use at this time. Moralists and educationists disliked such games because of their use for gambling, but they could not stop the practice. In playing these games and playing them for money, the gentry resembled the rest of society, but one game – chess – was especially associated with them because it was relatively expensive to buy and (like other costly things) was therefore a mark of distinction. Educationists approved of chess because they thought it encouraged quickness of wit and could be used for teaching purposes. Its pieces represented the orders of society: kings, knights, pawns and so on. One of Caxton's earliest printed books, *The Game and Play of the Chess*, produced at Bruges in 1474, was a translation of a Latin work on chess by the French friar Jacques de Cessoles, who used the pieces to reflect on the duties of the orders of society.[45]

Outdoor play also continued seamlessly from childhood to adulthood. Numerous open-air games were played by adults in late medieval England: 'closh' (a kind of croquet), 'camping' (a term that probably included both football and hockey) and 'kayles' (skittles).[46] These attracted criticism less for gambling than for supposedly distracting youths and men from military pursuits. The whole of male society was supposed to be able to fight, and the Statute of Winchester in 1285 obliged every man over the age of fifteen to possess weapons in accordance with his rank. By 1365 this obligation seemed to be undermined by the playing of ball-games and stone-throwing, and Edward III issued a proclamation ordering the male population to spend their holidays practising with bows and arrows. A series of parliamentary statutes after 1388 made similar demands, recalling the past achievements of the English with their bows on the battlefield and emphasising the nation's need for competent archers.

The statutes do not specify the training of children in this respect until an act of 1512, which laid down that every boy between the ages of seven and seventeen should be provided with a bow and two shafts and be taught the art of shooting. But children had been playing in this way for a long time, as we learn from evidence about accidents in which they were wounded or killed while playing with bows and arrows. Caxton wrote in 1489 that 'Englishmen are learned from their young age' in the longbow, and an Italian visitor to England noted the same a decade later: 'they are enthusiastically trained in it from their earliest youth'. Staves for making children's bows are mentioned as a commodity of trade in the fifteenth century, and the Princes in the Tower were last seen alive 'shooting and playing' in the summer of 1483. Even girls might shoot. Margaret, the elder daughter of Henry VII, must have learnt the skill as a girl because in 1503, when she was fourteen and was travelling to Scotland to marry James IV, she stopped at Alnwick in Northumberland and killed a buck in the park there, with her bow.[47]

Archery, then, like dice and cards, was something that the gentry had in common with those beneath them. Hunting, on the other hand, resembled chess in marking them out as different.[48] It was an elite sport, lawful only for the nobility and gentry in privileged places – forests and deer-parks – with lesser people merely assisting them as huntsmen and beaters. John Hopton, son of a Suffolk esquire, spent two days hunting deer with the vicar of Covehithe, Suffolk, in 1463–64, when he was a schoolboy. Thomas Cranmer, the future archbishop, was encouraged by his gentleman father to hunt in Nottinghamshire round about the year 1500, and Thomas Cromwell's son Gregory did so in the early 1520s when Thomas was still only a rising gentleman.[49] Girls might hunt, as Margaret did, by shooting at deer driven past, or go hawking. Medieval romances frequently talk of women doing so, implying that they had learnt the skills when young.[50]

There was more to hunting than the physical skills of riding and shooting. It was a well-developed sport in the modern sense, with its own rules, terminology and instruction books. The hunter had to know the habits of the beasts to be hunted and how to track them, how to signal to other hunters through horn blowing, and how to butcher the carcasses of the animals he killed. Several treatises were produced in England to teach these matters during the fourteenth and fifteenth centuries. The most popular was an English poem called *Tristram*, after the knight of twelfth-century romance who was regarded as the greatest hunter of the Arthurian world and the inventor of contemporary hunting procedures. The poem was written in the late fourteenth or early fifteenth centuries and presents itself as a work for teaching young people, since it claims to be written by a mother for her 'child', 'children', 'son' and 'sons', as the readership is defined in different parts of the work. It is chiefly a guide to the words you need to know: names of beasts, collective terms for them, the parts of an animal, and the words for flaying and stripping carcasses.[51]

Hunting was important for the gentry both recreationally and socially. As a recreation it provided a major form of exercise and diversion for people who were often confined to the countryside with few other amenities. Socially it provided the gentry with a common activity in which they could meet and entertain one another. The privilege of being able to hunt, and the common language of rules and words, made the activity a kind of freemasonry that distinguished its participants from other people. Sir Thomas Malory praised this aspect of hunting in his translation of the romance of *Tristram of Lyonesse*. After describing how Tristram invented the methods of blowing horns and all the terms of hawking and hunting, he observed,

> Wherefore, as me seemeth, all gentlemen that bear old arms ought of right to honour Sir Tristram for the goodly terms that gentlemen have and use [in hunting] and shall do unto the Day of Doom, that thereby in a manner all men of worship may discover a gentleman from a yeoman and a yeoman from a villein.[52]

He appears to mean that the technical terms of the sport enabled you to tell the difference between gentlemen (who knew them all) and yeomen (who might know some), and between yeomen and villeins or bondmen (who would know none).

Contemporaries saw another virtue in hunting, for both boys and men. It was a paramilitary sport, which toughened those who played it and trained them for fighting in war. John Hardyng, a chronicle writer in 1457, recommends that when boys reach the age of fourteen,

> they shall to field for sure,
> To hunt the deer and catch an hardiness,
> For deer to hunt and slay and se them bleed
> An hardiment [hardness] giveth to his courage,

> And also in his wit he taketh heed,
> Imagining to take them at advantage.[53]

Killing deer accustoms you to blood, and hunting develops your strategic skills: following your enemy and anticipating what he will do. Similar points are made by two writers of the early Tudor period. William Horman, writing for the schoolboys of Eton or Winchester in about 1500, described hunting as 'a plain recording [i.e. re-enactment] of war' and Sir Thomas Elyot in his treatise *The Governor* in 1531 called it 'the very imitation of battle, for not only doth it show the courage and strength as well of the horse as of him that rideth . . . but also it increaseth in them both agility and quickness, also sleight and policy to find such passages and straits where they may prevent or entrap their enemies'.[54] Hunting, he concluded, enables its practitioners to put up with the discomforts that they will suffer in war: hunger and thirst, cold and heat.

A number of commentators, from Giles of Rome onward, talk of youths being trained for warfare during their teens. This was probably most characteristic of the children of kings and the high aristocracy, whose leadership in war was a principal part of their adult life. Edward III commanded his first expedition against the Scots in 1327 when he was only fourteen, and his son the Black Prince famously won his spurs at Crécy in 1346 when he was sixteen. There is some evidence about the lesser aristocracy in the famous legal case of Scrope versus Grosvenor in 1386, at which a number of knights and squires appeared to support the claims of the two parties for the right to bear the same coat of arms. A knight named Sir John Bromwich claimed to have borne arms at the age of eleven in 1342 and, though this was unusual, plenty of other witnesses said that they had done so in their mid-teens. We must remember, however, that most of the English gentry in the fourteenth and fifteenth centuries took little part in fighting. For them, their military status was a matter of life-style. They owned arms and armour, they displayed coats of arms as their badges, they might share in militia training, and when they died they were represented in armour on their tombs. But they imagined themselves as warriors rather than functioning as such.[55]

Reflections

The gentry of the fifteenth century took education seriously. It figured as a topic in much of the material that they heard in sermons or read in literature, even in recreational reading such as romances. Books were produced on the subject, ranging from primers and prayer books through courtesy books to longer works like those of Bartholomew, Giles of Rome and *The Book of the Knight of the Tower*. The better-known educational books aimed at the gentry in the sixteenth century, Sir Thomas Elyot's *The Governor* and Roger Ascham's *The Schoolmaster*, followed a long tradition of such writing. There was a large number of agencies for dispensing education to the gentry: homes, great households, monasteries and nunneries, grammar schools, universities and the inns of court and chancery. Boys alone benefited from the more specialised institutions of education: schools, universities and the London inns, though some gentry boys may never have been educated outside households. Girls were confined to households and nunneries, and had a more informal (though not necessarily inferior) education. As wives and widows they often showed much capability in running families, households and property.

The education offered was a wide one. The notion of the 'universal man' is one that popular opinion associates with the Renaissance, but there was not much to separate well-educated gentlemen or gentlewomen of the fifteenth century from their sixteenth-century successors. The greatest difference was the latter's knowledge of classical (as opposed to medieval) Latin, and sometimes a greater amount of Latin knowledge. Late-medieval education was no less wide than that of the Renaissance. It covered language, meaning the ability to speak well; religion, meaning the beliefs and practices of Christianity; and good manners. It included the ability to read and (at least for boys) to write. It involved the cultural skills of music and dancing, and the physical ones of archery, hunting and (for boys) training in weapons. And besides these topics, experienced at first hand, reading opened one's eyes to many others, even if one only read in English: religious ideas, lives of saints, romances, science, history and geography.

It conferred a measure of privilege and power, as education often does. Boys and girls of the gentry grew up to understand, from their experience and their reading, that they belonged to a wealthy, privileged elite. Their reading skills put them ahead of many in the population, and those who learnt Latin drew level with the clergy in that respect. They could even claim benefit of clergy if they committed a crime, and receive more lenient treatment. Cultural and recreational skills also conferred power and exclusivity. Music, dancing and hunting enabled gentry to bond with one another socially. Military skills with horses, armour and knightly weapons marked off the gentry from their inferiors, and enabled them to act as leaders in war. How far education improved the gentry morally, as opposed to giving them skills and knowledge, is harder to say. Reading romances and chronicles did not teach one merely about chivalry, love and marriage.

The Arthurian romances told of Lancelot's adultery with Guenevere and the dissolution of the Round Table in civil war. The gentry of the fifteenth century, for all their education, included men and women who perverted the law, attacked one another's property and took part in the Wars of the Roses.

Historians of the early modern period have debated whether the gentry and nobility of the sixteenth and seventeenth centuries withdrew from a common culture, shared with the rest of society, into an elite culture that was special to themselves. Such a debate presupposes that there was a common culture in the fifteenth century, which is not entirely true. There were indeed ways in which the life of the gentry matched that of the rest of society. They went to church, shared many recreations and had the responsibility to fight when necessary. Late medieval households brought different ranks together more fully than in the more segregated households of Victorian times. Yet gentry did not necessarily do things in the same way as ordinary people, or in their company. They had superior sitting or standing places in church. Many of their recreations were probably taken with people of their own rank, and may have followed special forms in matters such as singing, dancing and chess. In war they were leaders, not followers. The culture of the fifteenth-century gentry was therefore ambivalent socially. On the one hand its members were anxious to preserve and emphasise their status; on the other they were leaders of fashions imitated by those beneath them. Education shared this ambivalence. It tried to teach the gentry to respect and care for their inferiors, but it also reminded them that they were different and charged with superior roles.

Notes

1 'Sir Gawain and the Green Knight', in *Poems of the Pearl Manuscript*, eds Andrew and Waldron, pp. 241-2 (lines 915-19). 'Vch segge ful softly sayde to his fere, / "Now schal we semlych se sleytez of thewez / And the teccheles termes of talkyng noble. / Wich spede is in speche vnspurd may we lerne, / Syn we haf fonged that fyne fader of nurture."' [Translation from *Sir Gawain*, eds Tolkien *et al.*].

2 MED, 'educaten'; OED, 'educate', 'education'.

3 MED, 'scolen', 'scoling'; OED, 'school', 'schooling', 'train'.

4 MED, 'foster', 'fostren', 'fostring', 'norture', 'norturen'; *OED*, 'foster', 'fostering', 'nurture'.

5 MED, 'theu', 'theuen'; OED, 'thew'.

6 Shakespeare, *As You Like It*, II. vii.139-66, in *Riverside Shakespeare*, pp. 381-2.

7 *Riverside Chaucer*, pp. 24-5 (lines 91, 94-6, 99-100).

8 *Ibid.*, p. 190 (lines 43-8, 55-8).

9   Orme, *From Childhood*, pp. 88–9.

10 Caxton, *Book of the Knight*; Orme, *From Childhood*, pp. 107–9.

11 Trevisa, *On the properties of things*; Orme, *From Childhood*, pp. 91, 95–6.

12 Orme, *From Childhood*, pp. 93–4, 95–7.

13 *Ibid.*, pp. 84–5.

14 On family size and infancy, see Orme, *Medieval Children*, pp. 52–68.

15 Caxton, *Book of the Knight*, pp. 16–17; *Babees Book*, p. 266.

16 Orme, *Medieval Children*, p. 207.

17 *Beowulf*, ed. Alexander, p. 160 (lines 2428–31).

18 Trevisano, *A Relation . . . of the Island of England*, pp. 24–6.

19 'Meglio a vivere', translated by the editor as 'learn better manners'.

20 Fortescue, *De Laudibus*, pp. 108–11.

21 Orme, *Medieval Children*, pp. 84–5, 306.

22 Orme, *From Childhood*, pp. 51–3.

23 Myers (ed.), *Household of Edward IV*, pp. 126–7, 137–8.

24 *Ibid.*

25 Orme, *From Childhood*, pp. 55–8.

26 *Ibid.*, pp. 58–60; *Paston Letters*, ed. Davis, I, pp. 42, 339, 348; II, pp. 350–1.

27 Orme, *From Childhood*, pp. 60–5.

28 *Riverside Chaucer*, p. 25 (lines 118–62).

29 *Ibid.*, p. 25 (lines 3921–4324).

30 Dickinson, *Ecclesiastical History*, p. 387: Orme, *From Childhood*, p. 64.

31 On schools in general, see Orme, *Medieval Schools*, and *Education and Society*.

32 Stevenson, *Report*, p. 346.

33 *Kingsford's Stonor Letters*, ed. Carpenter, p. 109 (no. 30).

34 Hooker, *Life and Times*, pp. 3–5.

35 Orme, *English Schools*, pp. 102–6, 113.

36 Orme, *From Childhood*, pp. 153–6.

37 *Ibid.*, p. 70.

38 *Ibid.*, pp. 72–3.

39 Ives, 'Common lawyers in pre-Reformation England'; by the same author, 'Common lawyers', in Clough (ed.), *Profession, Vocation and Culture*; Orme, *From Childhood*, pp. 74–9.

40 Fortescue, *De Laudibus*, pp. 118–19.

41 *Paston Letters*, ed. Davis, I, p. 27.

42 Fortescue, *De Laudibus*, pp. 118–19.

43 On toys and games, see Orme, *Medieval Children*, pp. 164–97.

44 Orme, *From Childhood*, pp. 163–74, 178–80; Orme, *Medieval Children*, pp. 165, 176–8.

45 On indoor games see Orme, *Medieval Children*, pp. 178–80.

46 On outdoor games, see Orme, *From Childhood*, pp. 205–10, and Orme, *Medieval Children*, pp. 178–81.

47 On war-games and archery, see Orme, *From Childhood*, pp. 182–91, 198–205, and *Medieval Children*, pp. 181–3.

48 On hunting, see Orme, 'Medieval hunting'.

49 *Original Letters*, ed. Ellis, I, p. 339.
50 Orme, *From Childhood*, pp. 191–8.
51 Hands (ed.), *English Hawking*.
52 Malory, *Works*, p. 375.
53 Hardyng, *Chronicle*, pp. i–ii.
54 Horman, *Vulgaria*, p. 277; Elyot, *Book Named the Gouernour*, Book I, ch. 18.
55 Orme, *From Childhood*, pp. 182–91.

5

Literacy

Alison Truelove

Levels of literacy among members of the fifteenth-century English gentry are often assumed to have been high. Several factors, such as their relatively privileged access to education, the survival of their own written documentation, and evidence of their book ownership, contribute to the impression that their ability to read and write proficiently may be taken for granted. Yet establishing the true relationship between documents and their authors and readers is a complex process, and conclusive statements regarding the literacy of this social group are not reached easily. The chance survival of family archives such as those of the Paston and Stonor families cannot be taken as firm evidence that all gentry families were highly literate. Indeed, as this chapter will demonstrate, levels of literacy within these well-known households, let alone more widely among the gentry, varied considerably.

In his study of early medieval literacy, Michael Clanchy noted that because medievalists 'rely largely on individual cases, which cannot be proved to be typical', they have often given little consideration in general histories to the development of literacy, 'even though this omission gives the impression that literacy was of little importance or was not wide-spread'.[1] Late medieval literacy, on the other hand, has attracted wider attention, and has a larger body of surviving evidence, but still there remains no book-length general survey of the subject.[2] Moreover, as with earlier periods, it remains the case that even though they are more plentiful, the individual cases available to study may or may not be typical. J. B. Trapp recently summarised the methodological difficulties of quantifying literacy during this period:

> The attempt may perhaps carry more conviction if generalisation and inference are reduced to a minimum and the enquiry is conducted on

the basis of the few specific contemporary statements that exist, and some examples. There is no reason to suppose that the statements that exist are utterly to be relied upon; they are, for one thing, made in the heat of controversy, or at least à parti pris. The rest of the evidence, besides being largely random, requires much circumspection in interpretation.[3]

Mindful of the need to avoid generalisations, and to approach the available evidence cautiously, this chapter draws on the surviving letter collections of the late medieval English gentry in an attempt to gain insight into the writers' literacy. Of all the late medieval social groups, evidence of the reading and writing skills of the gentry is the most accessible. Even if they possessed literacy skills, members of the nobility rarely put them into practice in ways that produced evidence accessible to us today, and although evidence of their education and book ownership is available, it rarely provides direct proof of their ability to read or write. At the opposite end of the social hierarchy, those below the gentry had fewer opportunities for acquiring literacy skills and, perhaps more importantly, had less of a need for them in what was still a highly oral culture.[4]

Before turning to a close analysis of this material, it is useful to understand why reading and writing became so central to gentry life, and why so much documentation was produced by this group. The advantages of acquiring developed literacy skills grew throughout the late medieval period, as the gentry's involvement in local and national bureaucracy, as well as in commercial activities, increased. There also seems to have been an increasingly strong desire to establish a group identity through 'literary' cultural pursuits, such as recreational reading and writing, sometimes in an attempt to emulate the activities of the nobility. In addition, the ability to write allowed individuals to engage more freely in private correspondence, reducing their reliance on secretaries, and enabled this increasingly litigious sector of society to conduct legal negotiations more covertly.[5] Such practical concerns, which also included the management of their often extensive estates, were undoubtedly the greatest stimulus to the development of reading and writing skills amongst the gentry. The plethora of surviving documentation regarding household and estate management, legal disputes, and commercial transactions testifies to the assiduousness with which this class maintained records of their activities. An increasing trust in written documentation, along with a recognition of the potential of using documentary proof, encouraged the trend for record-keeping. In such a litigious society, it was clearly advantageous to retain evidence of transactions in case of later disputes, and indeed the very survival of the documents today is often due to the seizure of private archives as evidence. Hence literacy was a necessity rather than a luxury for these gentry families. Even if there was some prestige value in being able to read and write, facilitating aspirational cultural activities, it was for pragmatic reasons that many in this social group developed these skills. As Clanchy has stated with reference to an earlier period, 'lay literacy grew out of bureaucracy, rather than from any abstract desire for education or literature'.[6]

The concept of 'being literate' changed considerably throughout the Middle Ages, and to confuse matters modern scholars have defined literacy in many different ways. In general, early in the period a literate person was regarded as someone who had received a formal education, and hence could read and write Latin, and had a familiarity with literature. From the fourteenth century, a person charged with felony was able to claim 'benefit of clergy' if he could demonstrate that he could read a prescribed verse from the Psalter, thus escaping the death penalty by proving himself *litteratus*.[7] By the end of the fifteenth century, the emphasis had moved away from knowledge of Latin, and individuals were sometimes classed as 'literate' simply if they were able to sign their own names. Using this particular measure, David Cressy has estimated that at the turn of the sixteenth century 10 per cent of men and 1 per cent of women met this definition of literacy.[8] Yet others have been more generous, though less specific, in their estimates; G. A. Lester, for example, has asserted that by the second half of the fifteenth century 'people of almost all ranks were capable of reading, writing, and enjoying books'.[9]

Hence when considering late medieval literacy it is essential to be precise in establishing the kind of skills we are looking for. Although there is evidence that during the late-fourteenth and early-fifteenth centuries members of the gentry, particularly those in its upper ranks, used French (or, more precisely, Anglo-Norman) for their personal correspondence, and most likely listened to and read literature in that language, by the middle of the fifteenth century English was undoubtedly their chosen medium for most purposes. In matters of worship and in recreational use of literature, there is no doubt that knowledge of Latin and French remained valuable and indeed, for some, necessary. The involvement of many within this wide social group in foreign affairs, whether military or commercial, also brought them into contact with other languages, but English was by the end of the medieval period the primary language of the English gentry. Hence this chapter focuses on the gentry's command of the English language, and deals predominantly with writing skills; reading abilities may be inferred, but direct evidence of these is less forthcoming.

Our knowledge of gentry literacy depends heavily upon the unusual survival of the correspondence of the Paston and Stonor families.[10] They are particularly valuable in providing evidence not only of those within these households, but also of their friends and associates, many of whom were among the professionals who gradually became accepted as part of the gentry. Yet the generalisations that are sometimes made regarding their literacy are not always well-founded. In the introduction to his 1904 edition of the Paston letters, Gairdner remarked that '[n]o person of any rank or station in society above mere labouring men seems to have been wholly illiterate. All could write letters; most persons could express themselves in writing with ease and fluency.'[11] At the very least this is an oversimplification: it simply cannot be proved that everyone 'above mere labouring men' could write letters. Yet the publication of the Stonor family's letters and papers in 1919 did little to dispel this view.[12] In the introduction to his edited collection, Kingsford affirmed that Gairdner's 'judgment is fully confirmed by the Stonor letters', stating confidently that:

> Sir William Stonor, his father, and brothers ... wrote their own letters and spelt passably well. Jane Stonor wrote tolerably but spelt atrociously. Her daughter-in-law Elizabeth generally employed an amanuensis, but could write well enough if she pleased ... Generally the country squires of Oxfordshire and their women folk, and the better class merchants of London could write with ease.[13]

Careful study of the letters reveals some of Kingsford's judgements to be unfounded: for instance, all four of Jane Stonor's surviving letters are written in different hands, so it is certain that she used secretaries, and the brief examples of Elizabeth's own handwriting show that her abilities were very limited. She could certainly not 'write with ease', and on close examination there is just one female correspondent in the collection (Margery Hampden) whose skills might fall into this category.

When Norman Davis published the first volume of his new edition of the Paston letters and papers in 1971, he made a much more detailed and accurate assessment of the writers' literacy skills.[14] His conclusion that all the Paston men 'could write, with differing degrees of competence and elegance', while the women 'were not, or not completely, literate', was based on more careful judgements of whether or not letters were autograph.[15] His subsequent work on the language of the letters has done much to clarify our understanding of gentry literacy, and has drawn attention to the ways in which abilities varied amongst this particular social group.[16]

Yet it remains the case that clear criteria by which we might judge these

87

varying levels of literacy are still to some extent lacking. A standard form of English was far from a reality even at the end of the fifteenth century, despite tangible evidence of a trend towards some degree of standardisation, so it is difficult to justify using this as a measure by which to judge any writing.[17] Moreover, in a culture that often still valued oral communication as highly as (if not more highly than) that which was written, we must be careful to avoid equating an ability to read and write proficiently with being educated and cultured. As might be seen in letters written by members of the nobility, privilege and advanced levels of education did not necessarily result in an ability to write with any degree of skill.[18] Although we have some idea of the kind of education some members of the gentry may have received, and evidence of their ownership and use of literary manuscripts and books, this is unreliable evidence of their particular literacy skills. Books, for example, were regarded as valuable prestige items, the ownership of such not necessarily denoting an ability to read them.[19]

So, it is the gentry's own hand-produced documents to which we must turn if we are to approach an accurate picture of their literacy. The numerous surviving letters, accounts, deeds and memoranda provide ample evidence that some degree of literacy was taken for granted by a large number of these individuals. Yet knowledge of exactly how widespread, and how advanced, their skills of reading and writing might have been is more difficult to obtain. The use of secretaries, whether for reasons of convenience, illiteracy or prestige, means that we can never take for granted that a signatory actually wrote a document. An author[20] may have had any level of participation in its production, ranging from autograph composition to merely outlining the intended content to a secretary, who would then proceed to compose the document and even sometimes to forge his or her employer's signature. However, evaluating authorial participation in any particular document can be a complex process. In straightforward cases, we may be able to recognise an autograph composition from a clear reference in the text itself, sometimes found within a valediction phrase at the end of a letter. Several of the Stonor family's correspondents, including Richard Page, Henry Dogett, Walter Elmes and Simon Stallworth, drew attention to the fact that their letters were autograph, typically using the phrase 'written with the hand of your servant' followed by a signature. Likewise, William Paston III signed off several of his letters with the phrase 'with the hand of your brother'.[21]

Elsewhere, writers can be found denouncing their scribal abilities at the same time as foregrounding them, such as when John Yaxlee, a legal advisor to the Stonors, wrote at the end of a letter, 'wreten ... with the rude hand of your feythefull scruaunt' (*KSL* 292), or when William Worcester asked John Paston I to 'foryefe me of my leude lettre wrytyng, and I pray yow laugh at it' (*PL* 566). In some of these cases, of course, this is false modesty, formulated as a rhetorical device employed to encourage a favourable response from the recipient. It certainly seems that some writers felt that writing a letter themselves, especially if they had access to secretarial assistance, demonstrated to the recipient a certain humility and respect, such as when John Paston III signed a letter in 1476 to his social superior, Lord Hastings, 'wyth the hand of your most humble seruaunt and beedman' (*PL* 370).

Undoubtedly, an autograph document was regarded as an authoritative and trustworthy record of a writer's intentions. Indeed, an acknowledgement of authorship could sometimes play an important role in allowing the document to act as a substitute for the actual presence of the author, recalling the original function of the epistolary form.[22] For example, William Stonor used phrases such as 'thys bylle wryt with my hond shalle be your dyscharge of the sum reseyuyd' (*KSL* 193), and 'thys wryt with my ovne hand schalle be hys sufficient dyscharge' (*KSL* 296) when writing to his servants and associates. Similarly, when in 1465 John Paston I was attempting to resolve confusion relating to an agreement with John Russe, he gave instructions to 'take ... a writyng of his hand that he dischargyth me of the grant' (*PL* 75). In 1469, John Paston III wrote to his brother that 'Dawbeney set in hys dettys that ye owt hym xij li. and x s. Whedyr it be so or nowt hys byllys of hys owne hand wyll not lye' (*PL* 335), and in *c.* 1476 to an unidentified lady, 'I send yow thys bylle wretyn wyth my lewd hand and sealyd wyth my sygnet to remayn wyth yow for a wytnesse ayenst me' (*PL* 373). The gentry had certainly come to accept written documentation as legally binding, and held literacy skills in high regard when it came to dispensing orders or trusting in the veracity of a document. As is clear from another of John Paston II's letters to his brother, recognition of an individual's handwriting could also have the benefit of allowing for greater privacy in communication: 'Ye knowe thys hande, therfore nedythe no mencion from whom it comythe' (*PL* 244).

Explicit indicators that an author is also the writer of a document are, however, the exception among the surviving gentry correspondence, and more usually we must look for other clues. For example, if a series of documents exist for an author, we can look for scribal, stylistic and orthographical consistency, and if this is combined with external references to the writing abilities of an individual, we can usually discount the possibility that the consistency was due to the same secretary being used on each occasion. Most of the letters written by John Paston II, for instance, are in the same hand, suggesting that these are autograph, and we can call upon other evidence to confirm his ability to write: after his death, William Paston III wrote a letter to his elder brother, John III, referring to John II's will 'that he wrote wyth hys owne hande' (*PL* 408). Almost all of John III's letters are in a single, autograph hand, identifiable as his own through the aforementioned subscription in the letter to Lord Hastings, and another in a letter to his mother (*PL* 386).

Of the other Paston men featuring prominently in the surviving correspondence, only one of William Paston's letters is autograph, his hand identified through his corrections to drafts of other documents. John Paston I's letters are mostly written by secretaries, though he does sign these, with just a few entirely autograph documents (*PL* 37, 73 and 74); Davis has described his handwriting as 'energetic, but extremely coarse and careless, with many letters ill formed and some left out altogether'.[23] Almost all of the letters of William II, Clement, Edmund II, Walter and William III are likely to be autograph due to the consistency of the handwriting, though there is no external evidence to corroborate this.[24] Of the Stonor men, all of the immediate family members seem to have been able to write their own letters, though the evidence is much slimmer than for the Pastons. Very few of the Stonor family's own letters have survived, the archive consisting mostly of correspondence entering the household from elsewhere. There are considerable variations in the quality of their handwriting, but one notable feature is the confidence with which some wielded a pen. The letters of Thomas Stonor III, for instance, demonstrate a practised ability to write fluently and at speed, but consequently some individual letters and words are poorly formed, potentially jeopardising their comprehensibility.[25]

There is plentiful evidence, then, that gentry men were increasingly likely to write their own letters throughout the fifteenth century. Though the older generation tended to rely upon secretaries more frequently than their younger relatives, they could certainly read and correct these dictated documents, and on occasion produce letters without assistance. It is hard to assess whether they chose to dictate for convenience or prestige, or simply due to a lack of sufficiently developed writing skills, but the choice existed nevertheless. While certain types of correspondence benefited from being autograph, it appears that the use of secretaries was accepted fully by the gentry as a legitimate means of producing a letter, and under most circumstances the practice did not provoke censure of any kind. The use of a secretary is only rarely made explicit within a letter, however, such as when one of the Stonor correspondents included the line, 'and the wrytter herr-off comawnd hym on-to yow' (*KSL* 134). More often, their participation is made evident with a change of hand for the signature, and sometimes the addition of an autograph subscription by the author. Three of the letters of Margery Paston (*PL* 417, 418, 420) contain subscriptions in the same shaky and unpractised hand, and as Davis has pointed out, the fact that she wished for another of her letters (*PL* 415), one of the famous 'Valentines' of 1477, not to be 'seyn of non erthely creature safe only your-selfe' indicates that if her writing abilities had only been better, she would surely have avoided the use of a secretary.²⁶

Like Margery, William Stonor's first wife, Elizabeth, also relied on secretaries while possessing a rudimentary ability to write; she used no fewer than nine different scribes to produce her thirteen surviving letters, but signed them herself and sometimes added a postscript. Her handwriting is unaccomplished, seemingly executed with a great deal of effort, but the subject and tone of these brief lines indicate that when writing to her husband, she regarded such autograph participation as a valued means of conveying her affection for him. In choosing to write of certain matters herself, she was in effect foregrounding them, giving them a significance that distinguishes them from the diary-like content of the main bodies of her letters. We find expressions of regret for not writing sooner – 'And, cosen, ther as ye wryte to me that I had no leysyr, truly I haue ben crised and besy, orelys I wyld haue wryte to you or thys tym' (*KSL* 176) – and of concern for his health – 'My ovne cosyne, I sende you a bladyr with powdyr to drynke when he go to bed, ffor hit ys holsome ffor yo[u]' (*KSL* 172) – along with reassurances of her own well-being – 'Cossen, I was crasyd that the makyng off thys letter, but I thanke God I am ryght well amendyd, blesyd by Jhesu' (*KSL* 204). There are also more cryptic postscripts – 'My ovne good co[s]yne, I se well ye remember the pvttyng ovt ... ovt off the bedy whan you and I lay last to gedyr' (*KSL* 175), and 'My good cosen, I am crassed in my baket: you wat what I men' (*KSL* 180) – indicating a level of intimacy that she may not have regarded as appropriate for dictation to a scribe.

Gentry women such as Margery Paston and Elizabeth Stonor clearly recognised the value of being able to write, and used their albeit limited abilities to add a personal dimension to their correspondence. That their writing skills were not more developed, at least when compared to those of their male counterparts, should be regarded primarily as a matter of circumstance. Practice undoubtedly made perfect, and it seems that gentry women rarely needed to exercise their writing skills. Men, on the other hand, had reason to put pen to paper on a daily basis, partly due to their increasing involvement in local bureaucracy. A surviving entirely autograph letter by Margery Hampden, a kinswoman to the Stonors, is an encouraging indication that women of this class *were* educated in rudimentary writing skills, and could be confident in exercising them.[27]

So if we accept that they were less practised than the men in writing, can we nevertheless confirm that gentry women's reading skills were well-developed during this period? Unfortunately evidence is slim. John Paston II's tantalising comment to his younger brother in 1470 that he should 'schewe ore rede to my moodre suche thyngez as ye thynke is fore here to knowe, afftre yowre dyscression' (*PL* 248) is, unfortunately, misleading, as he probably intended 'show' to mean 'make known', and hence this offers no revealing insight into Margaret Paston's ability to read.[28] However, in 1474 John Paston III wrote to a kinswoman, 'I am prowd that ye can reed Inglyshe, wherfor I prey yow aqweynt yow wyth my lewd hand' (*PL* 362), firmly testifying to this particular woman's reading ability. That gentry women oversaw the running of their large households, often while their husbands were away from home, is surely an indicator that they were able to monitor written accounts and records.[29] Elizabeth Stonor's signed household account book of 1478–79 (*KSL* 233) indicates that she may have been able to read well enough to approve of its contents, but we should not discount the possibility that details were read aloud to her. Anne Paston owned a copy of *The Siege of Thebes*, lent in 1472 to Thomas Boyd, Earl of Arran (*PL* 352), though, as already noted, we must recognise that ownership of a book or manuscript does not automatically presuppose an ability to read it.

On the basis of their own surviving documentation, then, it is safe to assume that by the fifteenth century, most members of these gentry circles possessed some literacy skills.[30] It is rare to find no evidence of writing or reading skills for any particular author, as even if an individual used a secretary, an autograph signature invariably appears at the end of a letter. The handwriting varies considerably in quality, but as has been observed in the case of Thomas Stonor III, lack of clarity in handwriting may be due more to the speed with which a letter was written than to unfamiliarity with a pen. Equally, inconsistencies in orthography and the use of abbreviations, evident even in the writing of the more highly educated and prominent members of this social group, are due more to the highly fluid nature of the English language at this point in its development than to any deficiencies in the writers' abilities. Consequently, relying on observations of the quality of handwriting alone may lead to misleading conclusions regarding gentry literacy, as would judgements purely based on evidence regarding the use of secretaries. In order to progress in our assessment of gentry literacy, we must look beyond these features to consider the actual content of the documents.

Initial readings of many fifteenth-century epistolary documents can leave the modern reader perplexed and frustrated. Even if the difficulties of interpreting the unusual spellings and vocabulary are navigated, we are sometimes still left with only a vague sense of an author's intended message to his or her correspondent. This is not necessarily a result of unfamiliarity with late medieval language. In our efforts to judge whether a letter successfully conveys information from author to recipient, we need to be aware of the various modes of communication available to the late medieval gentry. Most importantly, it should be recognised that, like today, letters were not the only means of communicating at distance: the lawyer Thomas Mull's advice to Thomas Stonor to neither 'write nor sende' to a potential marriage partner (*KSL* 123) clearly implies an alternative to written communication, presumably using verbal messengers. In fact, it seems that most written communication would have been supplemented by accompanying verbal messages. This was facilitated by the means of delivery: entrusting a letter to a known individual for conveyance to the recipient. In this way, the sender could make use of the 'bearer' by providing him or her with additional information, to be passed on verbally at the destination. Inevitably, this meant that the content of any letter need not be comprehensive, since it would have been supplemented by verbally conveyed messages.

Evidence of this practice is plentiful within the letters themselves, which also throw light on its particular advantages. Most straightforwardly, the bearer of a letter could orally reinforce the content of the letter, such as when Alice, Lady Sudeley wrote to Thomas Stonor, 'wheche seid deedes the berer of this shall shewe vn-to you, as my full trust ys and hathe be vn-to you, like as the berer here of shall enfourme you, to whom y prey you geve credence' (*KSL* 53). Alternatively, the carrier might convey trivial news that did not seem to warrant writing down, or which did not require the authority of the written word, as seems to have been the case in communication directed to William Stonor in *c.* 1482: 'Your saide seruaunt, the berer herof, can enfourme you ferthre of suche novelles as ben here' (*KSL* 316). That some individuals were not adept at recalling their employers' messages is implied by a comment by Richard Page from about the same date: 'As for news, y haue told this berer to enforme yow. I fer me he cannot well shew them to your mastership' (*KSL* 309). Nevertheless, it is evident that messengers were sometimes trusted with information deemed too confidential or sensitive to be written down, where it might be at risk of being intercepted on its journey. In such cases, it might be assumed that the letter authenticated the verbal message conveyed by the carrier, and licensed him or her to speak on the sender's behalf. This certainly seems to be implied by John Paston III's comment in 1476 to a woman to whom he was at pains to recommend himself, perhaps as a potential marriage partner: 'my ryght trusty frend Rychard Stratton, berer her-of, to whom I beseche yow to geue credence in syche maters as he shall on my behalue comon wyth yow of, if it lyke you to lysten hym' (*PL* 373).

Whether or not their role is made explicit, it is likely that every time a messenger conveyed a letter some additional verbal information was carried also. Lack of clarity in the written document, therefore, cannot always be attributed to poorly developed literacy skills. We also need to recognise that the surviving correspondence probably forms only a small proportion of the total body of written communication between individuals. Moreover, in addition to the verbal information conveyed between correspondents, we might expect a whole array of collective knowledge to have existed, very little of which is accessible to the modern reader. In reality, it is usually a simple matter to distinguish deliberate vagueness from that which results from unaccomplished or clumsy use of language, but we can never be sure how much information was entrusted to the carrier, nor whether the recipient already possessed the details apparently lacking in a letter.

It remains the case, however, that most letters written in this period had a specific function, and were composed and sent in order to procure a rapid response to a matter of urgency. Although more casual, informal missives also exist, the majority of surviving fifteenth-century gentry correspondence involves requests for immediate action, and in such circumstances the primary concern of the writer would have been to convey his or her intent clearly and concisely. Elaborate stylistic flourishes might be impressive, but if they interfered with the purpose of the letter, the writer's linguistic sophistication might be seen to jeopardise his or her objectives in writing the letter. Conversely, the writer of a badly-composed letter that nevertheless conveys the force of a matter may be deemed 'less literate', but if he or she is more successful in procuring the desired response, this may be deemed a more proficient use of literacy. So in assessing levels of literacy, we should certainly pay attention to whether an author successfully communicates his or her intended message. However, just as when assessing the writing skills of the author, we need to be aware of contemporary practices in order to draw valid conclusions, and, if possible, to understand something of the relationship between the sender and the recipient of any letter.

One of the most interesting and valuable characteristics of late medieval gentry correspondence is the insight it offers into relationships between individuals, revealing how letters could play an important role in developing personal and political allegiances, in resolving – and sometimes inflaming – disputes, and ultimately in helping to shape group identities. The written language was a powerful medium through which writers could display their knowledge, form and manipulate opinion, or simply maintain contact with others. Anybody with access to a secretary could use letters for these purposes, but those with more developed literacy skills could seek to augment their status and increase the effectiveness of their communications by drawing on more sophisticated language resources.

Early commentators on the Paston and Stonor letters were eager to draw attention to their non-literary features, celebrating what they perceived as a lack of linguistic sophistication. H. S. Bennett wrote in 1947 that the writers' 'only endeavour was to state their ideas in a straight-forward fashion, almost as simply as if they were talking', echoing Fenn's late eighteenth-century view that the 'artless writers ... tell their tale in the plain and uncouth phrase of the time' and 'aim not at shining by art or eloquence, and bespeak credit by total carelessness of correction and ornament'.[31] It is true that some of the surviving letters provide valuable insights into spoken language, at times containing passages that are strikingly colloquial in tone and seem to have been transcribed directly from speech. Yet such an assessment fails to take into account widespread adherence to the formulaic traditions of letter-writing, or the highly fluent and sophisticated writing found in the correspondence of some of the writers.

In general, the most formal letters adhere most tightly to the formulaic conventions of epistolary composition, while the informal correspondence between close family members is more loosely structured, with only truncated forms of the traditional phrases that opened and closed a letter. Davis studied various constructions that reoccur in the letters in an attempt to show that usages which might appear to be colloquial may in fact have been conventional in written communication. He drew attention to the use of appositive participles, for instance, concluding that as 'they are so much more numerous in the fifteenth-century letters than anywhere else that they may fairly be attributed to the epistolary tradition in particular'.[32] There is little to differentiate their use in the letters of those authors who dictated from those who did not, suggesting that even those who did not possess developed writing skills were aware of a difference in register between spoken and written language. In the same study, Davis attempted to identify literary sources for phrases that occur with some regularity in the surviving letters; this might suggest, of course, the writers' familiarity with certain literary texts, and provide some indication of the extent of their reading literacy. Once again, the examples he used suggest a parity between those who habitually produced autograph letters and those who used secretaries. This may either hint at the persistent popularity of oral transmission of literary texts, or suggest that what seem to be literary influences are in fact colloquial phrases preserved by chance within surviving literary texts.

Commenting on Davis's study, Malcolm Parkes has suggested that '[t]he development in family letters of conscious *written* usage with subconscious literary echoes, as opposed to spoken usage, indicates a sophisticated rather than a rudimentary form of literacy'.[33] Yet if this is an accurate assessment, the presence of these 'literary echoes' in the letters of those with no attested ability to write forces us to reassess our definition of what it meant to be literate. Clearly, those who appear to have dictated their letters were aware of the need for a change in register between their spoken and written use of English: like their contemporaries who produced autograph documents, their letters too contained conscious or subconscious references to literary texts, as well as linguistic features particular to written usage and more specifically to the epistolary form. It seems obvious that these members of the gentry could possess a level of linguistic proficiency that surpassed their basic ability to write. Whether we choose to define their literacy skills as non-existent, rudimentary or sophisticated depends on the importance we attach to autograph composition.[34]

On the evidence of the Paston and Stonor correspondence, therefore, the gentry seem to have embraced fully the potential of written communication to demonstrate their awareness both of epistolary protocol, and of a distinct difference between the spoken and written language. Surviving correspondence by the mercantile class, such as the Celys of London, suggests that they too appropriated traditional forms of constructing letters, but were, in general, less adherent to structures inherited from the early medieval letter-manuals.[35] Undoubtedly, the late medieval gentry put their increasingly sophisticated literacy to use for the purpose of strengthening their group identity. They adopted forms of address and letter-structures that not only aligned their modes of communication with those of the nobility, but also affirmed their connection with tradition. Eager to advertise, and even exaggerate, details of their ancestry, high levels of literacy enabled the gentry to establish their place in society, and even to aspire to higher ranks.

Yet, as noted by Trapp, we cannot accurately judge overall levels of literacy from the limited range of surviving documentation available to us. Every conclusion must be tentative, and take full account of the difficulties inherent in using evidence that may not be wholly representative of the experiences of the diverse range of people that we might include within the gentry. In particular, when using personal correspondence as evidence for literacy, it is important to recognise that letters had functions beyond demonstrating an ability to write, and that usually practical concerns overtook any desire to flaunt advanced writing skills. For this reason, the most literate individuals may not have been those that used the most sophisticated language in their correspondence. It is impossible to quantify gentry literacy for this period, and hence each case must be taken individually and fully contextualised. Each member of the gentry possessed a level of literacy to suit his or her requirements. What distinguished members of this group from those below them on the social scale, and aligned them with the nobility, is that the means of acquiring literacy skills were more readily available to them; whether or not they chose to acquire them was a matter of personal circumstance, need or desire.

Notes

1 Clanchy, *From Memory*, p. 12. On early medieval literacy, also see McKitterick (ed.), *Uses of Literacy*, and Stock, *Implications of Literacy*.

2 On late medieval literacy, see, for example, Adamson, 'Extent of literacy'; Boffey, 'Women authors'; Bräuml, 'Varieties and consequences'; Coleman, *Public Reading*; Green, 'Orality and reading'; and Parkes, 'Literacy of the laity'.

3 Trapp, 'Literacy, books and readers', p. 31. Useful comments regarding the complexities of defining literacy in this period are also made in Moran Cruz, 'England: education and society', esp. pp. 465–6.

4 However, members of the increasingly influential merchant class, and professionals such as lawyers, are often seen to be on a par with the gentry in many respects, not least literacy. On this subject, see Thrupp, *Merchant Class*, ch. 6.

5 It should be noted, however, that even apparently personal correspondence was not always 'private', partly due to the methods of composition and delivery, and partly through being read aloud or collectively.

6 Clanchy, *From Memory*, p. 13. For a discussion of the development of pragmatic literacy during the Middle Ages, see Parkes, 'Literacy of the laity'.

7 Clanchy, *From Memory*, p. 234; Gabel, *Benefit of Clergy*.

8 Cressy, *Literacy and the Social Order*, pp. 176–7.

9 Lester, 'Books of a fifteenth-century gentleman', p. 216.

10 The Plumpton and Armburgh letters are of less value when considering gentry literacy; the original letters in these collections do not survive, and are only available to us through early seventeenth-century copies in a Letter Book and a Coucher Book (Plumpton), and on a fifteenth-century roll (Armburgh). See *Plumpton Letters*, ed. Kirby; *Armburgh Papers*, ed. Carpenter.

11 *Paston Letters*, ed. Gairdner, I, p. 318.

12 *Kingsford's Stonor Letters* (hereinafter *KSL*), ed. Carpenter, is a single-volume reprint of *Stonor Letters*, ed. Kingsford. Due to the unreliability of Kingsford's transcriptions, however, quotations in this chapter are taken from Truelove, 'Fifteenth-century English Stonor letters', but with yogh and thorn modernised, and with letter-number references to the published edition of the letters.

13 *KSL*, p. 75.

14 *Paston Letters*, ed. Davis (hereinafter *PL*, with references to letter-number).

15 See the section on 'Handwriting' in Davis's introduction to the letters: *PL*, I, pp. xxxv–xxxix.

16 See, for example, Davis, 'Language of the Pastons', 'Scribal variation', 'Text of Margaret Paston's letters', and 'Style and stereotype'.

17 On the development of Standard English see, for example, Fisher, *Emergence of Standard English*; Burnley, 'Sources of standardisation'; and Freeborn, *From Old English to Standard English*. See Truelove, 'Linguistic diversity', on the extent of standardisation in the language of some of the Stonor correspondents.

18 Gairdner was correct in stating that the handwriting and spelling in letters from the nobility were 'sometimes so outrageous, that it requires no small effort of imagination to comprehend the words, even if we could be sure of the letters' (*Paston Letters*, ed. Gairdner, I, p. 318).

19 On education and book-ownership, see Chapters 4 and 7, by Nicholas Orme and Deborah Youngs respectively, in the present volume.

20 In consideration of the widespread use of secretaries, it is more accurate to use the term 'author' than 'writer' when referring to the signatory of a letter.

21 *KSL* 220, 221, 229, 231, 245, 246, 256, 276, 282, 309, 310, 321, 322, 327; *PL* 406, 407, 409, 411, 414.

22 On the origins of letter-writing, see Camargo, 'Where's the brief'.

23 *PL*, I, p. 131 (headnote to *PL* 73).

24 For a more detailed analysis, see Davis's survey of the Pastons' handwriting (n. 16, above) and the headnotes to his transcriptions.

25 *KSL* 142, 151, 153; NA SC1/46/126 (unpublished fragment: see Truelove, 'Fifteenth-century English Stonor letters', I, p. 203).

26 *PL*, I, p. xxxvii.

27 *KSL* 186; she also wrote the postscript to a letter from her husband, Thomas, to Thomas Stonor (*KSL* 75). On the letters of the Stonor women generally, see Truelove, 'Commanding communications'.

28 Davis also draws attention to this in his survey of the Pastons' handwriting: *PL*, I, p. xxxviii.

29 On women as household managers, see Archer, '"How ladies ... who live on their manors"'.

30 This must by necessity be a very tentative conclusion: we must acknowledge the difficulty that those who were illiterate often left little or no documentary trail, and are therefore hidden from the historian's view.

31 Bennett, *Chaucer and the Fifteenth Century*, p. 180; *Original Letters*, ed. Fenn, I, p. xv; Davis, 'Style and stereotype', p. 7.

32 Davis, 'Style and stereotype', pp. 8–9.

33 Parkes, 'Literacy of the laity', p. 295.

34 On the interrelationship between orality and literacy, see Coleman, *Public Reading*, pp. 1–33.

35 Thomas, 'Business writing in history'; *Cely Letters*, ed. Hanham.

6

Literature

Raluca Radulescu

Any discussion of gentry culture in late medieval England, and of the specific phenomena that accompany the shaping of gentry cultural identity, necessarily requires an analysis of the literature read, and sometimes produced, by the gentry. The emulation of noble culture in gentry circles has been noted by many critics;[1] in recent years, however, more emphasis has been placed on the similarities between the culture of the country gentry and that of urban elites, especially regarding the texts they chose to read and circulate, and the manuscripts they commissioned. As Felicity Riddy points out, these 'gentry and urban elites ... converged ... especially in their private identities', and this phenomenon of convergence coincided with the composition of a particular type of literature, the Middle English romances, texts which became witnesses of a 'new "bourgeois-gentry" cultural formation'.[2]

Literature, here defined in an all-inclusive way, rather than material for entertainment purposes, is traditionally assessed in relation to authorship, authorial intention, audience and socio-political context, and thus an investigation into the influence of literature on the gentry needs to take into account all of these factors. By identifying ownership marks in manuscripts and wills, and then by analysing the vocabulary and ideas employed in texts included in manuscripts associated with the gentry, we can reach a better understanding of those concepts which allowed members of the gentry to define the cultural characteristics, and, in many cases, protect the exclusivity, of their social class. How reliable are inventories, wills and marginalia in manuscripts owned, commissioned or circulated among the gentry, when one tries to establish the categories of literature read in the gentry household?[3] It is not easy to decipher the motivations behind purchasing or reading particular tracts, let alone restricting the use of romances or historical or political literature to gentry and urban circles. Since romances were read alongside other literary, historical, political and religious texts, and since their audience was both noble and gentle, the main focus of this chapter will be to identify gentry concerns in the different texts available to them, rather than to provide an exhaustive survey of literature contained in gentry-owned manuscripts.

Out of the various texts available to the gentry which had a direct relevance in their shaping of cultural identity, several will be examined in this chapter, from books of nurture (teaching gentle manners) to romances, historical and political tracts. Gentry reading interests were also linked to their everyday concerns, present in the family correspondence of the Pastons, the Stonors, the Plumptons, and the Armburghs. In these letters members of gentry families expressed their concerns, mostly centred around the notion of preserving personal and the family's worship, cultivating gentle manners, including good governance of the household and political behaviour in the locality, as well as keeping and improving alliances through marriage and through business contracts. These interests can be summed up in the concepts of 'worship', 'friendship', 'fellowship', 'lordship' and 'governance', which appear time and again in gentry letters, indicating their importance in everyday gentry life.[4]

The same ideas are reflected in the literature read, and sometimes produced, in the gentry household. The preservation of worship was intimately linked with the performance of one's duties and appropriate behaviour in all circumstances; as a result, an increasing number of books of nurture were read and copied into miscellanies circulated in gentry circles in late medieval England. The same advice previously destined for royal ears (in mirrors for princes) appears in instructional literature read by the gentry, and manners suitable for areas as diverse as domestic activities (including behaviour at the table) and political interactions in the locality are given equal importance. The increasing number of fifteenth-century gentry who commissioned and used courtesy books was due to their desire to supply an educational programme for acquiring those 'social skills of the class to which they aspired for themselves or for their children'.[5] As shown elsewhere in this volume, Latin, French and English formed an integral part of the education of gentry children and of gentry culture; as a result, at least some of the gentry would have been able to engage with texts written in one of these languages, whether for instructional purposes or recreation, or in order to facilitate business or other types of communication.

Instructional texts appear in miscellaneous manuscripts alongside romances, religious tracts and other items, including recipes and medical remedies. Without containing texts exclusively associated with the gentry, many of these anthologies or mini-libraries address a practical interest in shaping a gentle identity. Because the contents of such miscellanies reflect a shared literary taste with a noble audience, literary critics have often neglected the importance of gentry agency in their production and circulation. Surviving evidence about members of the gentry with a developed literary taste, who wrote or copied various tracts, designing their tracts or anthologies for the use of all members of a household, proves that a more specific, gentry-oriented production of books was perceived as necessary. Robert Thornton, for example, was one gentleman who gathered and copied into his anthology not only literary texts which would have appealed to his noble and gentle friends, but also religious and medical material, which would have served the interests of other members of his audience, male and female, sometimes of a lower social status than that of the gentry.[6] Indeed the similarity between this manuscript and others has led Phillipa Hardman to conclude that 'the fundamental purpose of all … household miscellanies … was to construct and preserve the collective memory of the household'.[7]

The identification of similar contents in miscellaneous manuscripts cannot, however, always be taken to represent a sign of demand from a particular reading public; post-1980s research has shown that the available groupings of texts would have prompted frequent re-copying and thus a partial standardization of contents.[8] On the other hand, the readers of these booklets would have shared expectations about contents and material production with writers and booksellers, since, as Andrew Taylor points out, 'without such common norms, reading would lose much of its social prestige'.[9] The pragmatic circumstances for the copying of various tracts into miscellanies, as well as for the acquisition of newly printed books which promised instruction in the form of exemplary romance, were prompted both by their inexpensive price and their relative availability on the market.[10] Nevertheless, the circumstances in which many composite manuscripts were produced in gentry circles, whether in the local communities or in the urban milieu, are often comparable, reflecting, as Alexandra Gillespie points out, the personal choices made by individuals, 'whose tastes and interests determined the final form of the volume'.[11]

Gentility

Among the most well-known Middle English texts dealing with the topic of gentility are Chaucer's poem 'Gentilesse' and his 'Wife of Bath's Tale'. The portraits of the Knight and the Franklin in Chaucer's *Canterbury Tales* have also been used by literary critics and historians when discussing fourteenth-century society and its stratification in relation to Chaucer's own reflections on this topic. Elsewhere in this volume these two portraits, as well as that of the Squire and of female characters, are used as a bridge between an imagined social structure and the real hierarchy which members of the gentry experienced in late medieval England. In such discussions due attention is paid to the complex issue of authorial intention and projected/real audience, as well as to fourteenth- and fifteenth-century readers' sensitivity to Chaucer's use of irony.

Chaucer's poem 'Gentilesse' and the old hag's monologue on the same topic in the 'Wife of Bath's Tale' explore the concept of gentility from the classical viewpoint of Christian virtue, while also taking into account the debate about the primacy of nobility by birth over that acquired by cultivating virtues and good manners. This debate featured in medieval romances and other exemplary stories in various forms, and represented an issue of great interest for the gentry and those who aspired to their status. Chaucer's verses reflect contemporary anxieties associated with traditional views of nobility by virtue as well as the new emphasis on cultivating appropriate gentle behaviour by heeding the advice of the old texts:

> He is noght gentil, thogh he riche seme,
> Al were he mytre, croune, or diademe.
>
> Vyce may wel be heir to old richesse,
> But ther may no man, as men may wel see,
> Bequethe his heir his vertuous noblesse[12]

According to medieval philosophy the source of all virtues was Christ, while nobility was transmitted through generations. While a noble ancestry and personal wealth did not, however, guarantee virtuous behaviour, the display of gentlemanly manners was a prerequisite of 'gentilesse' and all those who learned manners and had the financial resources to maintain a gentlemanly lifestyle could aspire to gentle status. This controversy over the old and the new view of gentility is exemplified in the old hag's diatribe in the 'Wife of Bath's Tale':

> But, for ye speken of swich gentilesse
> As is descended out of old richesse,
> That therfore sholden ye be gentil men,
> Swich arrogance is nat worth an hen.[13]

Nigel Saul notes that in this poem 'Chaucer's avoidance of economic criteria to define gentility was wholly in accord with the contemporary outlook'; moreover '[g]entility was viewed at the time as a *quality*, and accordingly was assessed in qualitative terms'.[14] Chaucer's verses reflect his sensitivity to this new development in late medieval mentality and the social changes taking place in late fourteenth-century England. Whether they had access to Chaucer's work or not (or indeed to any other similar writings in the period), most members of the gentry would have sympathised with his views on gentility as expressed here; the idea of cultivating virtues in order to maintain or improve one's status could only reinforce the gentry's sense of their place in the local community, in the urban milieu and in court circles.

Romances

Medieval French and English romances were particularly attractive to gentry readers, as the heroes and heroines in these narratives display a constant preoccupation with learning appropriate behaviour and shaping their social and cultural identity. The myth of knighthood put forth in these romances was thus easily adaptable to gentry needs; Riddy states in her recent study that:

> The knight's horse and his social status are emblematic of mobility and freedom. Although he looks archaic, he is in many ways a new man in fourteenth-century England: an adventure-seeker and risk-taker, a uniquely accessible and adaptable locus of fantasy and desire. In late medieval English romances the knight can be seen as a 'bourgeois-gentry' myth of young manhood.[15]

Helen Cooper also highlights several developments typical of Middle English romances, which correspond to the demands of a different audience than that for their French sources:

> The shift away from courtliness and ideological and sexual fantasies is reflected in the different social and ethical priorities contained in much Middle English romance. Adultery is rare, genealogy and a sense of a plausible history of Britain are given a higher profile, ideals are more

practical, in terms of homosocial relations, courtship leading to marriage, and a piety characterised by devotional duty rather than mysticism; and adventures tend at least to be grounded in a sense of possible.[16]

Manuscripts of both French and English romances circulated widely in gentry circles, and William Caxton partly anticipated, partly stimulated the interest of a gentry audience for his printed books when he encouraged them to read, for example, his edition of Sir Thomas Malory's *Le Morte Darthur*, in which a reader would find examples of noble and virtuous deeds of ancient heroes.[17] In a shorter romance, *Blanchardyn and Eglantine*, Caxton urged the reader to look for similar values to those contained in pious devotional tracts; the piety and steadfastness of gentle ladies depicted in these romances, he argued, would provide a similar model for a female audience: 'it is requesyte otherwhyle to rede in auncyent historyes of noble fayttes and valyaunt actes of armes and warre … in lyke wyse for gentyl ladyes and damoyselles for to lerne to be stedfaste and constaunt in their part to theym that they ones have promysed and agreed to'.[18] Commenting on this passage, Taylor sees Caxton's agency in the 'formation of a readership [as] a deliberate commercial policy', with the 'central claim that reading is a prerequisite of gentility'.[19] It is of course evident that the printer appealed, and also responded, to the desires of his would-be gentry audience, who were looking for texts which would help to shape a convenient social identity. Equally important in this discussion are female gentry readers and the broad appeal of these texts to both country gentry and urban elites.[20] Indeed the available evidence about book circulation shows that these readers seemed to find useful any tracts dealing with gentility and the appropriate ways to display it.

Caxton's marketing appeal was, however, not unique; another well-known scribe and translator, John Shirley, displayed sensitivity to social change when he chose to address his audience as 'my gracious lordes and feyre laydes my maystres and specyalli freendes and gode felawes' in the introductory lines to his copy of the *Brut* chronicle in Harvard MS English 530 (fol. 180v).[21] Shirley created a personal, recognisable style in his prefaces, especially as he wanted to emphasise the importance of reading (or listening to) English history: 'Loo heer my lordes maystres and felawes may yee see a truwe and brief abstracte of the Cronycles of this reaume of England frome the tyme that euer ma[n]kynde enhabited hit into the tyme of the laste Edwarde: reedethe or heerethe the sothe here filowing' (fol. 59r). In another preface, this time to his copy of the *Canterbury Tales*, found in the composite manuscript BL Harley 7333, once again Shirley widens the social circle of his readers, including all those who might be of 'gentile birth or … condiciouns':

> O yee so noble and worthi pryncis and princesse *other estatis or degrees what euer yee* beo that haue disposicione or plesaunce to rede or here the stories of olde tymis passed to kepe yow frome ydelnesse and slowthe in escheuing other folies that might be cause of more harome filowing … the tales of Caunterburye wiche beon compilid in this boke filowing ffirst foundid ymagenid and made *bothe for disporte and leornyng of all thoo that beon gentile of birthe or of condiciouns* … (fol. 37r; my italics)

The 'socially-mixed clientele' Shirley envisaged for his manuscripts is also mentioned in his formulae in BL MS Additional 16165, where his readers are addressed as 'bothe the gret and the comune' (1.18), 'this companye' (1.101); he also talks about 'all yt in this company / ben knight squyer or lady / or other estat what euer they be' (2.91–3). It is thus very likely that Shirley 'prepared his manuscripts according to the tastes of his audience, not merely because of his own literary interests'.[22] Whether intended as a marketing strategy or not, Shirley's prefaces shared a similar audience with Caxton's for the *Morte Darthur*, also 'al noble lordes and ladyes wyth al other estates, of *what estate or degree hey been of*'.[23] Caxton similarly looked beyond a noble audience, including in his addressees the gentry and the merchants (and perhaps not least any other readers who might have liked to 'style' themselves as gentry), who were interested in chivalric tracts. His further attempt to standardize the use of English by choosing an idiom which (he hoped) would be understood by everyone, is also representative of his wish to reach out to the 'clerke' as much as to the 'noble gentylman'; such a reader, irrespective of his social background (but possessing enough 'gentility' to be able to recognize the virtues advocated in Caxton's edition of *Eneydos*, for example), 'feleth and understondeth in faytes of armes, in love, and in noble chyvalrye'.[24]

In Malory's *Morte*, 'The Tale of Sir Gareth', like *Sir Isumbras* and other romances which describe the journey of a male hero in search of his (social) identity, contains, in a nutshell, all the advice given to young members of the gentry, from courtly virtues and manners to hunting and governance of the household. Gareth displays all the qualities of one of noble birth but needs to go through tests which in fact prove the premise of the story, that 'manhode and worship [ys hyd] within a mannes person; and many a worshipfull knyght ys nat knowyn unto all peple'.[25] As a result, a knight's qualities, mainly prowess and gentleness, appear as something to be developed – a sensitive issue for gentry readers of the *Morte* who were preoccupied by shaping their identity. Gareth's romance, without a known source, combines the traditional elements of the 'Fair Unknown' type,[26] with a striking emphasis on the performance of 'jantyllmannys servyse'. The last element appears to guarantee, in Larry Benson's words, 'all a gentleman needs to found a noble fifteenth-century family': 'riches, a noble wife, and a mighty retinue of the sort so necessary to the great households of the time'; in short, 'an almost possible dream for fifteenth-century gentlemen'.[27] Moreover, critics have shown that the process of 'growing up' through tests, and later courtship and the winning of the lady, is expressed in terms that reflect fifteenth-century gentry concerns with marriage alliances, the most typical example being provided by the Paston correspondence.[28]

Gareth's hidden identity at the beginning of the story (he is the brother of Sir Gawain) creates a tension in the narrative, which is only enhanced in each episode when he displays gentlemanly qualities. A contrast to Sir Kay, whose abrupt manners portray him as an 'unjantyll knyght', Gareth presented an opportunity for Malory to show the most appropriate behaviour for a gentleman; this character exemplifies, to a certain extent, the notion of 'nobility by virtue' as much as that of 'nobility by descent', issues which lay at the core of the fifteenth-century debate over gentility.[29] As a result, Gareth embodies Malory's original comment in 'The Tale of Sir Tristram', that 'he that jantyll is woll drawe hym to jantyll tacchis and to folow the noble customys of jantylmen', itself taken as an argument for distinguishing 'a jantylman frome a yoman and a yoman frome a vylayne'.[30]

Another hero of Arthurian romance, Sir Tristram, is invested, in Malory's story, with the authorship of 'all the good termys of venery and of huntynge', which 'all maner jantylmen' should be grateful for.[31] Time and again Malory's original passages on gentlemanly topics have been regarded by critics as examples of an inflexible view of social distinctions.[32] Recent analyses of Malory's *Morte* show, however, that he chose to describe gentlemanly behaviour in terms that would have appealed to his fifteenth-century gentry readers; this points to the idea of advancement in society through the cultivation of manners (chivalric behaviour may be learned within the *Morte*, from Tristram's and Gareth's example) in a similar fashion as in contemporary England, while access to knighthood was denied to the lower classes.[33] As already mentioned, we cannot assume that all gentry readers were familiar with Chaucer's and Malory's portraits of knights and squires, yet most of the gentry had access to similar examples of gentlemanly behaviour contained in popular romances (sometimes

circulating orally), books of instruction and penitential literature. The
gentry's attitude to such examples would naturally have been one of
sympathy and admiration; John Paston III's enthusiasm for Arthurian
romance, for example, is reflected in his passionate description of the
Burgundian court.[34] John III's career at the court enabled him (and others
like him) to travel to Europe and thus also to familiarise himself with the
chivalric traditions circulating on the Continent.

In another romance, *Sir Isumbras*, gentry readers could find all the
attributes necessary for a happy life, including courtly manners, knightly
achievement, financial stability and a wise choice in marriage, as well as the
path to religious salvation. Isumbras is described, from the beginning of
the romance, as the epitome of gentility:

> A curteys man and hende he was,
> His name was kalled syr Isumbras,
> > Bothe curteys and fre.
> His gentylnesse nor his curtesye
> There kowthe no man hit discrye:
> A ffull good man was he.
> [...]
> Of curtesye he was kynge;
> His gentylnesse hadde non endyng,
> In worlde was none so fre.[35]

The same is true about *Sir Gowther* and *Sir Amadas*, which in one
manuscript are accompanied by courtesy books, the *Urbanitatis* and the
Little Children's Book, thus 'providing practical instruction on good conduct
and etiquette: the "nortur" necessary to train the young gentleman'.[36]
Moreover, the same terms of carving and hunting mentioned in Malory's
'Tale of Sir Tristram' are present in the romance of *Sir Isumbras*; this
appears to be a design that reflects an educational programme for gentry
readers of such texts.

Alongside examples of gentle manners, some medieval romances also
contained a pious element, which appealed to gentry readers. In *Sir
Gowther* the hero is expected to pass several tests in order to attain
salvation and expiate his sins. To give another example, Malory's sinful
knight, Lancelot, becomes a saint, in what is an uncommon version of the
Arthurian story: at Lancelot's death the bishop sees his body taken up by
angels and a sweet scent spreads in the room, both of which are signs
usually associated with sainthood.[37] The penitential tracts read by the
gentry equally emphasised these patterns of behaviour; it becomes obvious

that these examples converged into a model of gentle conduct which could only appeal to the late medieval English gentry.

Tracts of practical use

The importance of miscellanies containing practical advice for the gentleman has received attention in post-1980s studies, with particular emphasis on the shaping of socio-political and cultural identity.[38] George Keiser points to the popularity of tracts on hawking and hunting both before and after the beginning of the printing era, justified by the ownership of manuscript miscellanies containing them; there is proof that these miscellanies 'reached the readership to which they were directed, that is, the English landholding classes and those responsible to them'.[39] Some examples of miscellanies connected with the gentry containing books of nurture alongside other material are Yale University Beinecke Library MS 163, BL MS Sloane 2027, and BL MS Royal 17 D xv.[40] Evidence for the appeal of miscellanies well into the printing era is provided by John Fitzherbert's *Book of Husbandry* (one of the most published and informative tracts of this kind), in which the author encourages its use in the gentry household:

> I auyse hym [any gentleman] to gete a copy of the present boke and to rede it from the beginning vnto thendyng/ wherby he may percuyue the chapiters and contentes of the same/ and by reson of oft redynge he may waxe parfet what shuld be done at all seasons ... Ryght so a man shalbe made wyse/ nat all onely by himself but by his oft redyng. And so may this yonge gentylman: acording to the season of the yere/ rede to his seruauntes what chapyter he woll.[41]

The gentleman is here urged to become an educator in his household, and his duties are thus extended from governance and wise rule over his family and servants to their instruction.

Practical miscellanies did not only focus on education and hunting and husbandry; indeed many of the surviving composite manuscripts associated with the gentry contain military (and chivalric) material and mirrors for princes. One of the most popular military tracts in late medieval England and Europe was Flavius Renatus Vegetius's *De Re Militari* (also known as *Epitoma Rei Militari*); among mirrors, Thomas Hoccleve's *Regiment for Princes* and John Lydgate's translation of the text known as the *Secrets of the Philosophers* gained popularity among both the English nobility and the gentry.[42] Examples of miscellanies containing a combination of these texts with other types of material are BL MS Sloane 2027,[43] BL MS Additional 14408, BL MS Lansdowne 285 (associated with the Paston family, now known as Sir John Paston's 'grete boke'),[44] Oxford, Bodleian Library MS Laud Misc. 416, and New York, Pierpont Morgan Library MS 775 (Sir John Astley's chivalric miscellany, which served as a model for Paston's).[45] Sir John Paston admired Astley, a Knight of the Garter well established at the court and particularly skilled in royal tournaments. Astley's miscellany contains the oath and ceremonies of the Knights of the Bath, several chivalric tracts, including Vegetius' *De Re Militari* and Christine de Pisan's *Epistle of Othea* (a similar tract on strategic advice in the form of a mirror), the poem at King Henry VI's coronation and Lydgate's *Secrets*, while Paston's 'grete boke' contains the same material, with minor variations. Paston's 'grete boke' seems to have been intended as a 'home encyclopedia of coats of arms', while he seems to have been interested in gathering a 'reference library of descriptive and how-to books on chivalry', a collection, which, as Thomas Hahn states, 'must have held urgent interest for the first member of a socially mobile family elevated to a knighthood.'[46] Moreover, the literary tastes of those members of the gentry who, like Paston and Astley, enjoyed the privileges of an international career (through war service or involvement in politics) were, as already mentioned, influenced by their contacts with European culture.

Indeed in England the popularity of the *De Re Militari* was such that, apart from several prose translations, a verse one survives; the latter was presented to Henry VI between 1457 and 1460, and was printed by Caxton under the title *Knyghthode and Bataile*.[47] Similar manuscripts of *De Re Militari* appealed to gentlemen who commissioned coats of arms and lavish illustrations alongside the main text, for example in Oxford, Magdalen College MS 30, Bodleian Library Digby MS 233 and Douce MS 291, and BL Royal MS 18 A xii.[48] Such manuscripts displayed their owners' pride and their attempt to establish their chivalric identity and their partnership in the governance of the realm.

Advice literature

Those members of gentry circles who interacted in the process of borrowing, lending, reading and commissioning miscellanies containing literary material were equally fascinated by the topics of governance, the commonweal of the realm and national history. In the composite manuscripts many copies survive of the *Brut* chronicle, Hoccleve's *Regiment*,

Lydgate's *Secrets*, chronicles, genealogical chronicles and advice literature alongside romances. To what extent did the gentry really choose their reading material, and what particular relevance did didactic literature and historical tracts formerly addressed to princes have in their everyday life? There is a striking similarity between the language employed in books of nurture and mirrors for princes, especially in terms of advice on personal conduct. Prudent speech, or indeed knowing when to keep quiet, is recommended, for example, in Peter Idley's *Instructions to his Son*, in proverbial phrases of the type 'Restreyne and kepe well thy tonge' and 'Be not autour also of tales newe'.[49] Furthermore a lot of emphasis is placed on giving and receiving advice:

> While thy counceill is within thy breste,
> It is sure as within a castell walle;
> And whan it is out fro thy cheste,
> Then art thou to thy counceill thrall.
> Therfore I counceill the oonys for all:
> Kepe thy tonge and kepe thy frende
> In euery contree wher thou wende.[50]

Such instructions have a resonance in the gentry correspondence, where wise conduct is described, in its turn, in terms also employed in the didactic literature directed to the prince.[51] Philippa Maddern points out that John Russe advised John Paston I in the same terms as those by which fifteenth-century kings were addressed in mirrors for princes, and the resulting image is that of Paston 'as a little king, advised by his faithful servant'.[52] These phrases are combined with advice regarding public (and political) behaviour, as exemplified by the following passage from a poem containing similar advice:

> Yf that thow wolte speke A-ryght,
> Ssyx thynggys thow moste obserue then:
> What thow spekyst, and of what wyght,
> Whare, to whan, whye, and whenne.[53]

As Nicholas Perkins notes, these texts were not exclusively related to personal conduct in one's private life, but were rather seen as 'units of authority, applicable both to personal ethics and political governance', and thus easily applicable in a variety of circumstances, in order to 'reinforce a moral or political argument at any level'.[54] Indeed, in the same poem cited above, one is advised against 'hasty speech', since such words may have political repercussions:

> Yf euery man had thys woord in thowght
> Meny thynggis had neuer be by-gunne
> That ofte yn Ingelond hath be y-wroght.[55]

This is a type of advice repeated in popular political poetry as well as in alliterative poems such as *Piers Plowman, Mum and the Sothsegger*, and *Richard the Redeless*, which survive in manuscripts often circulated among, and owned by, the gentry. Initially designed as advice literature for the consumption of the royal house, Hoccleve's and Lydgate's works addressed a wider readership during the fifteenth century, at a time when the gentry perceived their increasing involvement in local and central politics as an incentive to shape their own political identity. As a result, this type of literature developed 'plural voices', since it was directed towards a diverse audience; Hoccleve's poem, for example, may be said to have 'plural destinations', expressing political concerns like counsel and governance for readers outside court circles, while also helping to establish a 'tradition of vernacular writing on issues of governance which gave an English vocabulary to the process of political engagement'.[56] The interest in these texts manifested by the gentry also had a link with the changes in royal governance during the reign of the Yorkist king Edward IV, known for his policy of looking for support less from the divided nobility and more from among the newly empowered members of the gentry.[57] Another gentleman, George Ashby, indeed advised the king to rely on the gentry:

> Make knyghtes, squiers & gentilmen riche,
> And the pore Comyns also welthy,
> But to youre richesse make neuer man liche,
> If he wol stande in peas and be set by.
> So wol god and polleci sykerly,
> Lyke as ye in estate other excelle,
> In propre richesse ye sholde bere the belle.[58]

The readership of Hoccleve's and Lydgate's texts also increased, since advice about political behaviour necessarily became part of the public sphere; the cultural impact of these works was as great as that of political writings by professionals such as Sir John Fortescue. All of these were 'open texts', and their gentry readers felt entitled to participate in the 'construction of their meaning' by reflecting upon problems of governance in their own experience of local and central politics.[59]

The particular appeal of the mirrors in the fifteenth century is not surprising, given the late medieval climate of political instability, accompanied by spiritual and social reform. While the heroes of romance offered ideal models of courtly behaviour in an environment removed from reality, instructional literature presented practical advice in recognizable circumstances, in an English idiom also employed in the public, political sphere. The consumption of this type of vernacular literature became, as Larry Scanlon cogently states, 'no less an exercise in cultural entitlement than the growing participation in political discourse'.[60] In fact this literature reflects a desire to maintain peace and order on a personal level as much as in society at large.

Instructional literature thus provided a vocabulary which could be used in the transmission of political ideas at all levels of society. The appropriation of the political concepts used by authors of advice literature into the public sphere is evident: political figures of the day used vocabulary derived from these texts, because advice literature provided, as Judith Ferster suggests, 'nuanced models of relationships between rulers and subjects'.[61]

Historical literature

As already mentioned, chronicles and genealogical material formed a large proportion of the texts commissioned, owned and read by the English gentry, who were preoccupied with history especially because of their involvement in local and central governance and political events. Their interest in the national past was manifested not least in commissioning, for example, family crests alongside the text of the *Brut* chronicle, in the gentry-owned manuscript now Oxford, Bodleian Library Digby MS 185, belonging to the family of Sir William Hopton of Swillington, in what Carol Meale has identified as a desire to portray the family's presence in historical events of national importance.[62] Moreover, as Maurice Keen points out, the importance given to knightly descent and participation in historical events was reflected in some gentry genealogies, real or fabricated, hence the hastiness with which members of the gentry attempted to construct a family history going as far back as possible, since the common opinion was, as Nicholas Upton put it in his *De Studio Militari*, 'he is gentyll that descendyth of gentyll stok'.[63] The Pastons produced a family genealogy going back to the Conquest, while Humphrey Newton, a gentleman from Cheshire, took an active interest in reconstructing his family's local history.[64]

Other members of the gentry and urban circles chose to copy historical narratives, mainly the *Brut* chronicle, into their miscellanies (as we have already seen), or to write short chronicles or poems which contain a personal view of contemporary events, thus providing invaluable evidence of gentry agency in the writing of literature and history.[65] Recent findings and investigations have revealed the importance of contextualising political texts. An example is provided by the collection now known as 'John Vale's Book' (now BL Additional 48031A), composed in the later part of the fifteenth century by a scribe in the household of Sir John Cook, alderman and mayor of London in the reign of Edward IV, in which Vale's own short chronicle of the events from 1431 to 1471 is present alongside political pamphlets, Lydgate's *Serpent of Division* and Fortescue's *Governance of England*. Other gentlemen in small local communities wrote political verses in the margins or on the back of other manuscripts, thus displaying their interest in contemporary political events.[66]

The reading of chronicles was, along with discussions of chivalric tracts, a favourite pastime for gentlemen in court circles, as attested by an oft-cited passage from the household book of Edward IV, in which the esquires in the king's entourage, purposefully chosen from among the gentry (so that, 'by the auyse of his counsayll to be chosen men of theyre possession, worship and wisdom; also to be of sundry sheres, by whome hit may be knowe the disposicion of the cuntries'), are presented:

> Thes esquires of housold of old be acustomed, wynter and somer, in after nonys and in euenynges, to drawe to lordez chambrez within courte, there to kepe honest company aftyr theyre cunyng, in talkyng of cronycles of kinges and of other polycyez, or in pypyng, or harpyng, synging, other actez marciablez, to help ocupy the court and acompany straungers, tyll the tym require of departing.[67]

The *Brut* chronicle, with approximately 240 surviving manuscripts, was one such widely-read chronicle, the equivalent of a modern 'best-seller', only surpassed in popularity by the Wycliffite Bible.[68] Among these manuscripts, a significant number were owned by, and circulated in, gentry circles; the manuscripts containing this chronicle are heavily annotated and frequently contain attempts at inscribing family events in the larger picture of national history.[69] It is not surprising to see a gentry interest in these tracts; Malory's own interest in history was deeply influenced by his experience of contemporary anxieties over the English possessions in France and the English kings' ambitions to rule Europe. In Riddy's words, Malory's version of King Arthur's war with the Roman emperor becomes a 'post-imperial, or even post-colonial, text, which speaks with the voices of these "noble and dyvers gentymen" of Malory's generation, for whom the loss of the French territories in 1453 had been a personal disaster, and who could not accommodate themselves to the diminished view of their country and of their own role and prospects'.[70] As a result, in this and other romances as well as in historical and political texts the gentry found a 'public treasury of familiar terms and concepts, a clear and coherent conceptual framework for politics and a language in which to express it'.[71] John Watts has analysed the ideas that underlay fifteenth-century governance and its manifestation at all levels of society; in his opinion, this 'matrix of ideas' influences politics 'because in order to promote and defend their activities in a particular public environment, politicians are forced to explain themselves with reference to its "accepted principles", and this consideration, in turn, shapes their behaviour'.[72] The gentry used such political discourse both in their correspondence about governance and political events and in their own writings, since they felt the need to 'draw attention to the ideas and principles which underpinned their actions' at a time when 'the disorderly political events … were accompanied by a rich debate over the rights and duties of rulers and subjects'.[73] Thus an understanding of fifteenth-century gentry culture, including their political culture, can only be reached by examining the political attitudes the gentry developed under the influence of the texts they read.

Conclusion

What would the gentry have learned and put into practice from the texts they read and discussed? From books of nurture and mirrors for princes: how to behave appropriately and how to govern well, from romances, how to perform in a courtly context, and from chronicles and historical material, how to discuss national history and integrate their family history in the larger narrative of the nation. Despite inevitable difficulties in assessing the extent to which any of these practices were directly influenced by the texts they read and sometimes wrote, one can safely conclude that the cultural identity of the late medieval English gentry was shaped through a complex process, modified by factors as diverse as the literature available to them.

Notes

I would like to thank Professors P. J. C. Field and V. J. Scattergood for their comments and advice on earlier drafts of this chapter.

1 Among other studies, see especially Duby, 'Diffusion of cultural patterns', and Coss, 'Aspects of cultural diffusion'.
2 Riddy, 'Middle English romance', p. 237.
3 See Cavanaugh, 'Study of books privately owned'; an up-to-date inventory of manuscripts owners in late medieval England is now available online at http://lamop.univ-paris1.fr; this is part of an on-going project directed by Professor Jean-Philippe Genet, University of Paris I (Sorbonne). The most comprehensive inventory of romances in medieval English manuscripts is Guddat-Figge's *Catalogue of Manuscripts*.
4 An extensive discussion of gentry values reflected in their correspondence is available in Radulescu, *Gentry Context*, ch. 1.
5 Riddy, *Sir Thomas Malory*, p. 71.
6 Robert Thornton and his activities are discussed by Deborah Youngs in Chapter 7 of the present volume, at pp. 122, 126–7.
7 Hardman, 'Evidence of readership', p. 27.
8 See for example Hanna, 'Miscellaneity and vernacularity'.
9 Taylor, 'Authors, scribes', p. 362.
10 Boffey and Thompson, 'Anthologies and miscellanies', p. 295.
11 Gillespie, 'Balliol MS 354', p. 48.
12 *Riverside Chaucer*, p. 654 (lines 13–17).
13 *Riverside Chaucer*, p. 120 (lines 1109–12).
14 Saul, 'Chaucer and gentility', p. 39.
15 Riddy, 'Middle English romance', p. 239.
16 Cooper, 'Lancelot-Grail cycle', p. 148.
17 Malory, *Works*, p. xl.
18 Blake, *Caxton's Own Prose*, pp. 57–8.
19 Taylor, 'Authors, scribes', p. 364.
20 See Meale, '… alle the bokes' and 'gode men/Wiues, maydens and alle men'; Riddy, 'Women talking', and Boffey, 'Women authors and women's literacy'.
21 The introductory headings are printed by Voigts, 'Handlist of Middle English manuscripts'. Harvard MS English 530 is a miscellany in two parts, written by several scribes, which contains other items of interest for a gentle audience, like the *Brut* chronicle and its continuations alongside Lydgate's prose tract *The Serpent of Division*. Some ideas and quotes in this chapter are taken from Radulescu, *Gentry Context*, ch. 2.
22 Connolly, *John Shirley*, p. 139. The passages are cited at pp. 174 and 194.
23 Malory, *Works*, p. xl (my italics).
24 Blake, *Caxton's Own Prose*, p. 80.
25 Malory, *Works*, p. 63 (this comment is present in the episode about another knight, sir Balin).

26 See Field, 'Source of Malory's "Tale of Gareth"', pp. 246–60.

27 Benson, *Malory's* Morte Darthur, p. 108.

28 See Cherewatuk, 'Pledging troth'.

29 See Riddy, *Sir Thomas Malory*, p. 62. The debate over nobility of birth versus nobility of virtue was contained in *Knyghthode and Bataile*. The problem of nobility preoccupied Sir John Tiptoft, the fifteenth-century politician and humanist, whose translation of Buonaccorso da Mantemagno's tract on 'The Declamation of Nobility' contains arguments for and against nobility by birth (see Mitchell, *John Tiptoft*).

30 Malory, *Works*, p. 375. See also Riddy, *Sir Thomas Malory*, chapter on Sir Gareth.

31 Malory, *Works*, pp. 682–3.

32 Riddy, *Sir Thomas Malory*, p. 95.

33 For a review of criticism, see Radulescu, 'Introduction', in *Gentry Context*.

34 *Paston Letters*, ed. Davis, I, p. 539.

35 *Sir Isumbras*, in *Six Middle English Romances*, ed. Mills, p. 125 (lines 19–24 and 28–30).

36 Hardman, 'Compiling the nation'. The discussion in this paragraph is based on Hardman's analysis.

37 See Radulescu, '"now I take uppon me the adventures"' and Cherewatuk, 'Saint's life of sir Lancelot'.

38 See for example Keiser, 'Practical books'; the examples cited in this paragraph are taken from Keiser.

39 Keiser, 'Practical books', pp. 471–2.

40 For an extensive discussion of these and other miscellanies associated with the gentry, see Radulescu, *Gentry Context*, ch. 2.

41 *Short Title Catalogue*, 10994, fol. H3r–v.

42 For a discussion of manuscripts, see Seymour, 'Manuscripts of Hoccleve's *Regiment*' and *Lydgate and Burgh's* Secrees.

43 For a new investigation (2003) of the gentry ownership of this miscellany, see Radulescu, *Gentry Context*, pp. 47–8.

44 For a discussion of the contents of this manuscript, see Lester, *Sir John Paston's* Grete Boke.

45 This manuscript is discussed in detail in Cherewatuk, 'Malory's book of chivalry' and '"Gentyl audiences"'.

46 Hahn, 'Gawain', p. 226.

47 Vegetius, *Knyghthode and Bataile*, p. 11.

48 Schrader, 'Handlist of manuscripts', pp. 302–4.

49 *Peter Idley's* Instructions, lines 69, 76.

50 *Peter Idley's* Instructions, lines 330–6. The topic of counsel takes up a significant space in Book I (lines 330–574).

51 See *Paston Letters*, ed. Davis, II, p. 282. The same care for good governance and keeping convenient company may be found in a letter from John I to Margaret, his wife, in 1465 (*Paston Letters*, ed. Davis, I, pp. 127–8). For a thorough analysis of many other examples of this kind, see Radulescu, *Gentry Context*, ch. 1.

52 Maddern, 'Honour among the Pastons', p. 363.

53 Passage from the poem 'Whate-ever thow sey, avyse thee Welle', in *Babees Book*, pp. 356–8 (lines 57–60).

54 Perkins, *Hoccleve's* Regiment, p. 16.

55 'Whate-ever thow sey, avyse thee Welle', in *Babees Book*, pp. 356–8 (lines 50–2).

56 Perkins, *Hoccleve's* Regiment, p. 194.

57 For a discussion of this issue, see Ross, *Edward IV*, pp. 308–10. For the advancement of the gentry in central politics and especially within the body of the king's council, see Lander, 'Yorkist council and administration' and 'Council, administration and councillors'.

58 Ashby, 'Active policy of a prince', in *George Ashby's Poems*, ed. Bateson, lines 639–45.

59 See Lawton, 'Dullness and the fifteenth century', p. 790.

60 Scanlon, 'King's two voices', pp. 227–8.

61 Ferster, *Fictions of Advice*, p. 88.

62 Meale, 'Politics of book ownership'.

63 Keen, 'Heraldry and hierarchy'. The quotation from Upton is taken from the English translation of his tract by John Blount, found in Oxford, Bodleian Library MS English misc. D227 (fol. 53r).

64 These examples are discussed in detail by Deborah Youngs at pp. 124–7 in Chapter 7 of the present volume.

65 A gentry-owned composite manuscript including such a short chronicle is BL Harley 116, discussed in Radulescu, 'Yorkist propaganda'.

66 See Beadle, 'Fifteenth-century political verses'.

67 Myers (ed.), *Household of Edward IV*, pp. 127, 129.

68 See Matheson, *The Prose* Brut. For a survey of historical literature and the importance of linking the Arthurian past to national history, see Kennedy, 'Introduction', in Kennedy (ed.), *King Arthur*, pp. xiii–xlviii.

69 For a survey and discussion of gentry-owned *Brut* manuscripts and their readership, see Radulescu, '"Talkyng of cronycles of kynges"'; also Marx and Radulescu, *Readers and Writers*.

70 Riddy, 'Contextualizing *Le Morte Darthur*', p. 71.

71 Watts, *Henry VI*, p. 53.

72 Watts, 'Polemic and politics', p. 5.

73 Watts, 'Ideas, principles and politics', p. 111.

7

Cultural networks

Deborah Youngs

M odern writers have not only adopted the collective term 'gentry', but also have sought to uncover the various small groups or networks to which the gentry belonged. The motive is an important one: to understand the frameworks within which the gentry's political, social and cultural identities were formed. This can establish the relative importance of vertical (patron-client) and horizontal (friendship) ties in the lives of the gentry, as well as the extent and limitations of their horizons. Key approaches in the past have drawn on mainly legal and administrative records and focused on the county administration and the noble retinue, but an alternative approach is offered by a greater use of literary sources and a cultural perspective, which considers the gentry's book-reading interests.

Historians have begun looking at wills and inventories for book-owning gentry in order to examine groups with shared cultural interests, and to identify routes through which ideas could pass. Literary scholars, in their search for audiences and the social context in which manuscripts or early printed books were produced, have drawn attention to the gentry's role in forming textual communities or sub-cultures for particular literary genres. All offer useful insight into the nature of gentry horizons, and the potential influence of regional activities on gentry culture. The purpose of this chapter is to survey and assess the studies undertaken so far on what might be called literary or reading networks.

There are several reasons for trying to identify reading networks among the late medieval gentry. Firstly, the book was an important accessory to the gentry lifestyle. Despite the commercialisation of the manuscript/book trade in the fifteenth century, the book remained a luxury good and a symbol of affluence. Wealthy churchmen rarely owned more than one hundred books and aristocratic owners far fewer; the fifteenth-century landowner and sergeant-at-law Sir Roger Townshend was exceptional in owning around 40 books at his death.[1] As the majority of books owned by the gentry were for leisure rather than work purposes, buying books can be seen as an act of conspicuous consumption, possibly 'class privilege'; at the very least country gentlemen felt that a few books were 'a thing demanded by their position'.[2] Secondly, books were a channel through which gentry culture could travel and hence they contributed to moulding a group consciousness. Joan Thirsk's comments on sixteenth-century books and the gentry can be applied to later medieval England: as a storehouse of information, books were 'powerful agents fashioning the gentry, shaping their attitudes, giving them a philosophy of life, and directing their actions'. This meant that the gentry 'were being fashioned, not only as individuals, but as likeminded groups'.[3] This idea of 'cultivating' a person is close to fifteenth- and early sixteenth-century definitions of the term 'culture' as a process of development.[4]

Thirdly, a related issue is that books allowed members of a circle to keep in touch with one another for, as Martin Lowry has observed, 'the book was a symbol of friendship, and its circulation was a vital part of the more general exchange of information'.[5] As such, tracing a literary network provides a route map for other ties. Before printing, obtaining a text meant procuring an exemplar from which a copy could be taken, and this often depended on lines of communication formed by personal relationships among members of a book-owning network. The relatively small numbers of manuscripts in circulation meant that the book trade was largely a second-hand market, with an emphasis on informal lending and borrowing. This appears to have remained the case even with early printed books. Margaret Ford's recent study demonstrates the interconnectedness of early owners, what she calls a 'network of overlapping spheres', in which readers were related though kinship or social association.[6]

In order to illustrate the type of reading network with which this chapter is concerned, we can turn to a highly literate group of book owners and writers connected with the household of Sir John Fastolf (d. 1459) at Caister Castle, Norfolk. Fastolf's stepson, Stephen Scrope, esquire, of Castlecombe, translated Christine de Pisan's *The Epistle of Othea* (1440), and *The Dicts and Sayings of Philosophers* (1450) during his residency at Caister in the 1440s and 1450s. A co-resident was William Worcester, secretary and surveyor to Fastolf 1438–59, who combined his administrative work with collecting, copying, translating and writing literature. His works include an English translation of a French version of Cicero's

De Senectute and an analysis of English failure in Normandy known as *The Boke of Noblesse*.[7]

Cultural activity operated at a collective level too. Worcester collaborated with three other Fastolf employees to compile an account of Fastolf's military action on the fields of France, and he 'correctid and examyned' Scrope's *Dicts and Sayings* in 1472. This example of shared literary interest can be extended to the Paston family of Norfolk, whose connections with Fastolf and Caister are well documented. Sir John Paston II (d. 1479) was a major bibliophile, and an inventory drawn up between 1475 and 1479 reveals an impressive book collection covering a broad spectrum of history, romance, moral and spiritual material. Like Worcester, he owned Cicero's *De Senectute*; his text of *De Amicitia* was 'leffte with William Worcester'; he had a copy of Scrope's *Epistle of Othea*; and his 'Grete Boke', commissioned in the late 1460s, contains ordinances of war dating from Fastolf's service. He was also fascinated with epigrams and proverbs, an interest he shared with Fastolf's deputy receiver and auditor in the late 1440s and the 1450s, Geoffrey Spireling (b. *c.* 1426), who would later turn his talents to making a copy of Geoffrey Chaucer's *Canterbury Tales*. Significantly, women formed part of this literary coterie. Anne Harling (*c.* 1426–98), Fastolf's great-niece and ward, borrowed John Paston II's copy of *Troilus* and shared an interest in the *Epistle of Othea*. Moreover, a collection of Middle English religious treatises commissioned by Anne in the 1460s was written by the scribe who had previously penned a number of letters on Fastolf's behalf, all written from Caister in 1455–56. The network therefore may not have simply advised on topics to read, but recommended scribes to be trusted to produce a good copy.[8]

We can, therefore, identify a literate community engaged in book-lending and borrowing that shared literary interests, a common idiom, and scribes. Other ties bound the group together, but literature provided an additional link that cut across rank and gender distinctions: for example, unlike networks identified through administrative records and county communities, this literary network allowed women an active role. What is also notable is that the Fastolf network was based in a particular household, in East Anglia, a region which has been described as 'distinctive and self-sufficient, impatient, even suspicious' of customs in the rest of Britain.[9] Its rich cultural production ranged from a remarkable collection of illuminated psalters of the late thirteenth and early fourteenth centuries to the flowering of religious architecture and art, devotional literature, and drama in the fifteenth century. The gentry appear to have played some role in the cultural development of the region. To Samuel Moore it was the ties of kinship, marriage, neighbourhood and cultural interest among the gentry of Suffolk and Norfolk that provided the 'notable stimulus to the local production of literature'.[10] In fifteenth-century East Anglia important writers such as John Lydgate, John Methan, Osbern Bokenham and John Capgrave were all encouraged to write by local gentry patrons and bibliophiles; Methan's patron, for example, was Miles Stapleton of Ingham (d. 1466), a visitor to Caister (only nine miles away) and a kinsman of Fastolf.

The richness of the information on the Fastolf household and East Anglian culture is well known and may lead to doubts that such an approach to literary and regional networks can be adopted for other lesser known groups and areas. But that has not proved the case. Current trends in academic study have enhanced greatly our understanding of both the provincial gentry and regional culture. Historians have headed into the provinces to provide a number of studies of the regional gentry. From the literary side, there has been a growing interest in manuscripts and their provenance, especially in relation to placing literature within context, and attempts at mapping literary geographies.[11] This research has demonstrated that the provincial gentry did not need to search far to obtain a significant collection of texts. Gentry living in the environs of Pott Shrigley, Cheshire, had access to a gentleman's lending library at the local church, where they could borrow books either to read or to make their own copy. An inventory of the library (dating *c.* 1492) lists nineteen books, including one intriguingly called 'gode maners'.[12] Yorkshire parish churches, too, had well-stocked libraries, and impressive personal collections were gathered by the wealthy of the north-east. Between 1425 and 1450 Robert Thornton, lord of the manor of East Newton in Yorkshire, was able to compile two manuscripts from exemplars circulating in his locality. Both manuscripts are marked by a variety of devotional and literary texts and suggest that Thornton had access to around fifteen to twenty separate manuscripts. All were written in local dialect, and reflect northern spiritual trends, and a study of late medieval Yorkshire wills reveals that many of the religious and some romance items in the Thornton manuscripts were circulating in the region during the time of the manuscripts' making. How Thornton obtained his texts is unknown, but it is suggestive that one of the exemplars he used was later the basis for a transcription made for his friends and neighbours, the Pickerings of Oswaldkirk. Other texts appear to have been adapted for an audience of religious women, possibly from the nearby nunnery of Nun Monkton.[13]

While the extent of the gentry's role in promoting regional culture requires further consideration, Peter Coss's study of romances and Thorlac

Turville-Petre's work on alliterative literature have already suggested that the Caister household was not unusual. Coss argues that the provincial gentry household provided a focus for small-group literary activity, as guests were entertained and literature read, and became pivotal in the transmission of vernacular literature.[14] Piecing together the evidence often has to rely on fragments. One fruitful line of enquiry is the 'micro-study' of one or more manuscripts associated with the gentry. This can involve examining the way decorative devices such as heraldry were used to celebrate particular regional and political connections, or tracing the signatures appearing in manuscripts. Recent attention to the category of 'household' book has served to emphasise that books were not necessarily created for a single reader or for private reading, but rather to be consulted by various members of a household, as well as by friends and neighbours.[15] This type of 'textual community' is reflected in the anthology of secular verse associated with the Findern family of Findern, Derbyshire. Five women's names are present in the manuscript, and preliminary work traces them to families living in close proximity to the Findern family residence. Around two dozen amateur hands contributed to the manuscript, and the suggestion is that these neighbouring women copied selections of poetry into the manuscript on their visits to Findern.[16] Sarah McNamer takes the argument further by suggesting that the women composed at least fifteen of the lyrics. Her proposition rests on emphasising a shared outlook among the group, for she sees the lyrics, with their motif of departing, as resonating with a group of women whose menfolk were away on business or war.[17] Not everyone would attribute the poems to the women themselves,[18] but nevertheless this is an interesting way to uncover a literary network and understand a group mentality among neighbours of a small provincial household.

Poetry itself could be written to acknowledge and celebrate local associations of the gentry. The knightly prowess of provincial lords was commemorated in verse, while gentry-owned manuscripts contain works that would only make sense to an audience of locals. The early sixteenth-century literary collection known as the 'Wellys anthology' contains two poems that feature local acquaintances of the compiler, Humphrey Wellys, a Staffordshire gentleman. Of particular note is the poem in the form of a letter sent to Anthony Chetwynd, Wellys's brother-in-law, and a member of a prominent Staffordshire family living at Ingestre. Several names in the poem can be traced to the vicinity of Ingestre and have been identified with men connected to Wellys and Chetwynd, thus placing the poem within a local Staffordshire milieu.[19]

Another approach to uncovering literary networks has been to identify the readership of a particular text or literary genre. One of the most successful investigations has been in relation to alliterative verse, which found favour among a group of Cheshire and Lancashire gentry at the end of the Middle Ages. The commonplace book of Humphrey Newton of Newton and Pownall, gentleman (1466–1536) contains a poem which Russell Robbins called a 'Gawain epigone' because of its similarities to the late fourteenth-century alliterative poem *Sir Gawain and the Green Knight*.[20] The alliterative poem *St Erkenwald* was copied in 1477 into a Cheshire manuscript associated with the Booths of Dunham Massey. A member of the Legh of Bagueley family is favoured as the author of the alliterative poem *Scottish Field*, which celebrates the military prowess of Cheshire and Lancashire men in the English defeat of the Scots at Flodden in 1513. The main heroes of that poem are James Stanley (d. 1515), warden of Manchester College and bishop of Ely, and his son Sir John Stanley of Handforth, Cheshire, scions of the most powerful family in the region, who are celebrated in a number of other poems.[21]

Several connections based on social and kinship ties can be made between these families, and individual members acted alongside each other in local land transactions. For example, in 1518, Humphrey Newton and John Stanley conveyed lands in Dunham Massey to William Booth, which were to finance an obit to commemorate the death of Bishop James Stanley. Men of the North-West were brought together through leisure as well as deeds. James Stanley joined fellow heroes of the Flodden literature for cockfights at Winwick, near Wigan. This may have been the type of occasion where local literature celebrating the local elite was read. Alternatively, curiosity may have drawn them to the manuscript collections of their neighbours. Humphrey Newton travelled to several gentry households in north Cheshire and south Lancashire to look at, and copy, land deeds and genealogies from their family archives. Among the list of households he visited was that of the Booths of Dunham Massey, where he made genealogical notes out of a 'Remembrance Book'. Such an 'open book' policy and sharing of information may show the routes through which Newton accessed the literary material in his manuscript, and how others in the group may have come to share an interest in alliterative poetry.[22] The choice of literature is significant. By the later fifteenth century the taste for alliterative verse appears to have been confined geographically to the North-West; other examples such as the *Awntyrs off Arthure* and *The Destruction of Troy* are linked to contemporary gentry living in the Manchester region. Such thriving local interest can be seen either positively in terms of glorifying a strong, vital palatinate community, or more negatively, as does Michael Bennett, who describes the 'Stanley' poems as 'crude, regional chauvinism'.[23] Both, nevertheless, underline the literary significance of the region.

The examples discussed so far indicate how poetry and manuscript/book-making created horizontal ties among the gentry by helping to forge or cement links between them. In addition, it was a means to connect the local elite to their regional surroundings. How far this connection should be emphasised is open to debate. Those studying regional culture have sometimes emphasised parochialism to the point of exclusion. Gibson believes the culture of East Anglia 'had small need for the fashions of London or of other outlanders'.[24] Does the evidence suggest that the gentry were suspicious of culture beyond their locality?

As D. A. L. Morgan has famously argued, the English gentry regularly took themselves out of their localities. Humphrey Newton did not sit at home in Cheshire waiting for his books to come to him. On a visit to the parish church of Newark (possibly Nottingham) he copied out a number of prayers from a chained volume of Marian miracles.[25] A greater attraction was London, which acted as a meeting place for gentry from other parts of England and Wales. A few attended Parliament, which provided the opportunity for leisurely gatherings that, according to Geraldine Barnes, were 'conducive to the publication of romance'.[26] Others may have used the city 'as a kind of literary clearinghouse' where contacts could be made with those of similar taste and regional literature could gain a wider audience.[27] The Pastons, as Colin Richmond has recently shown, went for any reason, being eager for 'London news, opinion, and rumour' and the opportunities to cultivate patrons, friendships, marriage partners, careers and book borrowing.[28] One or two of the London inns they frequented may have gained a reputation for literary social gatherings. A tempting example is the *George* in Lombard Street, mentioned in the Paston letters in relation to books of entertainment. John Paston II obtained a book of chronicles and romances from the hostess at the inn, while the Earl of Arran was staying at the *George* when he promised John Paston III that he would return the book he had borrowed from John's sister Anne.[29] Coss wonders: 'Did people choose this particular inn because of the literary leanings of host and hostesses, or because they were likely to find others with similar interests there, or indeed both?'[30] It was certainly well placed, as early printers are known to have lodged in Lombard Street. These examples hint at the potential two-way traffic of literary culture between London and the regions. They also suggest the existence of fluid networks of people coming together through shared interests on a temporary basis.

Given the mobility of the gentry, it is not unusual to find that the contents of gentry manuscripts were not exclusively regional. Both Newton's commonplace book and the Findern anthology contain a range of texts that were far from provincial in character, including works by Lydgate and Chaucer. A recent study of one of Robert Thornton's manuscripts argues that its contents embody a 'national consciousness': an English rather than a regional identity.[31] But gentry cultural experiences were not confined to English or British shores. The Anglo-French wars exposed English and Welsh soldiers to the broader horizons of French and Burgundian culture, and conquest brought booty in the form of cheap books. In 1425 Fastolf was involved in the buying of the French royal library. Most went to form the core of a library at Rouen where Fastolf was captain, but a few books made their way back to Caister.[32]

Geographical proximity brought the gentry of Kent in contact with France and the Low Countries. Members of the 'Haute circle', discussed by Peter Fleming, commissioned a number of Flemish artists.[33] Calais has been studied recently as an important centre of cultural interchange, with Anne Sutton and Livia Visser-Fuchs drawing attention to what they have termed the 'Calais group' of book-owners. Although that group was of the higher aristocracy, they were based in a cosmopolitan, commercial centre where they formed a reading network with diplomats, clerics and merchants.[34] Recently, Julia Boffey has extended the study to find evidence of a shared cultural interest in works on statecraft and military strategy among a broad cross-section of literate society.[35] Richmond too believes a fraternity was forged among the gentry of the Calais garrison and Edward IV's household, as common experience bound together men from different geographical and social backgrounds. Shared literary interests might have given new meaning to experience, if Richmond is right in thinking that the fraternity came to see themselves as modern-day knights of the Round Table. John Paston III certainly saw Arthur as a reference point when he compared the duke of Burgundy's court to ' king Artourys cort'.[36]

The gentry therefore made cultural contacts beyond their locality. They were influenced by a mix of worlds, not a small world. But was this mix a peculiarly gentry phenomenon, developing from their shared experiences? Did the gentry create and circulate among themselves their own particular literary interests? There is a strong trend in contemporary analysis to answer both questions in the negative, particularly as regards the boundaries between gentry and noble culture. One of the forces acting for a shared gentry/noble culture is the strongly held view that culture per-colates downward: the gentry copied the nobility. Coss argues that the gentry emulated the aristocracy in culture, using their contacts among the nobility to borrow manuscripts. As such, he believes, the 'gentry and higher nobility enjoyed a broad common culture'.[37] Richard Green thinks that the literary interests of John Paston II 'were completely moulded by the fashions of an aristocratic milieu'. In emphasising the derivative nature of middle-class culture, Green argues that 'any attempt to differentiate between the reading habits of the bourgeoisie and the court ... will be like trying to distinguish between the reading habits of majors and lieutenant-colonels'.[38]

Emulation can be illustrated by manuscript evidence. Fifteenth-century book producers were keen to exploit social aspiration. The London scribe John Shirley sought to reassure a non-aristocratic audience that they were reading works which were popular among the nobility.[39] His rubrics are full of name-dropping and reminders of the context of courtly culture, helping to create what might be called an imagined noble community. That Shirley's manuscripts were headed for a sub-aristocratic audience is indicated by their 'downmarket' quality. Despite some reservations, an association is frequently made between manuscript quality and social status, with the poorer-quality work suggesting the gentry rather than the nobility. A well-known example is the manuscript containing *Sir Gawain and the Green Knight*, whose workmanlike reproduction has been used to support the view that the verses it contains must have been commissioned in a provincial gentry household rather than in a noble or courtly setting. Likewise, anthologies and miscellanies such as those by Newton and Thornton are considered largely the work of the gentry or urban classes. They reflect the cheap and easy option for households where books could not be afforded in large numbers.[40]

For some gentry, emulation occurred through direct contact with the noble milieu. Noble households remained influential in the literary deci-sions of the gentry, particularly at a time when the communal aspect of reading was strong. The event of hearing and discussing literature in the great households (amongst other cultural activities) is illustrated in the well-known extract from the household book of Edward IV in which the esquires of the household are described 'talkyng of cronycles of kinges and of other polycyes'.[41] Those sitting down to supper with Cecily Neville, duchess of York, would discuss the works Cecily had heard read to her over dinner. Such discussions, or events like it in the household, may have encouraged Sir Henry Heydon of Norfolk (d. 1503), steward of the duchess, to commission translations of Alain Chartier's works; or they may have influenced Richard Guildford, controller of Cecily's household, whose family, part of the Haute circle, is highlighted by Fleming for its 'impressive cultural activities'.[42] In a similar way, the 'De Vere circle', most recently studied by A. S. G. Edwards and Ralph Hanna, connects the Earls of Oxford, themselves keen book-owners and patrons, to the cultural activity of the East Anglian gentry associated with them. Elizabeth, wife of the twelfth earl, was a dedicatee of Osbern Bokenham's *Life of St Elizabeth* and could count among her circle the Pastons, Fastolf and Miles Stapleton, while her son entertained local gentry at his household over Christmas in 1490.[43] A final example is the affinity of Richard Beauchamp, earl of Warwick (d. 1439), which had 'a remarkably strong literary component'. The London scriptorium of the earl's secretary, John Shirley, produced several manuscripts containing poems by the earl and the gentlemen who served him.[44]

Introducing the nobility into the discussion raises the question of whether these networks show the book to be a horizontal tie or yet another way to emphasise the vertical ties of patronage and social aspiration. Patronage could be said to lie behind much of the gentry's literary output and ownership. Arguing against an emphasis on the provincial gentry household, Michael Bennett places the production of *Sir Gawain and the Green Knight* in the context of the retinue of Richard II and his Cheshire courtiers based in the royal household. Staying in Cheshire, Lawton viewed the alliterative poetry of the early Tudor period as 'testifying to the Stanley hegemony in the area and the intricate inter-connections of a gentry community around them'.[45] Creative initiative is often given to wealthy patrons. For Turville-Petre, the translation of *William of Palerne* into English was requested by Humphrey de Bohun, Earl of Hereford and Essex (1336–61), in order 'to polish the rough diamonds of Gloucestershire', meaning the gentry. The passing of books from the nobility to the gentry may also be seen as part of household largesse rather than the mark of a personal tie, such as when members of Edward III's court received a number of 'romances' in 1327.[46]

On the other hand, should it be assumed that the gentry were always passive recipients of hand-me-down noble culture? Is culture always transmitted top down? Although Georges Duby saw the imitation of aristocratic models as a key, the main thrust of his argument is that culture was a two-way process.[47] Research has established that vernacular romances, the work by Chaucer and Gower, and the early printed books of William Caxton were first read and demanded by members of the gentry or by educated townspeople.[48] When the Beauchamp affinity collapsed, the administrative officials, who provided the focus for Lowry's study of this circle, remained, and they continued their literary associations. It is not obviously the case that because works are dedicated to the nobility, the nobles commissioned them. Coss does not believe that *William of Palerne* was commissioned by the earl of Hereford, to whom the poem is dedicated. Rather, he suggests that it was written by a local man wanting to curry favour with his lord, but writing ultimately to satisfy local demand. In addition, books not only passed down the social scale. It will be recalled that the Earl of Arran borrowed a book from Anne Paston. More work is required in order to understand the nature of lending and borrowing between the nobility and the gentry, whether it reinforces a common culture, or whether more emphasis needs to be given to the gentry's regional interests and particular patronage of Middle English works.

At the same time, examining reading networks demonstrates that gentry culture should not be considered only in relation to the nobility. It will not have gone unnoticed that in discussions of book ownership and reading sub-cultures, the gentry are often paired with merchants or the urban elite. Together they formed Caxton's target audience: his translation of Cicero's *De Senectute* was directed at 'noble, wyse & grete lordes gentilmen & marchauntes' who 'occupied in maters towchyng the publyque weal'.[49] Studies on audiences and owners of late medieval literature often demonstrate the common outlook of a 'middling group' of owners. This group, defined by a non-aristocratic status and including the landed gentry, civil servants, lawyers, merchants and aldermen, has been collectively called, in different contexts, the professions (Clough), a fourth estate (Strohm), a civil service sub-culture (Riddy), and 'public servants' (Barnes).[50] Connections have been made between gentry and merchants in terms of blood ties and professional and social associations, and there appears to have been little difference between merchant and gentle in terms of literary interests. One recent attempt to make the distinction, but from the merchant's angle, is Carol Meale's study of the *Libelle of Englyshe Polycye*, in which she tries to identify those merchant interests that distinguish them from other sub-cultures. Further study is required to see how far the argument can be taken.[51] A related issue is whether it is possible to distinguish the cultural networks of the religious and the laity. In terms of the literary circles of female readers, the answer appears to be in the negative. Studies of female literary networks show the permeability of cloister walls. Ford's account of the Englefield-Fetiplace-Elyot connection, in which she traces fifteenth- and early sixteenth-century owners of early printed books, includes gentlemen, sergeants-at-law, a Brigittine nun and a Syon vowess. Mary Erler identifies what she terms 'a type of devout society' or 'local Norwich sub-culture' within the city's community as she illustrates the way devotional books were passed among both clerical and lay friends.[52] Male literary networks lack a comparable study, but with Thornton using texts designed for a local nunnery, it seems that a study of male gentry networks should probably take greater note of clerical connections.

When Raymond Williams stated that 'culture is one of the two or three most complicated words in the English language', he probably did not have 'gentry' and 'networks' in his mind as the other two.[53] Yet this chapter has highlighted the problematic nature of those three words, separately and in combination. Focusing on the book means that we are dealing with an artefact that in itself does not help to define the gentry. Books cannot be counted like manors to ascertain the extent of power, although poor quality appears to suggest a sub-aristocratic owner. Hence 'outside' markers are required to identify the gentry before seeing what they read and communicated to others. It might also be argued that examining networks with literary evidence, as compared to administrative records, offers a less clear, more temporary and shape-shifting picture of gentry connections. Anthony Gross sees a problem in relation to discussions of the county because 'with the weakening of the administrative emphasis the meaning of the county comes to rest on a gamut of volatile social bonds'.[54] Yet this would be to confuse the permanency of an institution with the permanency of a bond. County work changed from year to year; not everyone would be in post for several consecutive years; not everyone would turn up. While literary circles appear fragile, they may well have had a more long-lasting impact as a framework, particularly if the gentry framed their lives in regard to the literature they read. But it is more likely that the frameworks within which the gentry lived should be seen as unstable or at least fluid. The fixation with 'communities' has been criticised for implying agreement and stasis, underplaying their conflicting and porous nature.[55] Reading networks are recognisably more open-ended affiliations, but are nevertheless based on meaningful actions.

There are now several useful studies available that reveal the gentry as belonging to groups such as the Haute circle, the Fastolf circle, the De Vere circle, the Calais group and a civil-service sub-culture; all members are shown sharing a particular cultural outlook. They do not supplant other types of network, but they can be used either to add depth to a known connection (the Caister household, the Beauchamp affinity), or to map possible paths for future research (the women in the Findern manuscript or the owners of early printed books). Focusing on gentry-owned anthologies and miscellanies is particularly useful because they appear in the hands of those of lesser rank. Because the Thornton, Findern and Newton families were not much known outside their localities and were probably not leading lights in their own region, they appear rarely in the administrative documents upon which more historical and political accounts of the gentry are generally based. But their manuscripts point, in varying degrees, to their associations, and similar work could be undertaken on manuscripts associated with other less wealthy gentry. Studies of reading circles also offer interesting comments on group mentality. Literature can reflect a shared experience of war or garrison or business. The locality also played its part here. Gentry were celebrated in local verse, read literature in the local dialect and shared in a local culture with neighbours of various ranks. While research so far has drawn attention to the importance of culture in the formation of a regional identity, more work is required on the gentry's role in local cultural patronage.

Nevertheless, reading networks show that the gentry were not parochial in terms of their horizons and interests. While it is useful to construct sub-cultures in later medieval England, which rest on differences of gender, profession, status and geography, textual communities can cross these boundaries. The English prose *Brut* was owned throughout England by nobility, gentry, merchants, clerics and academics;[56] devotional reading was 'everyone's' reading; and distinctions in the cultural interests of gentle and noblewomen are difficult to draw.[57] What we see by focusing on the borrowing of manuscripts and the exchanging of ideas is the gentry forming part of a broad literate network and part of a leisured society. Medievalists must strike a balance between assigning the gentry to small groups (including 'the gentry') and allowing for movement between such groups. Eric Acheson puts it well: 'It need not be that the gentry saw themselves as members of one community rather than another... Rather like the ellipses in a venn diagram, the social circles of the fifteenth-century gentry sometimes overlapped and sometimes one circle engulfed another'.[58] Reading networks provide yet another circle.

Notes

1 Pearsall, 'Introduction', in Griffiths and Pearsall (eds), *Book Production and Publishing*, pp. 1–10 (p. 7); Moreton, '"Library" of a fifteenth-century lawyer', p. 339.

2 Ford, 'Private ownership', p. 218. Bennett, 'Author and his public', pp. 22–3.

3 Thirsk, 'Fashioning of the Tudor/Stuart gentry', p. 72.

4 Williams, *Keywords*, p. 87.

5 Lowry, 'John Rous', p. 331.

6 Ford, 'Private ownership', p. 218. See also Riddy, *Sir Thomas Malory*, p. 10.

7 Hughes, 'Stephen Scrope', pp. 109–46.

8 McFarlane, 'William Worcester', pp. 210–11; Lester, *Sir John Paston's* Grete Boke, p. 45; Wilson, 'Middle English manuscript', pp. 299–300; Dutton, 'Piety, politics and persona'.

9 Gibson, *Theater of Devotion*, p. 19.

10 Moore, 'Patrons of letters', p. 102.

11 Bennett, *Community, Class and Careerism*; Turville-Petre, 'Some medieval English manuscripts'; and Beadle, 'Prolegomena to a literary geography'.

12 Dodgson, 'Library at Pott Chapel'.

13 Keiser, 'Lincoln Cathedral Library', p. 159; Keiser, 'MS Rawlinson A. 393', pp. 445–8; Keiser, 'More light on the life', p. 118; Hanna, 'Growth of Robert Thornton's books', p. 61.

14 Turville-Petre, *Alliterative Revival*, p. 46; Coss, 'Aspects of cultural diffusion', pp. 42–5.

15 Meale and Boffey, 'Gentlewomen's reading', p. 537.

16 Harris, 'Origins and make-up', p. 327.

17 McNamer, 'Female authors', pp. 282, 290.

18 Boffey, 'Women authors', p. 170.

19 Wilson, 'Local inhabitants'.

20 Robbins, 'Gawain epigone'.

21 Luttrell, 'Three north-west Midland manuscripts'; Lawton, '*Scottish Field*'.

22 Lawton, '*Scottish Field*', pp. 44–5, 51; Marsh, 'I see by sizt', pp. 79–81.

23 Bennett, *Community, Class and Careerism*, p. 250.

24 Gibson, *Theater of Devotion*, p. 23.

25 Morgan, 'Individual style', p. 27. Marsh, 'I see by sizt', p. 89.

26 Barnes, *Counsel and Strategy*, pp. 21, 27–8.

27 Hanna, 'Sir Thomas Berkeley', p. 912.

28 Richmond, 'Pastons and London', p. 216.

29 *Paston Letters*, ed. Davis, I, p. 575.

30 Coss, 'Aspects of cultural diffusion', p. 56; Doyle, 'English books in and out of Court', p. 179.

31 Hardman, 'Compiling the nation'.

32 Hughes, 'Stephen Scrope', p. 129.

33 Fleming, 'Hautes and their "circle"', pp. 97–8.

34 Sutton and Visser-Fuchs, 'Choosing a book'.

35 Boffey, 'Books and readers'.

36 Richmond, 'Books and pictures', pp. 399–400, 407, and Lester, *Sir John Paston's* Grete Boke, pp. 43–4.

37 Coss, 'Aspects of cultural diffusion', p. 44.

38 Green, *Poets and Princepleasers*, pp. 9–10.

39 Edwards, 'John Shirley'.

40 Doyle, 'English books in and out of Court', p. 166; Boffey and Thompson, 'Anthologies and miscellanies', p. 293.

41 Coleman, *Public Reading*, p. 109; Myers (ed.), *Household Book of Edward IV*, p. 129.

42 Armstrong, 'Piety of Cicely, Duchess of York', pp. 79–80; Coleman, *Public Reading*, p. 139; Fleming, 'Hautes and their "circle"', p. 99.

43 Edwards, 'Transmission and audience', esp. p. 166; Hanna and Edwards, 'Rotheley, the De Vere Circle'.

44 Lowry, 'John Rous', pp. 331–2.

45 Bennett, 'Court of Richard II'; Lawton, *'Scottish Field'*, p. 51.

46 Turville-Petre, *Alliterative Revival*, p. 41; Doyle, 'English books in and out of Court', p. 174.

47 Duby, 'Diffusion of cultural patterns'.

48 Scattergood, 'Literary culture', pp. 38–41; Riddy, *Sir Thomas Malory*, p. 13; Pearsall, 'Cultural and social setting', p. 17; Ford, 'Private ownership', p. 227.

49 Ford, 'Private ownership', p. 213.

50 Clough (ed.), *Profession, Vocation and Culture*; Strohm, *Social Chaucer*; Riddy, *Sir Thomas Malory*; Barnes, *Counsel and Strategy*.

51 Meale, *'Libelle of Englysshe Polycye'*.

52 Ford, 'Private ownership', pp. 215–17; Erler, 'Devotional literature', pp. 523–4. See also essays by Riddy and Boffey, in Meale (ed.), *Women and Literature*.

53 Williams, *Keywords*, p. 87.

54 Gross, 'Regionalism and revision', p. 7.

55 Rubin, 'Small groups', p. 134.

56 On this topic, see the chapter by Raluca Radulescu in the present volume, pp. 100–18.

57 Erler, 'Devotional literature', p. 295; Meale and Boffey, 'Gentlewomen's reading', p. 526.

58 Acheson, *Gentry Community*, p. 93.

8

Religion

Christine Carpenter

I f this chapter had been written a mere quarter-century ago, it would
have contained an almost entirely different account both of gentry
religion and of the Church which ministered to the late medieval English
laity. For in the mid-1970s the reaction against the longstanding 'Protestant'
account of the Church and lay piety was only just beginning. The late medieval English Church, according to the 'Protestant' version, was permeated
at every level by corruption, pluralism and spiritual neglect of its flock,
while the laity, offered 'superstition' rather than spiritual sustenance, and
imbued with a deep anticlericalism and anti-papalism, were only too ready
to respond when they were offered the vital new religion of the Reformation. The perceived popularity in late medieval England of the heretical
ideas of John Wyclif, the so-called 'Morning-Star of the Reformation', was
testament to the laity's disenchantment with orthodox Catholicism.[1]

Re-evaluation began with the Church rather than with lay piety but,
although there were two early seminal revisionist studies,[2] it was not until
there was general recognition that the laity were mostly content with the
Church and its teachings that the evidence for the essential health of the
institution could be seen clearly for what it was. The conclusions of this
work on the Church will now be briefly summarised as a context for lay
piety.[3] The quality and education of the secular clergy – even of the parish
clergy – are now known to be far better than had been supposed, while the
Church's role in encouraging better education and training amongst its
servants, through formal education, legislation and manuals of instruction,
is recognised. Even the much-maligned religious orders, including the
allegedly despised friars, have been at least partially rehabilitated. It is now
understood, moreover, that many of the Church's problems, rather than
signifying corruption and decay, were structural, often springing from its

own success. Because it had become a great international institution with a sophisticated administration and vast lands and wealth, Church leaders tended to be administrators rather than spiritual figures. In England the Church was very close to the Crown, which valued the higher clergy for their administrative expertise and often found them wealthy benefices as a reward for good service. The grant of multiple benefices to reward the clerical administrators of Church and state caused pluralism and absenteeism, but even so the Church was attempting to enforce residence in benefices with cure of souls. Difficulties in finding enough educated parochial clergy were due partly to the intrinsic problems of having a celibate and therefore non-hereditary priesthood in a pre-mass-education age, but were also attributable to the number of parishes with inadequate financial support for their priests. Above all, if the laity were becoming more critical of the Church, this was because they were better educated in religion, and it was the Church's own systematic campaign to educate the laity in Church doctrine which had brought this situation about.

Meanwhile, the revision of late medieval lay belief has proceeded apace, encouraged and complemented by a new historiography of the English Reformation, which depicts it as much more protracted in its implementation and hostile in its reception than had been supposed.[4] Historians have ceased to assume that the comments of late medieval and early Tudor critics and satirists represented the views of the mass of lay men and women. First, in the 1970s and 1980s, the religion of the nobility and gentry was reassessed, especially the latter, using mainly wills and the evidence of lay ecclesiastical foundations. Then, via the magisterial work of Eamon Duffy, published in 1992, the focus moved to popular piety, explored through churchwardens' accounts and the material evidence of parish churches and their furnishings. A vibrant parish religion has been uncovered, in which religious festivals and the celebration of saints are seen as central elements rather than ignorant superstitions. In the Church as a whole, communitarianism is emphasised; in the parish, in the religious guilds, in the mass and in the medieval meaning of 'charity': living in Godly harmony with one's neighbours. The Reformation and Counter-Reformation are condemned in equal measure for their destruction of this communal identity. It can truly be said that a 'Protestant' orthodoxy has been replaced by a 'Catholic' orthodoxy.[5] If the religion of the gentry has been less explored in recent years, the gentry remain central to the subject, for the Reformation in England could never have occurred without their support in Parliament. But there are other reasons for taking another look at gentry piety. Where does it fit in with the new work on parochial religion and the allegedly communitarian faith? Given that the early work concentrated on the outward manifestations of gentry faith, can we say more about their inner beliefs? Now that Wyclif's followers have been found to be few in number, has the number and significance of his gentry adherents been over- or under-estimated?[6] How does the gentry contribution to late medieval religious culture relate to all these questions?

The best-explored sphere of gentry religion is charitable donations. Wills offer much of the evidence here but they can be supplemented with other written sources and with the evidence of buildings and church furnishings where these survive.[7] The overwhelming motive for the gentry's generosity was fear of the pains of Purgatory. The doctrine that there was a place which was neither Heaven nor Hell, to which Christian souls could go to be purged of their sins, was well established in the Church's teaching by 1300. Good works during one's life and prayers afterwards, sometimes stimulated by *post mortem* good works, could speed the sinner's path through Purgatory, an especially important notion for the wealthy and powerful, who were most exposed to such punishment.[8] This produced charitable works as various as educational endowments, roads and bridges, but the most obvious recourse was to pay for *post mortem* masses: these were almost universally requested in gentry wills, sometimes in very large numbers. Even better was to establish a chantry which supported a perpetual priest to say masses for the donor's soul and often the souls of members of his or her family, both living and dead. These were founded throughout the fourteenth and fifteenth centuries and indeed all the way up to the Reformation. Although chantry foundation seems to have declined after 1349, this did not betoken declining enthusiasm, for many families already had a chantry by then, while legislation made it harder to establish perpetual chantries after 1391, and so prayers for years rather than in perpetuity were often ordained. The grandest type of chantry was the college but it was more usually the nobility and higher clergy who could afford such an expensive foundation.[9] Gentry chantries were established above all in the church of the parish where they resided and it was the parish church that was the single greatest object of the gentry's generosity.

During the thirteenth century, there was a happy combination of the growth of belief in Purgatory, Church legislation that the nave be maintained by the parishioners and that each parish church be provided with a 'staggering list of objects' for worship,[10] and a growing self-consciousness among the gentry which determined that, like the nobility and their monasteries, they too wished to have a religious centre alongside the centre of their estate.[11] All these needs could be satisfied by the gentry moving into the parish church – literally in the sense of being buried there[12] – and rebuilding and beautifying it. Some of these churches in fact became gentry mausolea in which the chancel, full of family tombs and brasses, was effectively a family chantry. In some churches, a specially-built chantry chapel was inserted; this became so common a practice that from about 1350 firms specialised in constructing these.[13] It would be possible to cite a very large number of parish churches where the gentry founded chantries, placed tombs and built. One of the best-known is the church at Long Melford, whose grand rebuilding between the 1460s and 1495 was financed by John Clopton of Long Melford: the Clopton family and kin were remembered in inscriptions round the outside of the church and in the windows and a Clopton chantry was built inside the church.[14] Many parish churches, including Long Melford, benefited from lesser gifts: the provision of windows and other forms of decoration, of altar lights and of service books and vestments. Even those gifts to parish churches which were not made specifically to finance prayers were designed to keep the dead in the minds of the living whose prayers they sought, and so their names and/or their heraldry might be placed on the gift or depicted in the church in stone or glass; sometimes, as on the tomb of William Etchingham, a fourteenth-century Sussex knight, there might be an explicit request for prayers.[15] As with the churches themselves, some of this patronage could lead to work of a high artistic level. For example, under Henry VII, Sir Edward Guildford of Kent and Sir Henry Heydon of Norfolk used the Flemish 'Southwark School', responsible for the windows of King's College Cambridge, for the painted glass in their parish churches. The gentry may also have contributed to the development of church music in the parish, for in the later fifteenth century there is growing evidence of organs in parish churches and of the performance of polyphonic music there.[16]

Despite the focus on the parish church, the gentry did not entirely neglect the religious orders. Those families which retained links with a monastery, usually a local one, made grants to it and sometimes established their chantries in the monastic church, and almost all gentry testators left sums to the friars. It seems indeed that the hostility to the friars that we see in, for example, *Piers Plowman*, was more a matter of ideological debate within the Church and straightforward jealousy between secular clergy and mendicants than a reflection of lay attitudes towards them. Many landowners, both noble and gentle, had friars as chaplains and confessors. This was one cause of the seculars' hostility, for friars were thought to give absolution too readily in return for bequests.[17] Nunneries remained a preferred place to deposit unmarried daughters, while gentle-women were among the not insignificant number of 'vowed' laywomen who committed themselves to following a strict religious rule, sometimes within an institution.[18] Gentry children were sent to be educated in monasteries and nunneries.[19]

While supporting the parish church and the religious orders, gentry were also increasingly practising private devotions and playing some part in both the cultural and religious developments associated with these. Evidence for private altars and domestic chaplains in gentry and noble households begins to grow during the fourteenth century. The altar-piece commissioned *c.* 1480 by Sir John Donne from no less a painter than Hans Memling may have been intended for household worship. Although the great developments in English choirs and choral music in the later Middle Ages came mostly in the household chapels and collegiate churches of royalty, nobility and higher clergy, there is evidence that the gentry played some part. For example, under Henry VI, Sir Andrew Ogard had his own chapel choir, while Sir William Haute of Kent (d. 1492) was involved with a London guild which trained choristers and was himself a composer of carols and religious polyphony. By the fourteenth century, so many prayer books, known as 'Books of Hours' (sometimes called primers), were required for private lay use that they began to be mass-produced.[20] There was a burgeoning market for religious works in general, some of them in English, and there is evidence in wills and inventories and sometimes in surviving manuscripts themselves that members of the gentry owned and commissioned them. These were not just the cheaper mass-produced works: for example the Oxfordshire knight Edmund Rede (*c.* 1438–70) owned a high-quality manuscript which included a work by the thirteenth-century archbishop, Edmund Rich. With the development of private chambers and altars in noble and gentry households, there was space for private devotion and worship among the laity, emulating the *lectio divina* of the monks.[21] Not surprisingly in view of the leisure required for intense spiritual exercises, the most famous of these devout landowners were women, but noblewomen rather than gentry.[22] However, we know of at least one example of a devout layman, probably a member of the gentry, being advised, after his dinner to 'go up into your cell and pray', and we shall see that gentry as well as nobility were participating enthusiastically in the development of their own spirituality.[23]

All the same, despite the evolution of a more personal spirituality, the religion of the gentry, with few exceptions, was remorselessly orthodox, and this was hardly surprising since care was taken to bring them up in orthodox belief. An agreement of 1432 for the upbringing of Isabel Stonor specifically states that she is to be offered 'doctrina' as well as food and clothing.[24] It seems that much religious instruction was imparted in the family, by the paterfamilias, who might read at mealtimes from an improving book and perhaps expound it, and teaching by the laity within the home was encouraged by the Church. The chaplains in gentry households would be a further source of instruction. The gentry wills which release debtors and leave money for prisoners show how well they had absorbed one of the central texts in the Church's educational programme, the 'Seven Corporal Works of Mercy'.[25] Certainly, some gentry at least were acquainted with religious literature in English beyond the standard works, as we can see from the Cloptons' placing of quotations from the works of the eminent fifteenth-century poet and monk, John Lydgate, in their chantry. However, the Latin texts with which the gentry were familiar would in most cases have been the basic texts of the 'Book of Hours' and, although they learned to read through the medium of Latin, it must be doubted whether most could master the sophisticated Latin of theological treatises. Indeed, since primers were available in English from the later thirteenth century and some of these were certainly owned by gentry, even rudimentary Latin may have been deemed unnecessary. Moreover, many of the other religious books they owned were liturgical or conventional didactic works like the Golden Legend.[26] Similarly, as Wyclif and his followers complained, most sermons preached to the laity were extremely limited in their scope.[27]

Accordingly, although we can see the late medieval gentry putting their religious education to use in some very precise religious dispositions, often exhibiting their close knowledge of the liturgy, these choices were almost invariably made within an extremely conventional framework. Most wills begin merely with a commendation of the testator's soul to Jesus, Mary and the 'company of heaven', but some testators were naming their own favourite saints, and there was a growing tendency for individuals or families to associate themselves with particular saints. These may feature as dedicatees in wills and foundations, on tombs and among family names; one fifteenth-century example is the Cloptons of Long Melford and St Anne. Funerals and immediate *post mortem* prayers began to be specified in detail in wills, sometimes very elaborately. Some gentry (like several nobles) even dictated the order of service in the chantries they established.[28] That none of this precision savours of unorthodoxy is closely related to the way in which the gentry's religious beliefs and social mentalities were deeply intertwined.[29] The power and riches of heaven were seen very much in terms of lordship and wealth on earth: the jewel-like quality of the illustrations in many late medieval religious manuscripts is one obvious exemplar. There was a tension between a gentry testator's concern for his own soul and the damage that his dispersal of wealth, especially of land, to save it could do to his lineage. But it could be resolved if the family portraits on tombs and windows, and its heraldry on the church and its furnishings, were a reminder to the living not just to pray for the departed but also of the continuing greatness of their families and lineage. Support for the parish church where the gentry resided was an important aspect of this coalescence of the needs of this world and the next, but the connection between the geographies of religion and land went further than this. The grants of the gentry, including benefactions to religious houses, education, roads, bridges and the parish churches of secondary residences, can normally be closely connected to the distribution of their estates.

As this point implies, the pattern of donations also closely mirrored the position of a family within the hierarchy of gentility, for the greater gentry, having more widespread lands, generally distributed their generosity over a wider geographical area. Those with the largest body of lands were also best able to sacrifice some of it to found a chantry and, usually, the greater the family the better endowed the chantry. Very minor gentry would have to accept lesser, and less permanent, means of commemoration, like a finite number of masses, *obits* (prayers on the anniversary of their deaths), or the donation of an altar light, vestment or furnishing. Social hierarchy and religious dispositions may indeed be matched across the social spectrum: the greatest foundations were the colleges of the nobility, most of whom also already had a patronal tie with a monastery; then there were the gentry chantries and, for those below the gentry, the parish guilds or – the lowest level of commemorative prayers – inclusion in the parish bede roll. Noble religious foundations tended not only to be grander than those of the gentry but to last longer, because noble estates, and therefore their religious capitals, were large enough to retain their identity even when they were incorporated by marriage or inheritance into another noble family's lands. Gentry estates by contrast tended to be absorbed completely into the existing structure of a new owner's properties, their political and religious centres neglected entirely or, alternatively, becoming a new centre for the new owner, at the expense of the old one. Gentry bequests can also be distinguished from those of prosperous townsmen: gentry, having more land for permanent endowment but less in the way of liquid assets, tended to be more parsimonious than townsmen in immediate *post mortem* expenditure. However, we should not be over-schematic: donations of church furnishings were made at all social levels, many of the 'parish' gentry availed themselves of the cheaper form of commemoration provided by the religious guild, and the parvenu gentry broke all the rules. They adopted ancestral religious centres with which they had very little connection or none at all and, while almost invariably founding a chantry because the family lacked one, happily threw money at things that made an immediate and strong impact, such as funerals, masses, roads and bridges.

With the relationship of social hierarchy and religious practice, we come to one of the most vexed areas in the present historiography of late medieval religion. Building on earlier work which saw the European Reformation as cause of a widening gulf between an illiterate 'popular' religion rooted in folklore and superstition and an elite, educated religion, some historians have suggested that this division was already present in pre-Reformation England, and that it was the elite that dragged England down the path of reform. Colin Richmond characterises this elite piety as an individualistic, anti-communal 'me' faith, rather mechanical and superficial, and associates it strongly with the gentry.[30] This is essentially a debate amongst Catholic historians over the soul of their religion in the pre-Reformation period in England, and the strongest proponent of the belief that communalism was very much alive in this period is Duffy.[31] He argues that by the later Middle Ages the laity at all levels had a religious education which gave them much common ground. If the religious texts offered to the lower orders did not go far beyond the primer, then, as we have seen, the same could be said of much of what the gentry imbibed. Duffy's case may be weakened by the central place he gives to visual schemes in churches in the education of ordinary parishioners, since some historians would contrast a religion of the book found among the educated elite, which presaged the Protestant attitude to the Bible, with popular image worship. Nevertheless, although gentry and nobility were undoubtedly far more literate than peasants, images were meant to be prompts to worship, not objects of veneration in themselves, and they were used precisely for this purpose in the expensive Books of Hours of nobility and gentry.[32]

Turning from the methods of education to its content, the illiterate/educated contrast is still harder to sustain. The images in churches reflected much that was also to be found in the written word: for example, the cult of the Virgin, around which a large liturgy and numbers of stories had been built. Equally, 'superstitious' prayers for good outcomes and to ward off disasters were to be found in the primer. Moreover, gentry participation in all these practices, including the new cults, can be readily established. The cult of the Virgin, most evidently in Books of Hours, financing Lady Chapels and almost all testators' commitment of their soul, hardly needs mentioning and we have already noted an instance of the linked cult of St Anne, Mary's mother.[33] Other examples of new cults with a wide popular base followed by the gentry include those of St George and St Katherine.[34]

How far were the gentry part of the parochial 'community' that the Duffy school has celebrated? Without written evidence, it is rarely possible to be precise about who financed substantial building and furnishing schemes in rural parish churches, but it seems sometimes to have been the parish alone, sometimes a local member of the gentry or wealthy incumbent alone and sometimes a combination of these. Duffy offers late fifteenth- and early sixteenth-century examples of local gentry and ordinary parishioners joining in the major project of providing rood-screens. Corporate building and beautification of parish churches was often undertaken by religious guilds, to which lesser gentry often belonged. It is also the case that some very prominent gentry, and even nobles and members of the royal family, belonged to some of the more distinguished urban religious guilds, for example at Stratford-upon-Avon, Coventry and Norwich. Since guilds have been seen as important contributors to communal parochial religion, it is worth considering how far their upper-class members were participant in their activities in general. Several religious guilds were important in Corpus Christi celebrations. This festival was a major late medieval novelty and it certainly did not pass the gentry by. For example, in their Books of Hours there were prayers on the joys and sorrows of the Virgin very similar to those in Corpus Christi plays, while another urban guild with a distinguished membership was the Corpus Christi guild at York, which, like the Stratford guild, was becoming 'a county club' for local landowners during the fifteenth century. It is however very difficult to envisage gentry members processing with their urban or rural fellows in the annual celebration of guild feasts. In Stratford, only a small number of very local gentry, mostly of middling or lesser status, were much involved in guild affairs and their main contribution to the guild seems to have been to act as external arbiters in the case of division and as conduits to local nobles and the Crown.[35]

This raises the question of whether gentry religion can indeed be absorbed into the orthodoxy which places the parish at the heart of observance in late medieval England. We can certainly note not just the contributions to the parish church and membership of local guilds but also cultivation by the gentry of local saints and pilgrimages to local shrines. If some of them also made pilgrimages to the Holy Land, so did many of their inferiors.[36] But various members of gentry families with more widespread lands might patronise, and be buried in, churches in one or another of several counties; often were these counties at considerable distance from each other. Many of the gentry went to London or Westminster fairly frequently and consequently remembered London religious institutions in their wills, especially the friars, and might be buried in London. The wider debate on the localism of the gentry is apposite here and it seems clear that there was an ascending scale of localism matching a descending social scale, from the greatest noble to the least parish gentry. Even within the parish, the very least gentleman had a lordship over his tenants among the parishioners which must have set him to some extent apart.[37]

Indeed, Richmond argues that the gentry's elite individualism was visible in the very parish churches they helped construct and embellish. According to this view, burial within the church separated them from the faithful in the churchyard; as well as private spaces for the dead, they created private spaces for the living, with their chantries, their private pews and, sometimes, their annexation of the entire chancel as mausoleum and chantry; not content with this, they increasingly absented themselves from the parish church to pray in private chapels in their homes.[38] There are, however, obvious objections to this thesis. It is important not to confuse the expression of social hierarchy within the parish church, which began in the thirteenth century as the gentry became more self-assertive, with the creation of that hierarchy: it is hard to believe that lesser landowners treated ordinary parishioners as their equals in church before this time.[39] Church space as a whole was being divided up by pews in the fifteenth century as preaching became more important. Licences for private worship normally demanded a minimum attendance at the parish church and evidence suggests that they were intended to avoid the rigours of attendance in bad weather and to aid private devotions, rather than as a means for the gentry to withdraw from the parish church. Withdrawal would in fact have been unthinkable because the parish church was the place where the gentry proclaimed their standing among the people they claimed to rule. It was not enough to leave reminders of the dead; the living family needed to be present as well.[40] And we know from the Proofs of Age of landowners who had been in royal wardship how far the local church was a centre for both worship and secular business, including the local lord's.[41]

We must conclude that, while Duffy may overdo the communitarianism of gentry religious life, the argument that their faith was divorced from that of ordinary parishioners either ideologically or physically is far-fetched. But, even if we accept that many of the gentry participated, at least to some extent, in a vibrant communal faith, it may still be argued that their religion was growing more individualistic. A convincing case has been made that the development of confession, ordered for all laymen at the Fourth Lateran Council in 1215, the linked phenomenon of extending the teaching of the *ars moriendi* from clergy to laity, and the appearance of confession manuals in English in the later fourteenth century encouraged introspection and individualism among those people who could read the manuals and spend time with a private confessor. This was a contemplative, devout and questioning faith, nurtured in the fourteenth century by the ecclesiastical establishment, first Bishop Grandisson of Exeter and then the archbishops of York. It was given its most profound impetus by the northern mystics, especially Richard Rolle and Walter Hilton, who wrote in English as well as in Latin. Rolle and Hilton, hermits themselves eventually, advocated a solitary, ascetic life and it is suggested that, under their influence and that of like-minded confessors, inner meditation became more important than public worship to some nobility and gentry.

There is no doubting the immediate effect of such clerics on some of the northern nobility, nor that in the late fourteenth century the eremitic and ascetic Carthusians caught the imagination of the nobles. A persuasive case has also been made that noble enthusiasm for the Carthusians was encouraged by the development under Edward III and Henry V of a 'court devotion', linking inward ascetic faith with what has been called 'military puritanism'. Hilton's 'Epistle on the Mixed Life' was specifically addressed to a secular lord, teaching how, in his necessarily active life, he might also find room for contemplation. The evidence of links between the northern mystics and members of the gentry, of gentry ownership of penitentiaries and of books by Rolle, Hilton and other mystics, and of gentry patronage of hermits (one widowed lady even became one) suggests that gentry as well as nobility were attracted to this kind of devotion. So also do other indications: the preambles of some gentry wills, which exhibit the contempt for the body and awareness of human mutability which has been identified with this strain of faith; the cadavers on gentry tombs carrying the same message; and a surviving text, written apparently for a gentry family, which enjoins just such heart-searching and solitary prayer as was associated with this strand of religion. Moreover, we shall see that it may have been the gentry in the royal household who were most susceptible to these influences.[42]

Orthodox as this individualistic belief was, it was part of a development which represented a real danger to the faith. Academic theology had always been potentially subversive of orthodoxy but had been conducted within universities and in a language that few could understand.[43] Now, in the later fourteenth century, there was serious theological discussion in English, in works written in English, and at least one member of the gentry, the household knight John Clanvow (d. 1391), contributed to the religious literature in English. There were also translations of religious works from Latin, notably those by John Trevisa (d. 1402); that he also translated works on governance helped to take the whole edifice of Church and State into the domain of informed lay debate.[44] And it was just at this time that, in John Wyclif, England produced its first heretical academic, one who was prepared to take his ideas outside the academy and propound them in English. How many of the gentry followed Wyclif and became 'Lollard knights' is far from clear. Recent tendency has been to emphasise the role of the gentry among Wyclif's followers, even (perhaps slightly improbably) after Oldcastle's rebellion in 1414 had linked heresy with treason, and there is plenty of circumstantial evidence connecting gentry with Wyclif and his clerical adherents before 1414. It is not always self-evident, however, that these were fully-paid-up Wyclifites. Especially in view of the court connections of several of them, it is arguable that Wyclif, himself a product of northern devotional piety, appealed to the ascetic, self-denigrating, inward piety that characterised this milieu and that ironically was central to the beliefs of Henry V and his religious advisers who set about stamping out Lollardy after 1414. This clamping-down had already begun under Henry IV with the Constitutions of Archbishop Arundel – himself a key figure in the nurturing of piety in the north – which initiated a period of much tighter control over what might be read and debated in English, including restrictions on the ownership of bible translations. How tight this censorship really was and how far it forced even educated lay belief into a straitjacket has been much debated but it does appear that the earlier fostering of personal devotion among nobility and gentry by confessors and religious works was giving way to encouragement of group conformity.[45]

We could say more about these questions of individualism, superficiality and conformity if we could get beyond the outward expression of gentry belief, a difficult task, but one which can be attempted through study of their own words. Individualism is certainly there, for example in marginalia added to their religious books and occasionally in the phraseology which breaks into the usually rather conventional expression of their wills. Much of it is as 'me-focused' and mechanical as has been suggested: for example prayers and invocations to bring down enemies, prayers and good works for delivery from trouble or sickness, relics that heal particular parts of the body. Although it is now known that most religious developments formerly attributed to the Black Death – a deeper personal faith, sense of mutability and deep awareness of death – predated it, the greater probability of being struck down once the plague had arrived in Europe would almost certainly have contributed to the use of religion as a warding-off mechanism and would undoubtedly have encouraged an accountant's mentality with regard to Purgatory.[46] But there are also very different expressions of faith, even for time of trouble, for example that of the fifteenth-century Yorkshire knight, Brian Roucliffe: 'if ya be in dedely syn or in tribulaccon or in any deses goy to the kerke and fall on thy knes'. And even the educated faith of the later Middle Ages did not mean the loss of the numinous among the gentry, as we can see from the story of Sir James Berners, who, struck by lightning when accompanying Richard II's court on pilgrimage to Walsingham, was 'blinded and half-crazed' by a vision of the Last Judgement and restored by being taken to the shrine of St Etheldreda at Ely.[47] An exploration of the language used in the fifteenth-century gentry correspondences would offer valuable evidence of the true meaning of religion to the mass of the gentry, not just on their deathbeds but in the course of their daily lives.[48] Richmond has been dismissive of the religion of Margaret Paston, one of these gentry correspondents, adding her to his band of proto-Protestant late medieval gentry, but his comment that she 'took death as naturally as she took her Christian faith' may well be much more profound than he intended it to be.[49] For most of the gentry, religion probably was something entirely natural, even if it was gentlewomen, like Margaret, who had greater leisure to pursue a personal faith and perhaps less temptation to commit the worldly sins which put their souls at risk. All gentry men and women were well enough educated in the faith to express their own personal preferences in religion and develop their own favourite saints and rituals. Few would have had time or inclination to acquire a complex relationship with God, whether orthodox or unorthodox; and in the fifteenth century, when individual expression of faith was discouraged, perhaps fewer still would have been disposed to do so. Despite the growth of private altars, prayers and confession, all would have seen the parish church as a natural focus for their religious devotions and benefactions and shared many of the religious sympathies of their lesser fellow parishioners.

Where then did the Reformation in England come from? One answer may be from changing attitudes to Church property.[50] Partly this was simply the casting of envious eyes on ecclesiastical wealth by laymen, especially gentry, who were tired of paying for an unsuccessful war. It made the

Church particularly vulnerable in the later fourteenth century, when it was coupled with a deep suspicion of the pope, who was perceived to be in the pocket of the French, and a general suspicion of the international connections of the English Church. When Wyclif announced in the 1370s that the Church should be disendowed, greed became respectable. But there was another aspect, evident even at this time in the attempts at disendowment attributed to the Lollards, and which outlasted Wyclif's influence. Building on the European-wide debate about the Church's wealth which had begun in the late thirteenth century, this stressed the good works that might be done by the suppression of moribund religious institutions. It grew out of the landed laity's very knowledge of religion and involvement in its affairs and had already led to just such dissolution and foundation long before the dissolution of the monasteries.[51] When the king next found himself at odds with the pope, over his divorce, maybe the landed laity could be persuaded that it was time to embark on such root-and-branch reform. Certainly in the first decades of the sixteenth century there was a new vibrancy in the Church which could have been the seed-bed for reform from within but paradoxically may have been the passport to securing Reformation from without.[52] In the last analysis, a crucial context of the Reformation in England was that, for the gentry who voted in parliament in the 1530s for such radical reform with respect to the papacy and Church property, established religion was neither something they rejected nor something which they were coolly indifferent towards, but something that was integral to their lives. They received it in varying ways, and mostly more intensely at some times than at others, especially intensely of course in the face of death; but its centrality in their moral universe was inescapable.

Notes

1 For the 'Protestant' version, see Dickens, *English Reformation*. Dr Benjamin Thompson kindly commented on this chapter in draft form.

2 Thompson, *English Clergy*; Pantin, *English Church*.

3 See Bibliography and Further Reading for relevant works.

4 See Haigh, *English Reformations*.

5 Catto, 'Religion and the English nobility'; Hicks, 'Four studies in conventional piety'; Carpenter, 'Religion of the gentry'; Carpenter, *Locality and Polity*, ch. 6; Duffy, *Stripping of the Altars*; Brigden, 'Religion and social obligation'; 'Introduction', in French *et al.* (eds), *Parish in English Life*, pp. 3–14.

6 For changes in this historiography, see Hudson, *Premature Reformation*.

7 On problems in the use of will evidence, see Burgess, 'Late medieval wills', and

Carpenter, *Locality and Polity*, pp. 197, 223, 229 n. 149.

8 Swanson, *Religion and Devotion*, pp. 34–8; Owst, *Literature and Pulpit*, pp. 305–31.

9 For all general references to gentry donations, etc. in what follows, see Carpenter, 'Religion of the gentry' and *Locality and Polity*, ch. 6 and works mentioned there and, for more recent work, Saul, *Death, Art, and Memory* (but the major Cobhams belonged to the nobility) and Binski, *Medieval Death*. See also Kreider, *English Chantries*; Platt, *Architecture of Medieval Britain*, chs 5–7.

10 Duffy, *Stripping of the Altars*, pp. 132–3.

11 Carpenter, 'England: the nobility and the gentry', pp. 264, 274–5.

12 Platt, *Parish Churches*, pp. 44–5.

13 Morris, *Churches in the Landscape*, p. 366.

14 Gibson, *Theater of Devotion*, pp. 28, 79–90.

15 Saul, *Scenes from Provincial Life*, pp. 155–6; *Archdeaconry of Norwich*.

16 Fleming, 'Hautes and their "circle"', p. 98; Harrison, *Music in Medieval Britain*, ch. 4; Thomson, *Early Tudor Church*, pp. 304–7 (but note the grant of an organ associated with the Uffords before they were ennobled, in Middleton-Stewart, *Inward Purity*, pp. 175–8).

17 Swanson, *Church and Society*, p. 17; Hughes, *Pastors and Visionaries*, pp. 12, 49; Carpenter, 'Religion of the gentry', p. 63.

18 Ward, 'Noblewomen and piety'; Erler, 'English vowed women'.

19 Gardner, 'English nobility'.

20 Swanson, *Church and Society*, p. 49; Mertes, *English Noble Household*, pp. 46–7; Hughes, 'Ornaments to know a holy man', pp. 160–4, 166–7; McFarlane, *Hans Memling*, pp. 1–15; Bowers, 'Obligation, agency and laissez-faire'; Wathey, *Music in the Royal and Noble Households*, p. 52 and *passim*; Fleming, 'Hautes and their "circle"', p. 94; Duffy, *Stripping of the Altars*, pp. 210–12.

21 Carey, 'Devout literate laypeople'; Dutton, 'Passing the book'; Doyle, 'English books in and out of Court', pp. 175–6; Taylor, 'Into his secret chamber'.

22 Pantin, *English Church*, pp. 253–6.

23 Pantin, 'Instructions', p. 400; below, p. 144.

24 *Kingsford's Stonor Letters*, ed. Carpenter, p. 138 (no. 56).

25 Gibson, *Theater of Devotion*, pp. 86–90; Pantin, 'Instructions', pp. 399–400; *Peter Idley's* Instructions; Mertes, *English Noble Household*, pp. 173–4; Hughes, *Pastors and Visionaries*, pp. 85–6; Spencer, *English Preaching*, pp. 39–41; Hughes, 'Ornaments to know a holy man', p. 165; references in n. 28, below.

26 Swanson, *Catholic England*, pp. 23–4; *Peter Idley's* Instructions, ch. 2; Dutton, 'Passing the book'; Carey, 'Devout literate laypeople', pp. 365–71; Richmond, 'Margins and marginality'; Gibson, *Theater of Devotion*, p. 96; Hughes, 'Ornaments to know a holy man', pp. 160–4; Fleming, 'Hautes and their "circle"', p. 95.

27 Spencer, *English Preaching*, pp. 157–8.

28 Carpenter, 'Religion of the gentry' and *Locality and Polity*, ch. 6 (and extensive primary and secondary references in these); Steele, *Towards a Spirituality*, ch. 8; Middleton-Stewart, *Inward Purity*; Catto, 'Religion and the English nobility', pp. 45–6.

29 For what follows, see Carpenter, 'Religion of the gentry', *Locality and Polity*, ch. 6 and 'Fifteenth-century English gentry', pp. 53–6, and e.g. Gibson, *Theater of Devotion*; Binski, *Medieval Death*, ch. 2; Saul, *Death, Art and Memory*. Also Duffy, *Stripping of the Altars*, pp. 142–54 (guilds), 334–7 (bede roll).

30 'Introduction', in French *et al.* (eds), *Parish in English Life*, pp. 11–12; Richmond, 'Religion and the fifteenth-century English gentleman', 'English gentry and religion', and 'Margins and marginality'; Bossy, 'Christian life', and *Christianity in the West*.

31 For what follows, see Duffy, *Stripping of the Altars*.

32 Middleton-Stewart, *Inward Purity*, pp. 217–18.

33 Duffy, *Stripping of the Altars, passim* and pp. 181–3, 256–65; Morgan, 'Texts and images'; above, p. 00.

34 Duffy, *Stripping of the Altars*, p. 173; Dugdale, *Antiquities of Warwickshire*, p. 91; Carpenter, *Locality and Polity*, p. 227; Gibson, *Theater of Devotion*, p. 82; Middleton-Stewart, *Inward Purity*, p. 126.

35 Platt, *Architecture of Medieval Britain*, pp. 164–75; Brown, *Popular Piety*, ch. 5; 'Introduction', in French *et al.* (eds), *Parish in English Life*, pp. 3–14; Duffy, 'Parish, piety and patronage'; Rubin, *Corpus Christi*; Hughes, 'Ornaments to know a holy man', p. 168; for gentry and guilds and further reading on this, see Carpenter, 'Town and "country"'; Pollard, *North-Eastern England*, pp. 189–90.

36 Duffy, 'Dynamics of pilgrimage'; Morris, 'Pilgrimage to Jerusalem'.

37 Carpenter, 'Gentry and community' and *Locality and Polity*, chs 3, 6; above, p. 139.

38 Richmond, 'Religion and the fifteenth-century English gentleman', pp. 198–9.

39 Carpenter, 'England: the nobility and the gentry', pp. 262–4, 274–5.

40 Platt, *Architecture of Medieval Britain*, pp. 231–6; Spencer, *English Preaching*; Saul, *Scenes from Provincial Life*, p. 159; Brown, *Popular Piety*, p. 77; Pollard, *North-Eastern England*, pp. 183–4; Carpenter, *Locality and Polity*, pp. 242–3.

41 E.g. *Calendar of Inquisitions Post Mortem*, xix, nos 663, 664, 777–8, 781, 786, 901, and xx, nos 131, 263, 265.

42 Hughes, *Pastors and Visionaries*, 'Administration of confession', and 'Ornaments to know a holy man'; Swanson, *Religion and Devotion*, pp. 201–3; Binski, *Medieval Death*, p. 40 and ch. 3; Warren, *Anchorites and their Patrons*, pp. 208–21 and Plate 6; Carey, 'Devout literate laypeople'; Pantin, 'Instructions'; below, p. 145.

43 Ghosh, *Wycliffite Heresy*, pp. 209–16.

44 Thomson, 'Knightly piety', p. 97; Somerset, *Clerical Discourse*, ch. 3.

45 For Lollardy and the gentry, see Aston and Richmond (eds), *Lollardy and the Gentry, passim*, esp. Thomson, 'Knightly piety' and references there, and Catto, 'Fellows and helpers'; Catto, 'Religious change'; Hughes, 'Administration of confession', pp. 164–6, 246–7; Watson, 'Censorship and cultural change'.

46 Binski, *Medieval Death* and above, p. 136; Richmond, 'Margins and marginality'; Hughes, 'Ornaments to know a holy man', pp. 175–7; Bernard, 'Vitality and vulnerability', pp. 217–18.

47 Hughes, 'Ornaments to know a holy man', pp. 164–5, 172; Rawcliffe, 'Curing bodies', p. 131.

48 An interesting essay in this is A. Beckett, 'The religious beliefs of the English gentry in the fifteenth century' (BA dissertation, Cambridge University, 1999). See also *Kingsford's Stonor Letters*, ed. Carpenter, pp. 26–7.

49 Richmond, *Paston Family: Endings*, pp. 120–2; also p. 114 and the sermon preserved among the Paston papers, *Paston Letters*, ed. Davis, II, pp. 596–8.

50 This is a key idea in the work of Benjamin Thompson. See e.g. Thompson, '*Habendum et tenendum*'.

51 Heath, *Church and Realm*; Pantin, *English Church*, chs 4 and 5; Aston, 'Caim's castles'; Scarisbrick, *Reformation and the English People*, p. 54; Thompson, '*Habendum and tenendum*', pp. 224–33, 'Monasteries and their patrons', and 'Monasteries, society and reform'.

52 Swanson, *Church and Society*, pp. 314–18, *Catholic England*, p. 43.

9

Music

Tim Shaw

In his notable essay on the formation of the English gentry, Peter Coss suggests that, '[p]erhaps too much attention has been given to the problem of delineation of the gentry. Should we not ask, rather, what distinguishes the gentry as a social formation?'[1] Such social formation, Coss suggests, might include: close relationships with public authorities (local and distant); an influx of professionals; territorial behaviour to reinforce social status; and collective interests dependent on forums, networks and allegiances. If we are to view the gentry not just as a construct of the historian but as an active social impulse, then music, as a cultural practice or even a commodity in fifteenth-century England, is an undeniably attractive area for study.

As an index of taste and privilege, music may be seen as a vehicle to express ideas of territory, status and hegemony to society at large. To do so, however, requires very careful consideration of the nature of encounters between the gentry and music. Ongoing revision of the methodologies of music criticism has problematised terms such as 'consumer', 'audience' and 'patronage', thereby destabilising older Romantic ideas. Current studies now often place the musicians themselves as the principal consumers of musical works, where the 'institutions, patrons and listeners often 'consume' not so much the music itself as its contingent effects: splendour, prestige, devotion, pleasure, or even tradition and continuity'.[2]

Ideas of reception and meaning – that music could reflect particular aesthetic choices or associations, and even define territories within physical space and time – are of interest when it comes to considering how the organisation of music-making may contribute to the construction of gentry identity. That there is work to be done in this area is acknowledged in a recent bibliographical survey of 'Music in European cities and towns to c. 1650' which notes that, 'more could ... be done on audience reception and the communication of musical 'meanings' to the various social groups in urban communities'.[3]

In looking at how the gentry 'used' or 'did' music, there is potential to understand something of what music 'meant' to the gentry and their contemporaries, but there is a risk here of the tail wagging the dog. Music in fifteenth-century England appears to have been essentially a contingent rather than central aspect of daily life for the majority of members of the gentry, and much of its 'meaning' is therefore dependent upon being fleshed out by context. The issue of where and when gentry members may have gone beyond the role of providing resources for musical provision and crossed over to become performers of musical works themselves will be discussed below. In looking at music and the fifteenth-century English gentry we are looking at how music was embedded into the institutions and social networks that comprised gentry life, and attempting to discern how – if at all – their experience was distinct from that of their contemporaries.

What then of music culture at large? In the fifteenth century the sacred vocal polyphonic music of named English composers was included in continental manuscripts.[4] The universities of Oxford and Cambridge had moved to include the study of music alongside their formal curriculum, with students studying Boethius' *Musica*. Colleges supported choral institutions taking up trained choristers from the 'feeder' collegiate foundations and awarded degrees in music. Inventories of students' possessions, which included musical instruments, and college statutes (framed to curb excessive noise generated by such), also attest to recreational music-making.[5] The 'groundwork' for the 'new learning' of humanism was also being established through the channels of diplomatic travel and the interests of individual collectors and bibliophiles, such as Humphrey, duke of Gloucester, William Gray, bishop of Ely, and and Robert Fleming, Gray's contemporary at Oxford and later as students in Padua and Ferrara.[6]

The position of music as it was embedded in the daily lives of the English gentry in the fifteenth century, however, is not something that has enjoyed exhaustive critical survey to date. What follows takes the form of suggestions as to areas of research. In the field of musicology this shortcoming has been, in part, due to the nature of surviving evidence: a strong pull being exerted by royal and noble households and substantial institutions where archival materials are particularly rich. Additionally, some of the more technical and analytical traditions within musicology may have acted in the past to discourage cross-disciplinary engagement and dialogue. A critical shift occurred in the late 1980s and early 1990s, when 'the adoption of historical methodologies over technical ones' by some musicologists led to 'the equal treatment of the context of music with its content'.[7]

Recently a number of fields have opened up in the study of music culture in late medieval and early modern England, which are of potential interest for a study of the gentry. Principal among these is the body of recent (i.e. post-1980s) work on the English parish. Here, as members of the laity, the gentry would have been exposed to the music of the liturgy of the pre-Reformation church. In the parish church this meant song: male-voiced, mainly plainchant (sometimes polyphonic) setting Latin texts, sometimes accompanied by an organ located in a rood loft (above the screen separating the eastern end of the church from the nave). This took place in the choir of the church (separated from the congregational end of the church by a rood screen, pierced by a gate) and within the processions conducted by the clergy inside of the church, and outside along prescribed processional routes on key occasions during the liturgical year. Here, through endowments and through participation in guilds and fraternities, the gentry would have contributed to the fabric and resources of their churches, shaping the provision for the performance of the liturgy and within it the provision for music. What drove such generosity will be considered below.

Much of the post-1980s research concerned with the parish has resulted from the close collaboration of musicologists with religious and urban historians, concentrating largely on urban and metropolitan contexts.[8] This urban focus does not, however, exclude consideration of the position of the gentry. Writing outside of the specific concerns of any musicological debate, work by historians such as Rosemary Horrox, considering the 'urban gentry', and Coss, reappraising what it was to be recognised as a member of the late medieval gentry, provides a stimulating supplement to the recent work aimed towards mapping out the professional networks and practices of musicians on to the spaces of the late medieval town-scape.[9] A useful overview of such research (on which the following draws) is provided by Caroline Barron's interim report of research undertaken by a group of historians and musicologists exploring the evidence for urban parochial music, and by a separate overview of the historical context for the provision for music in the fifteenth- and sixteenth-century English parish by Beat Kümin.[10]

The growing study of music within communities inside urban settings, 'the "worlds within worlds" that characterised urban communities', and the use of music within religious, civic and royal ceremonial and drama (within urban space and time) means that increasingly the contribution of members of the gentry will be able to be read with greater understanding.[11] Barron notes that, given the amount of wealth being directed towards the pre-Reformation English Church, the consequences for musicological study are only just beginning to be fully examined: moving from the survey of 'institutions [as] isolated, constitutionally-defined entities' to examining the scope for 'interaction' especially within 'dense urban environments'.[12] The level of interconnection between the worlds of the urban and rural gentry makes this research into the late medieval town- and cityscape potentially rich ground for the type of micro history that the study of gentry culture will involve.

The stimulus for much of the work on the parish and other liturgical institutions has been the revision of the notion of a 'popular' Reformation in the mid-sixteenth century, which has, in turn, led to a fresh examination of the pre-Reformation Church.[13] Where older Anglican historiography viewed the pre-Reformation Church as racked by abuses, corruption and unpopularity, post-1980s reappraisal of parish history – examining surviving documents (especially the accounts of late medieval parish church-wardens and 'masters') and the buildings themselves – has revealed a thriving religious, liturgical culture, enthusiastically appropriated and elaborated by parishioners in urban and rural parishes alike. A key concept within this has been an acknowledgement of the potency of the desire for intercession by the laity, within the framework of the doctrine of Purgatory.[14]

The doctrine of Purgatory acted as part of an economy of Salvation. It provided both absolution for sin and the hard cash that drove the wheels of liturgical resource and growth. Penance not satisfied in life could, thanks to development of this doctrine in the twelfth and thirteenth centuries, be completed in this 'third place', the 'staging post' to Heaven. Purgatory established an important link between the living and the dead. The faithful could expiate their own progress, along with that of their families and the 'faithful departed', through good works: acts of charity to the poor, contributions to the fabric of their church, or the endowment of chantries. Establishing a chantry meant providing rents from land or property to fund a priest to recite prayers for the dead individual, his or her family or other individuals for a fixed period or in perpetuity. The more wealthy might have an individual chantry, or else individuals could club together to resource a guild or fraternity chantry, assisting their members and perhaps in turn also contributing another priest to serve the liturgical or educational needs of the parish and meet the demands of increasing liturgical provision.

The living beneficiaries of such good works were obliged to pray for and intercede on the donor's behalf – thus speeding the progress of the individual's soul through Purgatory. Beneficiaries might include the poor, or members of the parish whose liturgy had been embellished by gifts of vestments or materials for the performance of the divine service.

The scale of this influx of resources generated by the desire for intercession is noted by Burgess, who writes that 'England's wealthier classes were, in all probability, more generous towards the Church in the century or more preceding the Reformation than at any time since'.[15] It is here where we might look with profit for instances of gentry benefaction and perhaps question what, beyond the 'craving for intercession', may have prompted the particular character of their sponsorship of parts of the liturgy – through guild membership or specific contributions to the materials of the liturgy. That benefaction could follow liturgical initiatives, driven by lay ambitions and desires, has been documented.[16]

Just as the physical space laid out for the liturgy within churches was embellished by the addition of chantry, guild and fraternity chapels (leading to a proliferation of masses and prayer), so too the liturgy itself and provision for music within the liturgy could be elaborated. Drawing upon work on parishes in Bristol and highlighting the crucial role of lay benefaction in providing the resources necessary for 'the gradual elaboration of musical provision', Kümin characterises the way in which liturgical provision developed through lay benefaction. He writes:

> Late-medieval testators almost invariably specified a range of good works and intercessory services ... Prayers for the dead thus multiplied in a myriad of different forms, most prominently through the endowment of Votive Masses, and chantries, resulting in a great 'increase' in divine service and liturgical variety.[17]

From the choir stalls of the great abbeys to those of the rural parish church, the music of the late medieval liturgy was overwhelmingly that of monophonic plainsong. References to the books necessary for the performance of chant (chant books or antiphoners) are widespread in records of parish book ownership. Once acquired, antiphoners written for one institution could be reused by churches, where additional material, particular to the new parish, could be incorporated. A noted example of this is where in 1478 the rural parish of Ranworth, Norfolk, received an antiphoner created originally for Langley Abbey, Loddon. This antiphoner was, 'subsequently "customised" for its new community by the addition of services for the feast of St Helen, patron saint of the parish, and by annotations to the calendar containing obits for the local gentry'.[18] In this example, members of the gentry, as testators, have clearly left endowments to the parish in return for the performance of post-obituary services (*obits*).

One form embellishment of the music of the liturgy could take was through the performance of polyphony, or part song. This could take the form of either an 'improvised' form, *fauburden*, or could take the written form contained within 'pricksong' books – a generic term for polyphony, recorded in inventories within churchwardens' accounts.[19] Reflecting significant investment, in terms of personnel and material resources, provision for sung polyphony was once thought to be the preserve of only a limited number of large metropolitan churches, colleges and religious houses. As more research is carried out into the professional practices of musicians, the relationships between institutions (via personnel and the pre-print circulation of repertory through musicians' copies) and the practice of polyphony appear to have been more widespread. Consideration of now 'lost' books of polyphonic music shows, however, that out of 174 books, 30 were kept in churches in small urban settlements and village churches.[20]

There are some caveats. That a parish possessed 'pricksong' books does not automatically imply that polyphony constituted part of that parish liturgy. A manuscript could be gifted to a parish where changes over time could radically alter the resources available to a parish to perform such music in the liturgy. Work on a number of well-documented wealthy parishes with multiple well-resourced benefactions shows the ideal context for such elaboration.[21]

That the gentry took specific interest in the music of the liturgy, sometimes directly, is attested to in surviving wills. Horrox identifies the will (drawn up in 1492) of John Sturgeon, esquire of the parish of Hitchin, which as well as stipulating his desired location for burial in front of the 'image of the blessed lady before the high altar' demonstrates an interest in maintaining the quality of provision for the liturgy. Sturgeon requests that his executors provide for a mercer to move from another parish to 'sing in the choir and help to maintain God's service' and to 'sing and read in the parish church of Hitchin'.[22] It may be noted that the source is silent as to the type of repertory the mercer, 'Thomas Browne', might be expected to perform – whether chant or maybe improvised polyphony – and also there is no indication as to whether this intended move represents something new, or merely puts an existing arrangement onto a firmer footing.

Guild membership afforded members of the gentry another means of contributing to the resources for the liturgy and possibly, through 'elite' guilds, access to important social networks and to a corporate identity recognisable to their contemporaries. This corporate expression of lay devotional life could range from modest provision supporting ad hoc employment of additional singers or priests to celebrate the feast days of the guild and the obits of its members, to more spectacular outlay enhancing the liturgy of the incumbent church with supernumerary priests, and even singing clerks.[23] As Magnus Williamson notes in his survey of the role of religious guilds in the cultivation of ritual polyphony in north-east England, a key element of the resources generated by guilds was the way in which it allowed parishioners to 'emulate' the 'greater ecclesiastical institutions'.[24] Inventory evidence shows that of the polyphonic works most often held by parishes, amongst the most frequent were related to the liturgy of the festal and votive Mass. The festal Mass was that of a particular saint from the cycle of the Sanctorale; it was most likely the feast day of the titular or patronal saint of the parish. Votive Masses fell outside of the temporal calendar of the Church and allowed for the daily celebration of Mass for a specific need or intercession. Harper notes early votive Mass cycles for Holy Angels, Holy Cross, Holy Spirit, Holy Trinity, wisdom, charity and penitence (the votive Mass addressed to the Virgin is considered below).[25] That both of these types of Mass figure so significantly in what we know of the polyphonic repertory of late medieval parishes clearly demonstrates the importance of 'localised' ceremonial to the laity.

The question of what was driving such desires and where the models for liturgical enhancement might be found is interesting. Here it is possible to see members of the gentry as players in the transfer of liturgical ideas, not just in terms of the money wealthier members of the laity could provide, but also in terms of what liturgical models members of the gentry could expect to be exposed to in the maintenance of their duties as civic and legal administrators or as members of the Commons.

Work since the 1980s on the specialised liturgical institutions, the collegiate foundations of the fifteenth century, stresses the closeness of this type of highly organised liturgical life to the emergence of a public, national religion, parallel with that of structures of civil government.[26] Such work suggests that the prototype for such institutions (and indeed parish liturgy) was the monastic model, and that the two-gear approach for understanding closed and secular religious institutions is no longer appropriate. Monasteries – prolific in number and the first to fall in the sixteenth-century recasting of religious life – occupied the position of keystones for pre-Reformation liturgical life and experience. However, the model of liturgical practice offered for such emulation has still not been investigated in any detail.

Westminster Abbey was undergoing substantial structural expansion by the late fourteenth century, enlarging its sphere of influence to serve both its immediate surroundings (the Court and town), and also London. Indeed, it seems to have played an influential role in enriching Londoners' liturgical experience – the rise and fall of liturgical revenues from popular altar and shrine sites during Richard II's reign may be taken as an indication that Londoners ordinarily did attend the Abbey's services but, because of the strong association of Abbey and Crown, would absent themselves to express dissatisfaction with Richard's policies.[27] From at least the reign of Henry III onwards, Westminster Abbey was the proprietary house for the Plantagenet dynasty. Through the thirteenth and fourteenth centuries, the Benedictine monks celebrated a liturgy which served royal needs – both intercessory and as a means of projecting an image of Kingship. Late fourteenth-century evidence presents a picture of a self-consciously regal, and even imperial, development of the Abbey's liturgy dovetailed with conspicuous devotion to St Peter.

The Abbey did not operate in a vacuum. There is good evidence that it served not only the Court but also 'the good and the great' who regularly travelled to Westminster for both legal and 'parliamentary' purposes. It is also relevant to note that Londoners seem to have frequented the Abbey. Put these elements together, and there is every reason for believing that Westminster's liturgy would have been conspicuously influential – setting a template for innovatory liturgical practice in the capital and the localities.[28]

Returning to the parish, running alongside the cycle of the liturgical year was a season of more secular entertainment for which music appears to have constituted a part. Here REED, the Records of Early English Drama series, is particularly useful for individual case studies – although much source material discussed concerns the sixteenth century. Kümin notes a 'mixture of neighbourly conviviality and fundraising necessity' as providing the stimulus for a season of celebrations running from Easter to Midsummer, focussing on the festivals of Hocktide, May Day, Whitsun and Corpus Christi (in addition to the dedication and feast day of the church's titular saint). In particular, communal 'dancing days' associated with May Day appear to have relied upon the services of a piper or fiddler.[29] These 'secular holidays' coincided with important feast days in the liturgical calendar. This is not coincidental but rather, as Barron notes, reflects the trend beginning in the fourteenth century for English towns to develop civic ceremonial with the out-of-doors, perambulatory liturgical processions of town churches as their centrepiece.[30] Such processions, enshrined in English liturgical use from the eleventh century, were highly visual spectacles. They allowed for the display of the material riches of a church, reflecting back on the generosity of its lay benefactors. Furthermore, as chronicle and customary texts attest, they often featured the singing of antiphons, psalm texts and hymns, and could also feature choirs of boys at particular stations along a processional route.

Palm Sunday was such a feast day. It marked the beginning of the liturgy of Holy Week, the most solemn period of the liturgical calendar long anticipated in alterations to the liturgy during the penitential season. The Palm Sunday Procession celebrations, Barron notes, could include a procession 'in which a tabernacle containing the Host was carried outside the church by clerics, flanked by men and boys carrying flags, palms, crosses, incense relics and torches'. Barron describes the procession at Hereford where, imitating the arrival of Christ into Jerusalem 'in the mid fourteenth century, the sacrament and relics were taken outside the city walls … and were then brought back amidst chants, to be greeted by a small choir of boys on top of the city gate singing *Gloria Laus*'.[31] The procession of Corpus Christi was, to the same ends, another key event in the late medieval liturgical calendar. From the start of the fourteenth century, the extra-mural liturgical procession of the church was increasingly elaborated by lay participation and contributions accommodating civic concerns.[32] As noted above, the importance of this particular feast day to parishioners can be seen in the records of polyphonic votive Masses for the feast in accounts of churchwardens.

The music of liturgical ceremonial clearly provided a template for civic occasions. Indeed, so much so that Tim Carter notes that we

> now treat as a commonplace music's utility in terms of its potential to manifest civic, courtly or sacramental splendour as required by the ceremonies that punctuated the secular and sacred calendars of urban life. Music thus marks the significant rites of passage of both individual and state, while preserving continuities and traditions to grant an illusion of permanence in the face of the political, social and even personal uncertainties of a difficult world.[33]

Barron's account of the first recorded year in which music became a part of the annual mayoral election in London illustrates well Carter's perspective. In 1406 the outgoing mayor, John Wodecock, made the decision that 'the outgoing mayor, aldermen and "as many as possible of the wealthier and more substantial commoners of the city" should first attend Mass of the Holy Spirit to be celebrated with music in the Guildhall chapel'.[34] The success of this innovation, Barron notes, was demonstrated to contemporaries by the fact that the office was able to be filled 'without dispute', and that it was decided that this practice was to become the norm for all future elections.[35]

In a different arena, one performance which included both instrumental music and song and mixed the worlds of the liturgical and the secular, the clerical and the laity, is the English cycle and mystery plays. Here it is possible to identify gentry involvement through the guilds or occupational groups which traditionally held responsibilities for individual plays or pageants within the cycles. Horrox notes a reference in 1441 within the civic records for the Beverly *Pater noster* cycle of a pageant given over to the gentlemen (viciouse).[36] Such plays leant heavily on the resources and skills of the clerics and the religious. In the case of the Beverly plays, Richard Rastall notes that the banns of the play, written in 1423, and the subsequent revisions to the cycle in 1520, were both carried out by Dominicans – the latter by William Peers, the Earl of Northumberland's secretary.[37]

Education and service presented further opportunities for members of the gentry to be exposed to music and potentially to training in music. Much authoritative work has been written on late medieval education and on the song schools provided by parish and great religious house alike. The hard evidence siting the gentry within these various contexts, however, proves more difficult to locate.[38]

Service in great households (secular and religious) seems to have offered the principal means of education for the gentry. Nicholas Orme has noted that those considered gentle would have 'tried to place their children ... in ... careers which would give them a reasonable standard of life and the chance of self advancement', perhaps looking to the Church or the Law as a means to this.[39] Looking at evidence for the north of England, Jo Ann H. Moran Cruz considers that, 'because of the ubiquity of household training among the land-owning classes, before the late fifteenth century the sons of aristocrats and gentry were not likely to have been educated in the grammar school, and never in the local parish reading or song school'.[40] What opportunities for music education, then, might education in service offer to children of the gentry?

For the daughters of the gentry, education whilst in the household of a social superior or equal is often equated with some training in reading English, various domestic crafts and 'accomplishment in music'.[41] The exact nature of this musical accomplishment is often hard to pin down; when one reads the source materials this apparent orthodoxy appears to be built on very little evidence. This probably reflects a 'reading back' from source evidence such as the wills of aristocratic women in the sixteenth century – often rich in reference to music and music-making – and to the literature devoted to 'manners' and noble accomplishments. There is the potential danger here of viewing aspiration as a record of actual practice; the differences between a behavioural trope as found in courtesy literature, the aristocratic norms of the succeeding century, and contemporary reality for the children of the gentry in the fifteenth century might be quite marked.[42]

Given that explicit references to musical training for gentry children appear rarely, any such examples are of particular interest. One of note involves the son of William Marchall, a clerk of the Almonry of Chancery and a small landowner in Standlake and Woodstock in Oxfordshire. The source is a letter to William from a near relation, John Collas – who, it has been suggested, was in the service of the Bishop of Ely – who was, at the time of writing, living in London charged with the education of William's son, Thomas. Collas wrote telling the parents of his charge that 'the chylld [Thomas] ys rygth wele hentyrd in-to ys songe, that ys to say bouth playnsonge and prykyd sonnge'.[43] The letter, dating from the second half of the fifteenth century, suggests that Marchall's son is receiving the training of a boy chorister in a song school.[44] That the distinction between 'plainsong' and the polyphonic 'priked song' is made clear to Thomas' parents is of interest. In the context of the letter these technical references appear to show how Collas wishes the parents of Thomas to allow for their son to continue under his charge and not to be 'sent home'. Here, the detail of 'both plainsong and priked song' is being offered as a demonstration of Thomas' potential.

Richard Rastall, writing on notions of the professional and amateur musician for the period, notes that having mastered the plainsong repertory and its expressive system of notation, the 'most promising chorister' might graduate to learning the organ and to joining a group of singers trained in polyphony. The complexity of the system of notation required for this – in contrast to that of plainsong, to represent the duration of note values in mensural music – suggests for Rastall the exclusivity of this group. Complex traditions, such as the canon form exemplified in the Caius, Lambeth and Eton choirbooks, represented 'a tradition of learned complexity needed to maintain the special status of its intitates'.[45] The comments made to Thomas Marchall's parents would seem, then, to presuppose some familiarity on their part with the technical training of a liturgical musician and the transition from plainsong to polyphony – if Collas' reference was to have the effect he desired in maintaining the boy in his care in training, in London.

The music education of Thomas Marchall may reflect older patterns of household service or it may tie in with an educational trend identified separately by both Orme and Moran Cruz.[46] That trend was a shift in interest toward grammar and parish schools after 1450, and in particular post-1500, by the gentry. Moran Cruz identifies money directed towards the endowment and sometimes the founding of schools by landowners in the diocese of York as being stimulated by the model offered by notable local ecclesiastical foundations. In addition she notes that, 'by about 1,500 diocesan gentlemen were beginning to send their sons to local grammar schools, to provide funds for parish scholars, and, for the wealthier classes, to support large clerical retinues with household choirs and schooling'.[47] It is important to see such benefaction as being set against both the broad lay devotional trends discussed above, and the growth in administrative government, identified by Burgess, growing out of and inextricably linked with the organised liturgical lives of the collegiate foundations of the fifteenth century.

Sons and daughters of the gentry might also have found themselves as pupils of monastic or Almonry schools, boarding in abbeys or nunneries. This was clearly very different from being a novice. Alexander notes that before the Dissolution 'scores of female convents boarded young children from wealthy families' with a combined figure of around 2,500 pupils being educated yearly in both nunneries and monasteries. Orme describes how 'sons of the patron or of the neighbouring gentry' could receive a 'gentle' upbringing in the Abbot's household where either a tutor, engaged to go with the boys, or the monastery's own master, who provided the teaching in the Almonry school, would provide instruction. One liturgical development which placed a specific demand for the training of boys' voices was the desire for an increasingly elaborate daily polyphonic liturgy of the Virgin (votive Lady Mass) from the late fourteenth, and through the fifteenth, centuries in the great monastic and collegiate churches; the inclusion of sons of the gentry amongst those trained for this purpose awaits consideration, and Thomas Marchall may be just such an example.

Aside from temporary residence in regular religious institutions, work on the social status of office holders in a group of female religious houses in the diocese of Norwich between 1350 and 1540 has revealed a figure of around 64 per cent from the 'lower or parish gentry' within the population of these houses.[48] Here, gentry women would have been instructed to be able to perform the daily round of liturgical offices – choral plainchant from Latin texts – just as in a monastery. Evidence for the performance of vocal polyphony within the liturgy of English female convents is, however, more difficult to establish.[49]

Another avenue open to the male children of the gentry in terms of their education was the law. In the fifteenth century this meant attendance at one of London's Inns of Court. Traditionally the Inns have been viewed as accessible only to the sons of the nobility, a view stemming largely from the account given by Sir John Fortescue in his *De Laudibus Legum Anglie*, compiled for the instruction of Prince Edward of Lancaster in 1468.[50] Reappraisal of some of his statements have both scaled down the numbers thought to be attending the Inns annually and questioned the social status of those attending: Alexander suggests that 'the average law student was from a gentle background, not a noble one'.[51]

Furthermore, Alexander suggests that an education in the Inns offered a social exclusivity not afforded then by the universities (to which the sons of the gentry would not gain access fully until well into the sixteenth century), and additionally offered a secular ethos. Here students might be 'safe from the seductive appeal of theology [where they] could not be induced to become priests, or even worse, to join a monastic or mendicant order'.[52] Whilst few of the gentry might remain for the complete duration of the course leading to qualification as a barrister, the legal knowledge gained could be of use in defending the interests of family and estate.

The link between life in the Inns and music derives from Fortescue's accounts of the recreations of the Inns' members, where a 'smattering of a liberal education' could be gained. It was, Fortescue maintained, 'like a school of all manners that nobles learn. There they learn to sing and exercise themselves in every kind of harmony. They also practice dancing and all games proper to noblemen, just as those in the king's household are accustomed to practice them'.[53] Such accounts, as mentioned above, have to be treated with caution. It may be worth bearing this community of students of the Inns of Court in mind, however, when we look forward into the Tudor period and are looking for a secular audience for the 'broadside' songsheets and playful, suggestive (often highly technical) allusions to music, and, importantly, solmisation (the pedagogy of the singing master), in the popular urban theatre of Tudor London.[54]

Clearly there was a range of musical literacy within the gentry community, some of it dependent on gender. Within the parish a well-resourced church could hope to emulate the musical and liturgical models of the great monastic and secular churches and the household chapels of the elite. Here there is evidence of both male and female testatory generosity. It is attractive to speculate that, as a student at one of the Inns of Court, a son of the gentry might have received a grounding in music that would put him at his ease amongst his clerical contemporaries. A daughter of a gentry family admitted to a convent would, as a necessity, be trained to perform the round of liturgical plainsong, and a son such as Thomas Marshall, trained in polyphonic practice, would for all modern purposes, as Rastall argues, be classed as a professional musician.[55]

The character and volume of institutional archival evidence, when viewed in isolation, can unbalance our picture. Clearly the fifteenth-century soundscape was more varied than this range of institutional contexts would suggest, with more ephemeral popular practices, bells and criers, 'noise' and 'bad music' all within the range of the fifteenth-century ear. Unpacking what music meant to individuals, and thinking and writing about music as an aesthetic experience, is notoriously problematic. Given the potential for seeing 'gentility' as a construct, a bricolage of social actions, utterances and networks, it is perhaps tempting to look forward to the 'new learning' of humanism as an attractive context for engaging and stimulating gentry self-fashioning. The routes to music education for the gentry at least in fifteenth-century England appear, however, rather more traditional. This, at least, may have made them all the more desirable.

Notes

1 Coss, 'Formation of the English gentry', p. 47.
2 Carter, 'Sound of silence'.
3 Kisby, 'Music in European cities', p. 82.
4 Strohm, 'European politics'.
5 Carpenter, 'Medieval universities'. See also, for the subsequent lives of arts graduates, Kintzinger, 'Profession but not a career?'
6 Alexander, *Growth of English Education*, pp. 43–66.
7 For discussion of these points see 'Introduction' in Kisby (ed.), *Music and Musicians*, pp. 1–13 (esp. p. 5f).
8 In particular I refer to an AHRB project undertaken jointly by members of the Music and History departments at Royal Holloway College, University of London, working towards the publication of a four-part monograph. This will comprise 'Urban identity and urban geography' to be written by Andrew Wathey, 'The musical workforce in the parish church' by Clive Burgess, 'The practice of liturgy inside the parish church' by Fiona Kisby, and 'The impact of church music on urban spaces' by Caroline Barron.
9 Horrox, 'Urban gentry'; for Coss, see above, n. 1.
10 Barron, 'Church music'; Kümin, 'Masses, morris and metrical psalms'.
11 Kisby (ed.), *Music and Musicians*, p. 10f.
12 Barron, 'Church music', p. 85.
13 See here in particular Duffy, *Stripping of the Altars*. For a fuller discussion of the debate surrounding revisionism and the pre-Reformation Church, see Burgess and Wathey, 'Mapping the soundscape'.

14 Burgess and Wathey, *ibid.*, pp. 6–8.

15 *Ibid.*

16 For a fifteenth-century example of this in a parish guild in Louth, north-east England, see Williamson, 'Role of religious guilds'.

17 Kümin, 'Masses, morris and metrical psalms', p. 73.

18 *Ibid.*, p. 72.

19 See Kümin, *ibid.*, for bibliographical references to this improvisational technique. *Fauburden* was a practice for creating improvised polyphony around a chant line in the middle voice using intervals of thirds and sixths. The most notable late medieval literary reference is in Chaucer's 'General Prologue' to *The Canterbury Tales*: 'This Somonour bar to hym a stif burdoun' (*Riverside Chaucer*, p. 34, line 673). The bawdy interplay between reference to the performance and pedagogy of music and sex appears to be something of a literary trope closely wedded to clerical recreations. See Shaw, 'Contextualising the "Winchester Songbook"', for the binding of erotic cantilenas with early English vernacular liturgical and devotional songs.

20 Wathey, 'Lost books', cited in Kümin, 'Music in the English parish', p. 73.

21 For the London parish of St Mary at Hill, see Baillie, 'London church'; and more recently Lloyd, 'Music at the parish church'. See also Lloyd, 'Provision for music'. For the parish church of All Saints', Bristol, see Burgess (ed.), *Pre-Reformation Records*.

22 Prerogative court of Canterbury, Prob 11/9 fol. 143; Horrox, 'Urban gentry', p. 36.

23 Kümin, 'Masses, morris and metrical psalms', p. 76, notes the early sixteenth-century 'cathedral-size choir of some thirty men supported by a local guild' in the parish church of St Botolph, Boston, Lincolnshire.

24 Williamson, 'Role of religious guilds', p. 82. Here, Williamson is also keen to stress that regardless of size and wealth 'most [religious guilds] played little role in the cultivation of liturgical polyphony'.

25 For a detailed introduction to the various parts of the late medieval liturgy, see Harper, *Forms and Orders*, p. 134.

26 For an example of such research and a setting-out of the parameters of this debate, I refer to Clive Burgess, 'Liturgy and power in the fifteenth century', a lecture given at the Institute of Historical Research, London, on Tuesday 20 February 2001.

27 Shaw, 'Reading the liturgy', p. 273f.

28 Of key importance here, in Westminster itself, is the parish church of St Margaret and the guild of St Mary's Assumption; see Rosser, 'Essence of medieval urban communities'.

29 Kümin, 'Masses, morris and metrical psalms', p. 76. For Westminster and the parish of St Margarets see Holt and Rosser (eds), *English Medieval Town*, pp. 228–9. For parishes in south-eastern England see Johnston and MacLean, 'Reformation and resistance'. For a discussion of the profession of Minstrels, here specifically within the context of music to accompany drama, see Rastall, *Heaven Singing*, pp. 364–8.

30 Barron, 'Church music', p. 87f.

31 *Ibid.*, p. 88.

32 Rubin, *Corpus Christi*, cited in Barron, *ibid.*

33 Carter, 'Sound of silence', p. 13.

34 Barron, 'Church music', p. 88.

35 *Ibid.*, p. 89. Barron also gives here a detailed account of the history of the Guildhall chapel and its endowments, and additionally suggests a possible contemporary continental source for this use of music in civic ceremonial. Interestingly, referring to the peripatetic flexibility of the careers of singing clerks in London, musical practice is described by Barron as 'homogenised' (*ibid.*, p. 86).

36 Horrox, 'Urban gentry', p. 24. See also, Beadle (ed.), *Cambridge Companion to Medieval English Theatre*, pp. xx, 24; the earliest reference for the Beverly play is from 1377. No text of the play survives.

37 Rastall, *Heaven Singing*, p. 252.

38 Orme, *English Schools*, pp. 63–7, 245–8.

39 *Ibid.*, p. 30.

40 Moran Cruz, 'Education, economy, and clerical mobility', p. 200.

41 Jewell, *Women in Medieval England*, p. 145.

42 For reference to music and status for Tudor aristocratic women, see Harris, *English Aristocratic Women*. For discussion of courtesy literature, see Orme, *English Schools*, p. 30.

43 NA SC 1/46/268; published in Lyell (ed.), *Mediæval Post-Bag*, pp. 296–7. I am grateful to Alison Truelove for bringing this example to my attention.

44 Without a clearer picture of Collas' connections and circumstances it is unclear where this may have taken place. A song school was active at St Paul's at this time: Orme, *English Schools*, p. 63. For a description of St Paul's at the hub of liturgical music activity, see Baillie, 'London gild'. For a more recent appraisal see Barron, 'Church music', pp. 90–1.

45 Rastall, *Heaven Singing*, pp. 301–2. For a discussion of one of these songbooks see Williamson, 'Early Tudor court', p. 229.

46 Orme, *English Schools*, p. 30; Moran Cruz, 'Education, economy, and clerical mobility', p. 200.

47 *Ibid.*

48 Jewell, *Women in Medieval England*, p. 159.

49 For a discussion of this issue see Yardley, 'Ful weel she soong'.

50 Alexander, *Growth of English Education*, p. 24.

51 *Ibid.*

52 *Ibid.*

53 *Ibid.*, p. 26.

54 Milsom, 'Songs and society', p. 275f.

55 Rastall, *Heaven Singing*, p. 301. Looking forward to the first half of the sixteenth century, Rastall notes a shift in the status of some musicians (part sociological, part due to technical changes and the emergent print culture) which led to some being styled 'gentlemen'; *ibid.*, pp. 300–6.

10

Visual culture

Thomas Tolley

In the later Middle Ages visual culture – and access to it – was an expensive business. The end of the period witnessed the rise of a flourishing culture of reproduction, with widely affordable images in woodcuts and printed books.[1] But the most eye-catching developments in the visual arts remained the preserve of those with significant means – royalty and the upper nobility. Spectacular complexes involving a fusion of the arts (architecture, sculpture, painting and stained glass) – such as Edward III's completion of St Stephen's Chapel at Westminster (1350–63) or the Beauchamp tomb and chapel at St Mary's, Warwick (1441–52) – evidently required resources far beyond the means of most landed families.

The gentry, however, certainly aspired to such projects. Their interests were the conventional ones of the period – devotional, commemorative or charitable concerns, decorative schemes for the places where they lived and worshipped, and visual programmes for education or amusement – differentiated from those promoted by the higher nobility in scale alone. The gentry's ability to exercise patronage may have been limited, but this did not necessitate compromising standards. After all, they felt themselves, on account of their ancestry, to belong essentially to the same social fabric as the peerage; and they recognised that one of the most effective ways of expressing this was through material possessions. The visual arts therefore played a part in providing the gentry with an identity. Several factors contributed to forge this construction, distinguishing it from developments abroad.

In England, unlike in some Continental countries, there existed strong suspicions of the value of visual creativity, which arguably inhibited the development of a system of artistic patronage based on mutual respect between artist and patron. Any discourse on the visual arts, permitting assessments of the gentry's attitude to the visual arts and motivation for their artistic preferences, was limited; where it exists, it is often negative in character. Whilst pictures were traditionally recognised as useful for drawing the faithful closer to God and to educate the illiterate, imagery for its own sake, as in the sumptuous decoration of books or buildings, was often regarded as a dangerous diversion. The power of the eye, it was thought, had the potential to lead the beholder into temptation. Images were also mistrusted because they persuaded beholders to give to the Church, the more ornate the greater their authority.[2]

By the later fourteenth century these ideas had been given a coherent voice in arguments made by John Wyclif and his Lollard followers, with contemporaries considering that opposition to images was Lollardy's most conspicuous feature.[3] The Biblical prohibition of graven images prompted Wyclif to argue that an image could lead people astray when 'undue delight was taken in its *beauty, expense* or *connection to external circumstances*'.[4] Furthermore, there was the danger of mistaking the divinity of holy figures with the form of their pictorial representations, an error leading to idolatry. Most Lollards therefore avoided images and denied devotional practices associated with them, advocating the notion that expensive items, like sculptures, merely served to impede mankind's spiritual progress.

Although the Church condemned Lollardy, many knights and their followers were sympathetic, with consequences for artistic patronage.[5] Whilst holding to the path of orthodoxy, the gentry were often drawn to the movement's puritanical aspects partly because they provided sanction for economic restraint. A reluctance to engage with images when deemed unnecessary is therefore a prominent feature of English patronage. For example, except for commissions from leading nobles and clergy, books made in England tend to be sparingly decorated, with few pictures. The gentry were also unable to support a culture of panel painting, such as developed in the Netherlands. The correspondence of the Pastons provides useful insights into this deep-rooted prejudice. Only infrequently are artistic projects mentioned, occasionally hinting at a reluctance to engage with them – as in Sir John's embarrassing delay in ordering a tomb for his father, unimaginable in the higher nobility.[6]

On the other hand, Lollardy also had positive artistic consequences. Ecclesiastics sought to counter the heresy's appeal by devising ever more opulent schemes of decoration to reinforce the attraction of orthodoxy for the laity. One reflection of this is the large number of decorated missals commissioned in England during the period between *c.* 1380 and *c.* 1430. This had repercussions for the gentry who imitated the clergy's lead. The

Lapworth Missal (1398), given by Thomas Ashby (d. 1443) to the parish church of Lapworth in Warwickshire, is probably an example of this.[7] Its full-page Crucifixion miniature is close in style to illuminations in a yet more elaborate missal made for the London Carmelites in the 1390s.[8] Though this magnificent volume was for use in a religious house, it features donor representations of a kneeling couple, identifiable as gentry from their dress.

Such lavish commissions may be understood as one manifestation of an aesthetic ideal upholding the beautiful as an expression of divine grace, advanced by St Thomas Aquinas (d. 1274), the great Dominican. Later Dominicans continued to advocate it in their writings, largely because their order had been founded to eradicate heresy, and the principle provided tangible opposition to Lollard ideas. Since Dominicans frequently acted as spiritual advisers to prominent gentry the philosophy played a part in interpreting their visual experiences as well. By the later fifteenth century a secular equivalent to this line of argument had established itself in privileged society. The principle is articulated in Sir John Fortescue's *The Governance of England* (*c.* 1460–70), which describes the kinds of expenditure a king should make. These include: 'magnificence and liberalite' ('necessarie ffor the worship off his reaume'); new buildings; rich clothes; furs; jewels; and ornaments 'conuenyent to his estate roiall'. Should a king not display himself in this manner, 'he lyved then not like his estate, but rather in miserie, and in more subgeccion than doth *a private person*'.[9] Although Fortescue was concerned principally with perceptions of kingship, his theory of the social function of magnificence, stemming from notions of display at Continental courts, implies a kind of preordained gradation of show and splendour, needed across the whole spectrum for the stability of the realm. Fortescue partly had in mind the national conflicts of the 1460s. From the gentry's point of view display was indispensable, but only when set within bounds.

One sphere in which this operated was in entertaining. Feasts provided opportunities for displaying expensive plate, the value of its metal being one means of emphasising a household's status. Bequeathing items of plate was a way of ensuring that all loved ones benefited from the estate of a deceased, so that even sets of smaller items, such as spoons, were divided to satisfy this purpose. Only occasionally are such items described in wills to indicate appreciation of their artistry. In the will of Elizabeth Poynings (1487) all her plate and 'other juelles' were bequeathed to her daughter to help secure a husband.[10] Despite listing all items, few are described with decoration. One silver gilt cup was 'chased with plompes [plums]', and another 'chased with flowres'. The list runs directly into precious items of devotional significance. Here the descriptions are more revealing. There was, for instance, an 'Agnus [Dei] with a baleys, iij saphires, iij perlys, with an jmage of Saint Antony apon it'; and 'a tablet with the Salutacion of Our Lady [Annunciation] and the iij Kingis of Collayn [three Magi]'.[11] These items were clearly of religious value; but this was potentially the case with all items of plate. For Elizabeth, they contributed to the promotion of her daughter's marriage, a sacrament. Because feasting was an aspect of religious celebration, they also served to honour God and His saints.[12]

Sumptuary legislation of this period also attempted matching ranks of society with forms of consumption. More extensive legislation was frequently attempted for personal appearance.[13] The main consideration was that the dress of any particular social category should not surpass that worn by the category immediately above; all classes should be recognisable from their dress. Clothes were undoubtedly important to the gentry. An inventory (1484) of William Catesby, esquire, member of a Northamptonshire family who held office under Richard III, shows that much of his material wealth resided in his clothes; they are all listed at the beginning of the document.[14] The first item was 'a long gowne of purple velvet' lined with sheepskin, followed by several further velvet gowns in black and purple, all expensively trimmed. Catesby was at the peak of his career when these garments were listed and would have been asserting his standing to its limits. In 1465 legislation had been introduced ordaining that knights below the rank of lord should wear neither cloth of gold, nor any cloth decorated with gold, nor with sable (an exclusive fur), nor any kind of double velvet. Nor could they dress in purple. Those below the rank of knight were forbidden, on pain of a sizeable fine, to wear patterned velvet, satin, damask or any silk stuff made in imitation of such fabric unless they were royal officials or had possessions worth more than £40 a year. In 1483 legislation attempted still greater restrictions, forbidding all subjects (except royalty) to wear cloth of gold or purple silk. Excepting esquires of the king, no one below the rank of knight was permitted to wear velvet, damask or satin in his or her gowns.

Sumptuary legislation was not new in Catesby's time. An intricate law of 1363 details a series of prohibitions on types of clothing for different classes, an early instance of gentlemen being treated on a par with esquires. Interestingly, the legislation permitted wealthy merchants to dress like esquires and gentlemen. It cannot have been very effective since the statute was repealed in 1364. No further attempt to legislate for apparel was made until the reign of Henry IV. In the interim, dress became so extravagant that it often attracted unfavourable comment. 'The Parson's Tale', Chaucer's sermon on penitence and sin, includes a section on the 'superfluitee of clothying', listing many excesses of late fourteenth-century fashion that made (according to the text) clothes so expensive, 'to the harm of the peple'.[15] In 1402 the House of Commons instigated a petition to deal with the situation, advocating that only bannerets and above should be permitted to wear certain costly fabrics and great hanging sleeves. Chaucer's description of his Squire 'with sleves longe and wyde' is clearly apposite in this context.

In describing the Squire, Chaucer mentions his proficiency in music, dancing and writing – well-documented skills for the nobility by c. 1400 – and adds that the Squire could also 'weel purtreye'.[16] It has sometimes been assumed that this refers to some literary expertise in observation, but an alternative interpretation is that Chaucer meant that the Squire had learned to draw, an artistic skill. A sense that some gentry received training in basic draughtsmanship comes from a rough sketch of Thomas Froxmere and his wife (datable to c. 1484–98) with instructions for realising it in some unspecified memorial; the drawing is reasonably attributed to Froxmere himself.[17]

However, there is only limited evidence that the gentry were actively engaged in the practice of artistic creativity. An exception is the case of John Siferwas, one of the most prominent and best-connected illuminators in early fifteenth-century England. Manuscripts on which he worked may be identified today through his 'signatures', rare for artists during this period and suggestive in Siferwas's case of social confidence. In the most lavish manuscript he illuminated, the Sherborne Missal, he even included his personal coat-of-arms: '*azure*, two bars gemelles, a chief of the last *or*, all within a bordure engrailed *ermine*'.[18] Comparison of this with heraldry relating to the family in heraldic rolls suggests that the artist was a scion of a branch of the Siferwas family established in Buckinghamshire and Hampshire.[19] In 1380 Siferwas appears in the register of William of Wykeham, bishop of Winchester when, as a Dominican friar in their convent at Guildford, he was ordained acolyte in Farnham Castle. Later documents show him to have been a member of the Dominican house in London. With the London book industry located nearby (near St Paul's Cathedral), and also the King's Great Wardrobe, where artists were employed, it seems likely that Siferwas's artistic training was in this environment. Dominicans particularly promoted the use of pictorial material in furthering their aims. The decision to enter this order is therefore understandable for a son of the gentry showing aptitude in visual creativity. How such aptitude was identified at a formative age, however, is unclear.

One possibility is suggested by the connection with William of Wykeham, whose interests in education and visual creativity are well-documented.[20] Siferwas could not have attended Wykeham's College at Winchester (founded in 1382), but he may have benefited from Wykeham's educational schemes of the 1370s, qualifying for patronage as a junior member of his family. Wykeham treated artists who worked for him in ways uncharacteristically respectful, entertaining them alongside noble guests, and providing for their children's education. One beneficiary was the 'architect' William Wynford, probably the son of a manorial family in Somerset.[21] Siferwas's artistic inclinations were perhaps first encouraged within this circle.

One of Siferwas's artistic activities may have been the illumination of books of hours, or 'primers' as they were called in England. Unlike the Psalter, the standard devotional book customarily receiving illumination in the fourteenth century, primers were generally smaller, with shorter, more focused texts. They were better suited to personal use and the rise of more private forms of devotion favoured by the gentry. Primers are commonly mentioned in wills, though the only decoration usually described in these entries is the bindings, their most visible element, where perceptions of value often also lay. The heiress Anne Harling (d. 1499), for example, left one primer to her son 'whiche kynge Edward [IV] gauffe me', perhaps with royal arms on its cover, and another to her god-daughter 'clasped w^t silver and gylte, for a remembraunce, to pray for me'.[22] Pictorial decoration was integral to the main contents of books of hours. Given the likelihood that many among the gentry were unable to read Latin texts, it seems probable that pictures were crucial to the use of such volumes, stimulating devotional responses. One rare fourteenth-century survival, the Carew-Poyntz Hours, has an extensive and unique pictorial programme with many narrative scenes independent of the text.[23] The illumination is in various styles, suggesting several campaigns over a prolonged period. The earliest style, c. 1350, shows knowledge of contemporary work in France. A late fifteenth-century inscription apparently written by Elizabeth Poyntz mentions the name Carew, indicating that the book then belonged to the wife of Sir Edmund Carew. It seems likely that the manuscript, a valued item, was begun for the wife of Sir John Carew (d. c. 1363) and then passed down through the wives of his descendants. Iconographical choices reflect what may be surmised about the devotional interests of successive generations of Carews. Sir John, for instance, had been on campaigns in France and might have had the opportunity to develop Frenchified tastes reflected in the earliest work.

During the fifteenth century, however, whilst royalty and the upper nobility readily commissioned elaborate books of hours from English artists, others seldom followed their example. The main explanation for the paucity of surviving primers illuminated by English artists for the gentry lies in their expense; it was cheaper to import. More than 200 Flemish hours designed specifically for English use have survived, many made in Bruges during the first half of the century, and often revealing evidence of bulk production, the pictorial programmes being rather limited.[24] The English gentry, it seems, were more concerned with acquiring such books, which served to project their status, than with high standards of presentation. During the English occupation of northern France (1415–50), however, several distinguished French illuminators also produced hours for Englishmen.[25] Their clients were usually English knights serving in France who, perhaps through direct familiarity with French work, were more discriminating. One example is Sir John Fastolf, the celebrated soldier and leading figure of the gentry, who commissioned an artist temporarily active in English-occupied Rouen to illuminate a manuscript containing texts by Christine de Pisan.[26] The workshop of this particular artist, known as the Fastolf Master, illuminated a number of hours for English clients, including an ambitious volume for the Lincolnshire knight William Porter, probably before 1431.[27]

Heraldry was another preoccupation of the gentry that generated artistic activity.[28] The Sherborne Missal includes coats of arms signifying those responsible for its patronage, their allies, and also a series of blazons reproducing in effect an extensive heraldic roll, including monarchs and members of the English nobility.[29] Heraldic display, involving series of shields, suggests the solidarity of the armigerous classes throughout their ranks. It appears in many contexts, from large glazing programmes to most categories of illuminated manuscript.[30] Since knights, esquires and gentlemen were all entitled to coats of arms, they aligned themselves visually with the higher social classes wherever displaying their arms. Women were equally versed in the significance of heraldry, as the will of Anne Harling indicates. Items are repeatedly identified exclusively through reference to the family 'scochen' or 'armys'.[31] One example of Anne's patronage survives in the rebuilding and glazing of the church at East Harling (Norfolk). The glass, datable between the deaths of her first two husbands in 1462 and 1480, features figures of both husbands, dressed in military garb with heraldic trappings.[32] Nearby is the elaborate monument to Anne's first husband, like so many tombs of this period, covered in shields from top to bottom.[33]

The proliferation of heraldry that took place during this period meant that measures of control were soon felt necessary. In 1416 Henry V ordered that – with minor exceptions – only those with ancestral rights or by grant from someone with authority could now take arms.[34] But the chief purpose of the measure was to guard against the practice of any persons serving for the king devising arms for themselves, thus devaluing the entire system. This, of course, was intended to have social implications for those aspiring to gentry status, setting conditions for inclusion as perceived by the Crown. From then on heralds were required to register the arms of gentlemen in their provinces. In practice, however, many whose income justified such status were granted rights to arms in the fifteenth century, especially merchants (and their organisations).

The heralds who regulated this were themselves influential in promoting the development of heraldic display in artistic schemes. Sir William Bruges (d. 1450), the first Garter King of Arms, is a good example.[35] A representation of him kneeling before St George occurs in the book he had made to record portrayals and armorials of the original members of the Order of the Garter.[36] This book has been considered the prototype of several classes of heraldic manuscript developed later in the century. In St George's, Stamford, where Bruges was buried, he commissioned stained glass, including the life of St George, representations of himself and his family, and more representations of Garter knights, and his will reveals a painstaking attitude towards visual creativity.[37]

Another notable manuscript where heraldic devices prominently feature is a Gospel Lectionary commissioned by John, Lord Lovell (d. 1408), significant also for its inclusion of a large miniature depicting Lovell being presented with a book by the artist, himself identified by an inscription as Siferwas.[38] Presentation scenes are uncommon in English art; generally they depict authors before their patrons. Since this is the only known example involving an artist, Siferwas's family origins help to explain its acceptability. The image is arranged in such a way that it suggests Siferwas's lower status in relation to Lovell, a baron; but the mere fact that the artist was permitted to portray himself suggests some kind of closer relationship, at the level of family ties, between artist and patron. This is emphasised by the portrait-like characterisation of the two figures, opening up the possibility that physiognomical accuracy is a factor here. The features Siferwas gave himself show the same Dominican who appears in profile in the Sherborne Missal. If these are indeed examples of portraiture based on life, they are unusual for this period. Outside royal circles, lifelike portraiture within England seems to have been negligible, perhaps because few artists were trained to achieve it,[39] but this did not prevent Edward Grymston, esquire, of Suffolk, from being painted by a major artist, Petrus Christus, during a trade mission to the Continent in 1446, or the production c. 1478 of a triptych portraying Sir John Donne and his family.[40]

The circumstances of Siferwas's miniature depicting himself and Lovell show it to have been painted after Lovell's death. Siferwas presumably executed it at his widow's request after Lovell bequeathed the book to Salisbury; she belonged to a confraternity in the Cathedral. Widows, obliged by circumstances, were often responsible for commissioning works of commemoration for their husbands. War in France and civil conflict resulted in many knights, esquires and gentlemen losing their lives before making appropriate arrangements. Of course, religious and family requirements and traditions compelled those of this class to make such arrangements; and many certainly did so, or expected to do so, during their lifetimes. Sir Henry Pierrepoint, for instance, indicated in his will, made in 1489 a decade before his death, that he desired an alabaster tomb 'graven by the discressions of myne executors, *if I make it not in my lif daies*'.[41] In the standardised brasses that some chose for their memorials, the part of the inscription mentioning date of death is sometimes left blank or completed later, indicating that the monuments were ordered before death.

But often this was not possible. The contract for the alabaster effigies of Ralph Greene, esquire, and his wife Katherine, on their monument at Lowick in Northamptonshire show that they were commissioned from sculptors in Chellaston (Derbyshire), close to the alabaster quarries, two years after Ralph's death in 1417.[42] It was Katherine, with executors, who entered into the agreements and made the iconographical decisions stipulated in the contract. If this is representative, then women of Katherine's status were evidently skilled in negotiating and making artistic judgements. Several aspects of the development of funeral monuments may have been shaped by women's preoccupations. For instance, Katherine specifically requested that her own effigy and that of her husband should be shown holding hands, implying partnership between the two, abandoning older conventions implying the woman's subservience to her husband. By 1400 there were several variations on this theme, particularly in brass memorials.[43] At Little Shelford in Cambridgeshire brasses to two generations of Frevilles and their wives suggest, in an earlier pair (c. 1400), coy intimacy and, in a later pair, who turn to face each other, undisguised affection. The role of women in binding the family together perhaps also accounts for the appearance of children on gentry tombs. This type rarely occurs before the fifteenth century, but had became increasingly popular by c. 1500.[44]

'Family' memorials for the gentry were probably prompted by the grand tombs made for the upper nobility, where family members are represented through 'weeper' figures.[45] But it would be misleading to imply that a clear and consistent distinction in tomb types existed between the gentry and their social superiors. Although brasses were the favoured medium for gentry memorials, there is one royal brass (Queen Anne Neville, d. 1485), and they were sometimes the preferred option for noble families over generations, as in case of the Cobhams. Their mausoleum in the collegiate church at Cobham in Kent is essentially one formed by a family belonging to the peerage. A collateral branch of the family, which by the fifteenth century had declined to gentry status, established another mausoleum at Lingfield in Surrey, with a further set of family brasses. But the most elaborate monument at Lingfield is the very grand alabaster tomb of Sir Reginald Cobham (d. 1446), who left instructions in his will specifying this material for the monument and its position in front of the high altar.[46] His widow followed these directions precisely. Reginald clearly wished to distinguish himself, the ostentatious display compensating for his immediate family's social decline. Alabaster tombs were more expensive than brasses, at least those made in English centres of production such as London and York. Ralph Greene's alabaster tomb cost £40; the near-contemporary brass of Sir Arnold Savage at Bobbing in Kent, with two figures and a canopy, cost £13 6s 8d.[47] Brasses also became increasingly affordable, broadening the market but decreasing the prestige in ordering them.[48]

The concern gentry showed with positioning their tombs is as informative in assessing their visual alertness as their instructions for design and materials. Thomas Windsor, who held the manor at Stanwell (formerly Middlesex), requested in 1479 his memorial on the north side of the choir of the local parish church: 'afore the ymage of our lady wher the sepultur of our Lord stondith'.[49] He intended the tomb to double as an Easter sepulchre. John Baret made even more elaborate arrangements for his chantry and memorial in St Mary's in Bury St Edmunds, specifing burial 'before the ymage of oure Sauyour'.[50]

Such instructions are, of course, closely dependent on the piety of those concerned; but unlike the piety of the primer, this is a facet of its public manifestation – the kind of display that essentially encourages prayers for the deceased as an adjunct of devotion associated with a pre-existing image. Baret's delight in the visual aspects of his faith is evident from several bequests. One was for a new painted altarpiece showing 'the story of the Magnific[a]t (the Visitation)' explained with his own verses – he had in mind a folding triptych. Another identifies a particular 'ymage of oure lady' by the name of its painter, Robert Pygot, evidence that personal artistic creativity was taken seriously by those of Baret's status.[51]

The fashion for strategically placed tombs and chantries often necessitated extensions to the parish churches the gentry considered their spiritual homes, where their rights and patronage were locally taken for granted. A rare surviving contract (1476), between Sir John Say and Robert Stowell, mason, gives an indication how this was arranged.[52] Stowell was to extend an aisle of the church at Broxbourne (Hertfordshire) eastward, creating a new arch into the chancel, beneath which was to be a tomb-table. Proximity to the high altar, the focus of the spiritual life of the community, was clearly crucial. The work still exists, together with the brasses that were commissioned separately. An analogous arrangement survives at North Leigh (Oxfordshire), where Elizabeth, widow of Sir William Wilcote, received licence to found a chantry chapel in 1438.[53] She went to much trouble to secure a structure of the highest standards, including an intricate fan vault and elaborate mouldings, attributable to a leading mason, Richard Winchcombe.

Equally elaborate is the Easter sepulchre tomb surviving at Long Melford in Suffolk, an exceptionally well-documented church of the later fifteenth century, conceived to a large extent as a single entity, with important stained glass, brasses and other images.[54] Here the visual features and traditions of the church were so strong that after the Reformation one local gentleman recorded his recollections of them for posterity.[55] The Easter sepulchre tomb is that of John Clopton, the most generous of the local donors who contributed to the church and its decoration. Clopton was not nobly born, but a wealthy cloth merchant.[56] The evidence of his appointments, his associates and executors indicates, however, that in all key respects he behaved like, and was accepted as, country gentry. An insight into Clopton's piety and that of men like him comes from a series of thirty-two stanzas from two poems by John Lydgate, painted within his chantry.[57] One striking aspect of these verses is how they invoke the sense of sight in drawing spectators towards contemplation. 'Behold o man lefte up thyn eye & see/ what mortall peyne I suffred for your trespace' speaks Jesus to fix the audience's attention on his suffering. Several other poems by Lydgate invoke images even more directly. One, for example, deals with indulgences to be gained from worshipping in front of a copy of a painting in Rome of the Virgin, claimed to be by St Luke.[58] One indication that verses offering 'explanations' for pictures held special attraction for the gentry comes from the same poem: Lydgate says that it was made for 'a gentylman'.

Lydgate's secular verse also contains many powerful visual elements that probably appealed to the same audience. These works lent themselves well to illustration. A manuscript of Lydgate's *Troy Book* in Manchester, illuminated in the 1440s, is especially sumptuous.[59] The narratives, which spill across the margins of the page very effectively, are set against landscapes capped with hill-top castles, very similar in effect to pages in the Sherborne Missal. Lydgate began writing the *Troy Book* for the Prince of Wales in 1413, so the possibility exists that Siferwas may have illuminated a lost copy that acted as a model for the later artist. The Manchester manuscript bears the arms of two gentry families from the West Country and features in gentry wills of 1492 and 1503. Exclusive manuscripts like this, however, were more likely to be made for aristocratic patrons. The only other substantial manuscript illuminated by the same artist was made for a major magnate, Lord Grey of Ruthen.[60] In other words, the gentry often followed the higher nobility in taste in illuminated manuscripts when resources permitted; otherwise they acquired books better suited to reading than to looking.

A similar argument applies to the most costly of all secular projects, domestic residences. Castles were traditionally the power-bases of the nobility. From the later fourteenth century, licences to 'crenellate' (build) castles were also granted to wealthy knights. Their experience of serving in France resulted in several features derived from near-contemporary castles on the Continent.[61] Examples include Sir John Delamare's castle at Nunney (Somerset), begun in 1372, and Sir Edward Dalyngrigge's castle at Bodiam (Sussex), licenced in 1385 and built on a scale intended to rival that of the nobility.[62] Its symmetrical plan, its setting and its heraldic decoration all contribute to present Dalyngrigge as a man to be reckoned with. The same is true of Fastolf's castle at Caister (Norfolk) begun in 1432. Here the surviving accounts give insights into Fastolf's conception of the structure as a fortified residence, lavishly decorated, but offering all the comforts of the day, such as extensive provision for large fireplaces. Worcester described it as a 'ryche juelle'.[63]

These and other castles, built by former soldiers, naturally took account of military considerations in their planning.[64] But the fortified aspects of these mansions were subordinated to the comforts sought by the wealthy in old age, a trend followed in manors built by the lesser gentry. The most conspicuous aspect of this change was increasing emphasis on better fenestration, promoted by decreasing glass prices. For example, substantial bay windows were regularly included in the designs for the great hall, the focus of social activities such as feasting, to emphasise the area at the head of the

table. But even when larger windows became fashionable, panes continued to be removed when a building was not in use. An inventory of items
left by the Pastons at Caister at the time that the duke of Norfolk took it
over includes many '[removable] panes of glasse', several with heraldic
decoration.[65] At Ockwells Manor in Berkshire, built by Sir John Norreys
(d. 1467), the heraldic shields in the hall windows survive.[66] Fenestration
in halls was also carefully designed to allow for interior decoration. At
Wardour Castle, begun by Lord Lovell in 1393, the hall has a series of
untransomed windows set high to allow for hangings below, a feature
subsequently used in manors throughout the country.[67]

Unfortunately, hangings of English provenance from this period rarely
survive, and documentation provides limited information. Fastolf's
inventory, however, lists many hangings; some also feature in an inventory
drawn up by John Paston I in 1462.[68] Most of the items were probably
versions of designs originally created for commercial purposes, purchased
through merchants. Others were evidently acquired when Fastolf served
in France, spending part of his career in Arras, a leading centre for tapestry
production. Arras products were extremely costly and generally beyond
the means of most gentry. One of Fastolf's hangings, representing the
Siege of Falaise, a celebrated English victory, was possibly especially commissioned, an indication of the extent of his wealth. This is exceptional
since surviving tapestries designed for English clients were made for noble
or royal patrons.[69]

From this survey of late medieval visual culture it should be clear that
issues of identity and appearance were fundamental for the English gentry.
However, it is doubtful that anything intrinsically distinguished their uses
of the visual arts by comparison with those of their social superiors.
Aspirations were generally curtailed by limited resources and position, not
because gentry tastes were essentially different. When the means existed,
as in the case of Fastolf, the gentry promoted themselves as the nobility
did. When the opportunity arose, as during the English interventions in
France, they commissioned works from fashionable Continental artists, as
did members of the peerage; only the scale of commission implies any
distinction.

This is not to say, however, that an element did not exist in some gentry
resistant to lavish display, based on religious conviction and economics.
Such restraint rarely touched the nobility. On the other hand, interest in
Continental Humanism, which often informed the artistic interests of noble
and ecclesiastical patrons in fifteenth-century England, is seldom reflected
in the gentry's artistic inclinations. Occasionally evidence indicates the

gentry's direct involvement in artistic practice, as in the case of Siferwas. The gentry also evidently became more articulate in commissioning material goods, conveying a clearer sense of individual preferences.

In their conception of themselves, a key issue was to ensure that the gentry could never be confused with the lower social orders. Dress and heraldry were paramount in this. But as the more prosperous merchants were permitted to adopt the trappings of the gentry, it may be argued that a change took place in attitudes to visual culture. Merchants brought new skills to the gentry: an instinctive eye for value and quality, and an innate sense of acquisitiveness. In this respect, the wills of 'gentlemen' merchants, such as Baret, are informative. They offer detailed textual insights into visual culture of the period. Consumption became an objective in its own right, the gentry setting out to rival in expenditure and display the nobility and each other. Those most adept at keeping abreast of developments were also those socially most successful. If acquisitions and commissions ensured the gentry were noticed, then their chances of appointment to lucrative posts and of maintaining, or advancing, their social rank were increased. Alternatively, if the reward for profitable talents (military or diplomatic) was the ability to spend, then expenditure inevitably embraced the latest goods or the most advanced domestic comforts. Either way, the achievement depended on the gentry keeping firm control over their lands, while keeping a close eye on developments elsewhere, from their neighbours to the leading centres of commerce.

Notes

1 William Caxton, for instance, issued his first illustrated book in 1481.
2 See Stanbury, 'Vivacity of images', esp. pp. 145–6.
3 Jones, 'Lollards and images'; Aston, 'Lollards and images' and *England's Iconoclasts, I: Laws Against Images*, p. 97.
4 Ex. 20: 3–4; *Tractatus de Mandatis Divinis*, p. 156.
5 McFarlane, *Lancastrian Kings*.
6 See Bennett, *Pastons and their England*, pp. 203–4.
7 Oxford, Corpus Christi College MS 394, described in Alexander and Binski (eds), *Age of Chivalry*, no. 717; and in Scott, *Survey of Manuscripts*, no. 6.
8 BL Add. MSS 29704–05, 44892. This missal has been reconstructed from fragments; see Rickert, *Reconstructed Carmelite Missal*, and Scott, *Survey of Manuscripts*, no. 2.
9 Fortescue, *Governance of England*, pp. 123–6.
10 *Paston Letters*, ed. Davis, II, pp. 210–14 (no. 123).
11 For such Agnus Dei, see the article by E. Mangenot in *Dictionnaire de Théologie Catholique*, I, cols 605–13.

12 See Camille, *Mirror in Parchment*, pp. 88–9.

13 Baldwin, *Sumptuary Legislation*; Hunt, *Governance of the Consuming Passions*. For dress, see also Newton, *Fashion in the Age*.

14 Tudor-Craig, *Richard III*, pp. 97–8. For the Catesby family, see Williams, 'Catesbys 1485–1568'.

15 *Riverside Chaucer*, pp. 300–1 (lines 416–33).

16 *Riverside Chaucer*, p. 25 (line 96).

17 BL Landsdowne MS 874, fol. 191, described in Goodall, 'Two medieval drawings', pp. 160–2, pl. L(b).

18 BL Add. MS 74236, p. 81; Backhouse, *Sherborne Missal*, p. 7.

19 Cf., for example, Greening Lambourne, *Armorial Glass*, pp. 59, 80.

20 Hayter, *William of Wykeham*; Moberly, *Life of William of Wykeham*, pp. 209–10.

21 Harvey, *English Mediæval Architects*, pp. 352–6.

22 *Testamenta Eboracensia: A Selection of Wills from the Registry at York*, IV, ed. James Raine, Surtees Society, 53 (1868), p. 153. Gibson, *Theater of Devotion*, pp. 96–106. For primers in general featuring in the wills of the gentry, see Hoskins, *Horae Beatae Virginis*, pp. xv–xvii.

23 Cambridge, Fitzwilliam Museum, MS 48; James, *Descriptive Catalogue*, no. 48; Sandler, *Survey of Manuscripts*, no. 130; Dennison, 'Fitzwarin psalter'.

24 Arnould and Massing, *Splendours of Flanders*, pp. 113–31; Rogers, 'Patrons and purchasers'.

25 For a survey, see Reynolds, 'English patrons'.

26 Oxford, Bodleian Library, MS Laud misc. 570, described in Pächt and Alexander, *Illuminated Manuscripts*, no. 695.

27 New York, Pierpont Morgan Library, MS 105, described in Plummer, *Last Flowering*, no. 22; Alexander, 'Lost leaf' (with a preliminary list of manuscripts attributed to the Fastolf Master); Farquhar, *Creation and Imitation*, pp. 59–60, 82–8.

28 Friar, *Heraldry for the Local Historian*.

29 Tolley, 'Use of heraldry'.

30 For examples, see Kerr, 'East window', esp. pp. 125–6; Michael, 'Privilege of "proximity"'; Goodall, 'Heraldry in the decoration'.

31 Raine (ed.), *Testamenta Eboracensia*, no. LXXV.

32 Woodforde, *Norwich School*, pp. 42–55; Marks, *Stained Glass*, p. 198. Anne herself was originally included in the programme, but her figure is now lost.

33 This is the tomb of Sir William Chamberlain. See Pevsner, *Buildings of England*, p. 146.

34 Wagner, *Heralds of England*, p. 36.

35 London, *Life of William Bruges*.

36 BL Stowe MS 594, fol. 5v, described in Scott, *Survey of Manuscripts*, no. 84.

37 Hebgin-Barnes, *Medieval Stained Glass*, pp. 272–76; Riches, 'Lost St George cycle'.

38 BL Harley MS 7026, described in Scott, *Survey of Manuscripts*, no. 10.

39 Cf. Hepburn, *Portraits of the Later Plantagenets*.

40 London, National Gallery, on loan from the Earl of Verulam; Franks, 'Notes on

Edward Grimston'; Ainsworth and Martens, *Petrus Christus*, pp. 49–53; London, National Gallery: Campbell, *National Gallery Catalogues*, pp. 374–91.

41 Raine (ed.), *Testamenta Eboracensia*, IV, p. 44 (my italics). For related alabaster effigies, see Routh, *Medieval Effigial Alabaster Tombs*.

42 Hope, 'On the early working'. Cf. Ryde, 'Alabaster angel'; Bayliss, 'Indenture for two alabaster effigies'.

43 Coss, *Lady in Medieval England*, pp. 94–105.

44 Page-Philips, *Children on Brasses*; Greenhill, *Incised Effigial Slabs*, I, p. 2 (plate 66).

45 Gardner, *Alabaster Tombs*, pp. 13–26.

46 Saul, *Death, Art, and Memory*, pp. 136–9, 176–8.

47 Norris, *Monumental Brasses*, p. 52.

48 D'Elboux, 'Testamentary brasses'; Badham, 'Monumental brasses'.

49 Heales, 'Church of Stanwell', p. 120; Cherry, 'Some new types', p. 146.

50 Raine (ed.), *Testamenta Eboracensia*, IV, p. 15. For Baret, see Gibson, *Theater of Devotion*, pp. 72–9.

51 *Ibid.*

52 Salzman, *Building in England*, pp. 537–38 (no. 87).

53 Heard, 'Death and representation'.

54 Parker, *History of Long Melford*.

55 Kamerick, *Popular Piety*, pp. 68–105.

56 Gibson, *Theater of Devotion*, pp. 79–96.

57 Trapp, 'Verses by Lydgate'.

58 *Minor Poems of John Lydgate: I*, pp. 290–1. Cf. Pearsall, *John Lydgate*, pp. 181–3.

59 Manchester, John Rylands University Library, MS Eng. 1, described in Scott, *Survey of Manuscripts*, no. 93.

60 Nicholas Love's *The Myrrour of the Blessed Lyf of Jesu Christ* (Edinburgh, National Library of Scotland, MS Adv. 18.1.7), described in Scott, *Survey of Manuscripts*, no. 98.

61 Platt, *Castle in Medieval England*, pp. 112–25.

62 Turner, 'Bodiam, Sussex'.

63 Barnes and Simpson, 'Building accounts' and 'Caister Castle'.

64 Bodiam's licence mentions its purpose for 'defence of the adjacent countryside and for resistance against our enemies'.

65 *Paston Letters*, ed. Davis, I, pp. 434–6 (no. 259).

66 Evans, *English Art*, pp. 133–4; Marks, *Stained Glass*, pp. 96–7.

67 Wood, *English Mediæval House,* p. 358.

68 *Paston Letters*, ed. Gairdner, III, pp. 174–89 (no. 389); *Paston Letters*, ed. Davis, I, pp. 107–14 (no. 64).

69 MacKendrick, 'Tapestries from the Low Countries'.

BIBLIOGRAPHY

Endnote references in this book are given in short-title format, with full titles and publication details provided in the bibliography. Primary and secondary sources are listed together in alphabetical order by author's or editor's name, or, in exceptional cases, under the most well-known title of the work. Works by the same author are ordered by date, original works precede works edited by the same writer, and works by a single author precede joint works.

Acheson, E. *A Gentry Community: Leicestershire in the Fifteenth Century*, c. 1422–c. 1485 (Cambridge: Cambridge University Press, 1992).

Adamson, J. W. 'The extent of literacy in England in the fifteenth and sixteenth centuries: notes and conjectures', *The Library*, 4th ser., 10 (1929), 163–93.

Ainsworth, M. W. and M. P. J. Martens. *Petrus Christus: Renaissance Master of Bruges*, exh. cat. (New York: Metropolitan Museum of Art, 1994).

Alexander, J. and P. Binski (eds). *Age of Chivalry: Art in Plantagent England 1200–1400* (London: Weidenfeld and Nicolson, 1987).

Alexander, J. J. G. 'A lost leaf from a Bodleian book of hours', *Bodleian Library Record*, 8 (1971), 248–51.

Alexander, M. *The Growth of English Education, 1348–1648* (University Park, PA: Pennsylvania State University Press, 1990).

Alexander, M. (ed.). *Beowulf* (London: Penguin, 1995).

Allan, A. 'Yorkist propaganda: pedigree, prophecy and the "British history" in the reign of Edward IV', in C. Ross (ed.), *Patronage, Pedigree and Power in Late Medieval England* (Gloucester: Alan Sutton, 1979), pp. 171–92.

Allmand, C. T. *Lancastrian Normandy: The History of a Medieval Occupation, 1415–50* (Oxford: Clarendon Press, 1983).

Andrew, M. and R. Waldron (eds). *The Poems of the Pearl Manuscript*: Pearl, Cleanness, Patience, Sir Gawain and the Green Knight (Exeter: University of Exeter, rev. edn, 1987).

Anglicus, G. *Promptorium Parvulorum Sive Clericorum*, ed. A. Way, Camden Society OS 25, 2 vols (London: 1843, repr. Johnson Reprint Co., 1968).

Archdeaconry of Norwich: Inventory of Church Goods temp. Edward III: Part Two, ed. A. Watkin, Norfolk Record Society, 19 (1948).

Archer, R. '"How ladies ... who live on their manors ought to manage their households and estates": Women as landholders and administrators in the later Middle Ages', in P. J. P. Goldberg (ed.), *Woman is a Worthy Wight: Women in English Society*, c. 1200–1500 (Stroud: Sutton, 1992), pp. 149–81.

Archer, R. E. and S. Walker (eds). *Rulers and Ruled in Late Medieval England: Essays Presented to Gerald Harriss* (London and Rio Grande: Hambledon Press, 1995).

The Armburgh Papers: the Brokholes Inheritance in Warwickshire, Hertfordshire and Essex, c. 1417- c. 1453, ed. C. Carpenter (Woodbridge: Boydell, 1998).

Armstrong, C. A. J. 'The piety of Cicely, Duchess of York: a study in late medieval culture', in D. Woodruff (ed.), *For Hilaire Belloc* (London: Sheed and Ward, 1942), pp. 68–91.

Arnould, A. and J. M. Massing. *Splendours of Flanders* (Cambridge: Cambridge University Press, 1993).

Ashby, G. *George Ashby's Poems*, ed. M. Bateson, EETS, ES 76 (London: 1965).

Aston, M. 'Caim's castles: poverty, politics and disendowment', in B. Dobson (ed.), *The Church, Politics and Patronage in the Fifteenth Century* (Gloucester: A. Sutton, 1984), pp. 45–81.

Aston, M. 'Lollards and images', in M. Aston, *Lollards and Reformers: Images and Literacy in Late Medieval Religion* (London and Rio Grande: Hambledon Press, 1984), pp. 135–92.

Aston, M. *England's Iconoclasts, I: Laws Against Images* (Oxford: Oxford University Press, 1988).

Aston, M. and C. Richmond (eds). *Lollardy and the Gentry in the Later Middle Ages* (Stroud: Sutton, 1997).

Ayton, A. 'War and the English gentry under Edward III', *History Today*, 42 (1992), 34–40.

Ayton, A. 'Knights, esquires and military service: the evidence of armorial cases in the Court of Chivalry', in A. Ayton and J. L. Price (eds), *The Medieval Military Revolution: State, Society and Military Change in Medieval and Early Modern Europe* (London: Tauris Academic Studies, 1995), pp. 81–104.

The Babees Book: Early English Meals and Manners, ed. F. J. Furnivall, EETS OS 32 (London, 1868; repr. 1992).

Backhouse, J. *The Sherborne Missal* (London: British Library, 1999).

Badham, S. 'Monumental brasses and the Black Death – a reappraisal', *Antiquaries Journal*, 80 (2000), 207–47.

Baillie, H. 'A London church in Early Tudor times', *Music and Letters*, 36 (1955), 55–64.

Baillie, H. 'A London gild of musicians 1460–1530', *Proceedings of the Royal Musical Association*, 83 (1956), 15–28.

Baldwin, F. E. *Sumptuary Legislation and Personal Regulation in England* (Baltimore: Johns Hopkins University, 1926).

Barber, R. and J. Barker. *Tournaments: Jousts, Chivalry and Pageants in the Middle Ages* (Woodbridge: Boydell, 1989).

Barnes, G. *Counsel and Strategy in Middle English Romance* (Cambridge: D. S. Brewer, 1993).

Barnes, H. D. and W. Douglas Simpson. 'The building accounts of Caister castle AD 1432–1435', *Norfolk Archaeology*, 30 (1947–52), 178–88.

Barnes, H. D. and W. Douglas Simpson. 'Caister Castle', *Antiquaries Journal*, 32 (1952), 35–51.

Barron, C. 'Centres of conspicuous consumption: the aristocratic town house in London 1200–1550', *The London Journal*, 20 (1995), 1–16.

BIBLIOGRAPHY

Barron, C. M. 'Church music in English towns 1450–1550: an interim report', *Urban History*, 29:1 (2002), 83–91.

Barron, C. and N. Saul (eds). *England and the Low Countries in the Late Middle Ages* (Stroud: Sutton, 1995).

Barron, C. M. and A. F. Sutton (eds). *Medieval London Widows, 1300–1500* (London and Rio Grande: Hambledon Press, 1994).

Bayliss, J. 'An indenture for two alabaster effigies', *Church Monuments*, 16 (2001), 22–9.

Beadle, R. 'Prolegomena to a literary geography of later medieval Norfolk', in F. Riddy (ed.), *Regionalism in Late Medieval Manuscripts and Texts* (Cambridge: D. S. Brewer, 1991), pp. 89–108.

Beadle, R. 'Fifteenth-century political verses from the Holkham archives', *Medium Ævum*, 71:1 (2002), 101–21.

Beadle, R. (ed.). *The Cambridge Companion to Medieval English Theatre* (Cambridge: Cambridge University Press, 1994).

Bennett, H. S. *The Pastons and their England: Studies in an Age of Transition* (Cambridge: Cambridge University Press, 2nd edn, 1932).

Bennett, H. S. 'The author and his public in the fourteenth and fifteenth centuries', *Essays and Studies*, 23 (1937), 7–24.

Bennett, H. S. *Chaucer and the Fifteenth Century* (Oxford: Clarendon Press, 1947).

Bennett, M. J. *Community, Class and Careerism: Cheshire and Lancashire Society in the Age of* Sir Gawain and the Green Knight (Cambridge: Cambridge University Press, 1983).

Bennett, M. J. 'The court of Richard II and the promotion of literature', in B. Hanawalt (ed.), *Chaucer's England: Literature in Historical Context* (Minneapolis: University of Minnesota Press, 1994), pp. 3–20.

Bennett, M. *Richard II and the Revolution of 1399* (Stroud: Sutton, 1999).

Benson, L. D. *Malory's* Morte Darthur (Cambridge, MA and London: Harvard University Press, 1976).

Bernard, G. 'Vitality and vulnerability in the late medieval Church: pilgrimage on the eve of the break with Rome', in J. Watts (ed.), *The End of the Middle Ages? England in the Fifteenth and Sixteenth Centuries* (Stroud: Sutton, 1998), pp. 199–233.

Biggs, D. 'Henry IV and his JPs: the Lancasterization of justice, 1399–1413', in D. Biggs, S. Michalove and A. C. Reeves (eds), *Traditions and Transformations in Late Medieval England* (Leiden: Brill, 2002), pp. 59–80.

Binski, P. *Medieval Death: Ritual and Representation* (London: British Museum Press, 1996).

Blake, N. *Caxton's Own Prose* (London: Deutsch, 1973).

Boffey, J. *Manuscripts of English Courtly Love Lyrics in the Later Middle Ages* (Woodbridge: D. S. Brewer, 1985).

Boffey, J. 'Women authors and women's literacy in fourteenth- and fifteenth-century England', in Meale (ed.), *Women and Literature in Britain*, pp. 159–82.

Boffey, J. 'Books and readers in Calais: some notes', *The Ricardian*, 13 (2003), 67–74.

Boffey, J. and J. J. Thompson. 'Anthologies and miscellanies: production and choice of texts', in Griffiths and Pearsall (eds), *Book Production and Publishing*, pp. 279–315.

The Boke of Noblesse, ed. J. G. Nichols, Roxburghe Club (London: Nichols, 1860).

185

Bolton, J. '"The World Upside Down": plague as an agent of economic and social change', in W. Ormrod and P. G. Lindley (eds), *The Black Death in England* (Donington: Shaun Tyas, 2003), pp. 17–78.

Bossy, J. *Christianity in the West 1400–1700* (Oxford: Oxford University Press, 1985).

Bossy, J. 'Christian life in the later Middle Ages: prayers', *Transactions of the Royal Historical Society*, 6th ser., 1 (1991), 137–48.

Bowers, R. 'Obligation, agency and laissez-faire: the promotion of polyphonic composition for the Church in fifteenth-century England', in I. Fenlon (ed.), *Music in Medieval and Early Modern Europe: Patronage, Sources and Texts* (Cambridge: Cambridge University Press, 1981), pp. 1–19.

Bräuml, F. H. 'Varieties and consequences of medieval literacy and illiteracy', *Speculum*, 55 (1980), 237–65.

Brigden, S. 'Religion and social obligation in early sixteenth-century London', *Past and Present*, 103 (1984), 67–112.

Briggs, C. F. 'Literacy, reading and writing in the medieval West', *Journal of Medieval History*, 26 (2000), 397–420.

Brown, A. D. *Popular Piety in Late Medieval England: The Diocese of Salisbury 1250–1550* (Oxford: Clarendon Press, 1995).

Brown, A. L. *The Governance of Late Medieval England, 1272–1461* (London: Edward Arnold, 1989).

The Brut *or* The Chronicles of England, ed. F. W. D. Brie, EETS OS 131 and 136 (London, 1906 and 1908), rptd Part I (London: Oxford University Press, 1960) and Part II (Millwood: Kraus, 1987).

Bühler, C. F. The Epistle of Othea. *Translated from the French Text of Christine de Pisan by Stephen Scrope*, EETS OS 264 (London, 1970).

Burgess, C. 'Late medieval wills and pious convention: testamentary evidence reconsidered', in Hicks (ed.), *Profit, Piety and the Professions*, pp. 14–33.

Burgess, C. (ed.). *The Pre-Reformation Records of All Saints' Bristol: Part One*, Bristol Record Society, 46 (1995).

Burgess, C. and A. Wathey. 'Mapping the soundscape: church music in English towns, 1450–1550', *Early Music History*, 19 (2000), 1–46.

Burnley, J. D. 'Sources of standardisation in later Middle English', in J. B. Trahern, Jr (ed.), *Standardizing English: Essays in the History of Language Change* (Knoxville: University of Tennessee Press, 1989), pp. 23–41.

Calendar of Inquisitions Post Mortem, xix and xx (London: HMSO, 1992, 1995).

Camargo, M. 'Where's the brief: the *ars dictaminis* and the reading/writing between the lines', *Disputatio*, 1 (1996), 1–17.

Camille, M. *Mirror in Parchment: The Luttrell Psalter and the Making of Medieval England* (London: Reaktion Books, 1998).

Campbell, B. M. S. 'Population pressure, inheritance and the land market in a fourteenth-century peasant community', in R. M. Smith (ed.), *Land, Kinship and Life-cycle* (Cambridge: Cambridge University Press, 1984), pp. 87–134.

Campbell, L. *National Gallery Catalogues: The Fifteenth-Century Netherlandish Schools* (London: National Gallery Publications, 1998).

Carey, H. 'Devout literate laypeople and the pursuit of the mixed life in later medieval

England', *Journal of Religious History*, 14 (1986–7), 361–81.

Carpenter, C. 'The fifteenth-century English gentry and their estates', in Jones (ed.), *Gentry and Lesser Nobility*, pp. 36–60.

Carpenter, C. 'The religion of the gentry of fifteenth-century England', in Williams (ed.), *England in the Fifteenth Century*, pp. 53–74.

Carpenter, C. *Locality and Polity: A Study of Warwickshire Landed Society, 1401–1499* (Cambridge: Cambridge University Press, 1992).

Carpenter, C. 'Gentry and community in medieval England', *Journal of British Studies*, 33 (1994), 240–80.

Carpenter, C. 'Political and constitutional history: before and after McFarlane', in R. H. Britnell and A. J. Pollard (eds), *The McFarlane Legacy: Studies in Late Medieval Politics and Society* (Stroud: Alan Sutton, 1995), pp. 175–206.

Carpenter, C. 'The Stonor circle in the fifteenth century', in Archer and Walker (eds), *Rulers and Ruled in Late Medieval England*, pp. 175–200.

Carpenter, C. *The Wars of the Roses: Politics and the Constitution in England, c. 1437–1509* (Cambridge: Cambridge University Press, 1997).

Carpenter, C. 'Town and "country": the Stratford guild and political networks of fifteenth-century Warwickshire', in R. Bearman (ed.), *The History of an English Borough: Stratford-upon-Avon 1196–1996* (Stroud: Sutton and The Shakespeare Birthplace Trust, 1997), pp. 62–79.

Carpenter, C. 'England: the nobility and the gentry', in Rigby (ed.), *Companion to Britain in the Later Middle Ages*, pp. 261–82.

Carpenter, N. C. 'The medieval universities', in N. C. Carpenter, *Music in the Medieval and Renaissance Universities* (Norman: University of Oklahoma Press, 1958), pp. 76–92.

Carter, T. 'The sound of silence: models for an urban musicology', *Urban History*, 29:1 (2002), 8–18.

Castor, H. 'The duchy of Lancaster and the rule of East Anglia, 1399 to 1440: a prologue to the Paston Letters', in R. Archer (ed.), *Crown, Government and People in the Fifteenth Century* (Stroud: Alan Sutton, 1995), pp. 53–78.

Castor, H. *The King, the Crown and the Duchy of Lancaster: Public Authority and Private Power, 1399–1461* (Oxford: Oxford University Press, 2000).

Catto, J. 'Religion and the English nobility in the later Middle Ages', in H. Lloyd-Jones, V. Pearl and B. Worden (eds), *History and Imagination: Essays in Honour of H. R. Trevor-Roper* (London: Duckworth, 1981), pp. 43–55.

Catto, J. 'Religious change under Henry V', in G. L. Harriss (ed.), *Henry V: The Practice of Kingship* (Oxford: Oxford University Press, 1985), pp. 97–115.

Catto, J. 'Fellows and helpers: the religious identity of the followers of Wyclif', in P. Biller and B. Dobson (eds), *The Medieval Church: Universities, Heresy, and the Religious Life* (Woodbridge: Boydell for the Ecclesiastical History Society, 1999), pp. 141–61.

Cavanaugh, S. H., 'A study of books privately owned in England: 1300–1450', (Unpublished PhD thesis, University of Pennsylvania, 1980).

Caxton, W. *The Book of the Knight of the Tower*, ed. M. Y. Offord, EETS SS 2 (London, 1971).

The Cely Letters 1472–1488, ed. A. Hanham, EETS OS 273 (London, 1975).

Chaucer, G. *The Riverside Chaucer*, ed. L. D. Benson (Oxford: Oxford University Press, 3rd edn, 1988).

Cheetham, F. *English Medieval Alabasters: with a Catalogue of the Collection in the Victoria and Albert Museum* (Oxford: Phaidon, 1984).

Cherewatuk, K. 'Malory's book of chivalry: the *Morte Darthur* and manuals of chivalry' (Unpublished PhD thesis, Cornell University, 1986).

Cherewatuk, K. 'The saint's life of Sir Lancelot: hagiography and the conclusion of Malory's *Morte Darthur*', *Arthuriana*, 5:1 (1995), 62–78.

Cherewatuk, K. '"Gentyl audiences" and "grete bokes": chivalric manuals and the *Morte Darthur*', *Arthurian Literature*, 15 (1997), 205–16.

Cherewatuk, K. 'Pledging troth in Malory's "Tale of Sir Gareth"', *Journal of English and Germanic Philology*, 101 (2002), 19–40.

Cherry, B. 'Some new types of late medieval tombs in the London area', in L. Grant (ed.), *Medieval Art, Architecture and Archaeology in London*, British Archaeological Association Conference Transactions, 10 (1990 for 1984), pp. 140–54.

Cherry, M. 'The Courtenay earls of Devon: the formation and disintegration of a later medieval aristocratic affinity', *Southern History*, 1 (1979), 71–99.

Cherry, M. 'The struggle for power in mid-fifteenth-century Devonshire', in R. A. Griffiths (ed.), *Patronage, the Crown, and the Provinces in Later Medieval England* (Gloucester: Alan Sutton, 1981), pp. 123–44.

Clanchy, M. *From Memory to Written Record, England 1066–1307* (Oxford: Oxford University Press, 1993).

Clayton, D. J. *The Administration of the County Palatinate of Chester, 1442–1485*, Chetham Society, 3rd ser., 35 (1990).

Clough, C. H. (ed.). *Profession, Vocation and Culture in Later Medieval England: Essays Dedicated to the Memory of A. R. Myers* (Liverpool: Liverpool University Press, 1982).

Coleman, J. *Public Reading and the Reading Public in Late Medieval England and France* (Cambridge: Cambridge University Press, 1996).

The Complete Peerage of England, Scotland, Ireland, Great Britain, and the United Kingdom, eds G. E. Cokayne and P. W. Hammond, 14 vols in 7 (Gloucester: Alan Sutton, 1987; repr. of revised edn, 1910–59).

Connolly, M. *John Shirley: Book Production and the Noble Household in Fifteenth-Century England* (Aldershot: Ashgate, 1998).

Cooper, H. 'The Lancelot-Grail cycle in England: Malory and his predecessors', in C. Dover (ed.), *A Companion to the Lancelot-Grail Cycle* (Cambridge: D. S. Brewer, 2003), pp. 147–62.

Cooper, N. *Houses of the Gentry, 1480–1680* (London: Yale University Press, 1999).

Coss, P. R. 'Aspects of cultural diffusion in medieval England: the early romances, local society and Robin Hood', *Past and Present*, 108 (1985), 35–79.

Coss, P. R. 'Knights, esquires and the origins of social gradation in England', *Transactions of the Royal Historical Society*, 6:5 (1995), 155–78.

Coss, P. R. 'The formation of the English gentry', *Past and Present*, 147 (1995), 38–64.

Coss, P. *The Lady in Medieval England, 1000–1500* (Stroud: Sutton, 1998).

Coss, P. R. *The Origins of the English Gentry* (Cambridge: Cambridge University Press, 2003).

Coss, P. and M. Keen (eds). *Heraldry, Pageantry and Social Display in Medieval England* (Woodbridge: Boydell, 2002).

The Coventry Leet Book: Part One, ed. M. D. Harris, EETS OS 135 (London, 1907).

Cranmer, T. *Miscellaneous Writings and Letters of Thomas Cranmer*, ed. J. E. Cox (Cambridge: Parker Society, 1848).

Cressy, D. *Literacy and the Social Order: Reading and Writing in Tudor and Stuart England* (Cambridge: Cambridge University Press, 1980).

Davies, R. G. and J. H. Denton (eds). *The English Parliament in the Middle Ages* (Manchester: Manchester University Press, 1981).

Davies, R. T. (ed.). *Medieval English Lyrics: a Critical Anthology* (London: Faber & Faber, 1963).

Davis, N. 'The text of Margaret Paston's letters', *Medium Ævum*, 18 (1949), 12–28.

Davis, N. 'The language of the Pastons', *Proceedings of the British Academy*, 40 (1955), 119–44.

Davis, N. 'Scribal variation in late fifteenth-century English', in *Mélanges de Linguistique et de Philologie: Fernand Mossé in Memorium* (Paris: Didier, 1959), pp. 95–103.

Davis, N. 'Style and stereotype in early English letters', *Leeds Studies in English*, NS 1 (1967), 7–17.

Davis, N. 'The epistolary usages of William Worcester', in D. A. Pearsall and R. A. Waldron (eds), *Medieval Literature and Civilization: Studies in Memory of G. N. Garmonsway* (London: Athlone Press, 1969), pp. 249–74.

Daw, B. 'English knighthood in the fifteenth century, 1400–1500' (Unpublished M.Phil. dissertation, University of Manchester, 1997).

D'Elboux, R. H. 'Testamentary brasses', *Antiquaries Journal*, 29 (1949), 188–91.

Dennison, L. '"The Fitzwarin psalter and its allies": a reappraisal', in W. M. Ormrod (ed.), *England in the Fourteenth Century: Proceedings of the 1985 Harlaxton Symposium* (Woodbridge: Boydell, 1986), pp. 42–65.

A Descriptive Catalogue of Ancient Deeds in the Public Record Office (London: HMSO, 1900).

Dickens, A. G. *The English Reformation* (London: Batsford, 2nd edn, 1964).

Dickinson, J. C. *An Ecclesiastical History of England: the Later Middle Ages* (London: A. and C. Black, 1979).

Dictionary of Medieval Latin from British Sources, A-L, eds R. E. Latham *et al.* (Oxford: Oxford University Press, Published for the British Academy 1975–97).

Dictionnaire de Théologie Catholique, eds A. Vacant, E. Mangenot and E. Amann (Paris: Le Touzey et Ané, 1903–50).

Dillon, Viscount and W. H. St John Hope (eds). *Pageant of the Birth, Life and Death of Richard Beauchamp, Earl of Warwick* (London: Longmans Green, 1914).

Dodgson, J. McN. 'A library at Pott Chapel (Pott Shrigley, Cheshire) *c.* 1493', *The Library*, 5th ser., 15 (1960), 4–53.

Doyle, A. I. 'English books in and out of Court from Edward III to Henry VII', in Scattergood and Sherborne (eds), *English Court Culture*, pp. 163–81.

DuBoulay, F. R. H. *The Lordship of Canterbury*: *An Essay on Medieval Society* (London: Nelson, 1966).

Duby, G. 'The diffusion of cultural patterns in feudal society', *Past and Present*, 39 (1968), 3–10.

Dudley, E. *The Tree of Commonwealth* (Cambridge: Cambridge University Press, 1948).

Duffy, E. *The Stripping of the Altars: Traditional Religion in England,* c. *1400–c. 1580* (London and New Haven, CN: Yale University Press, 1992).

Duffy, E. 'The parish, piety and patronage in late medieval England: the evidence of rood screens', in French, Gibbs and Kümin (eds), *Parish in English Life*, pp. 133–62.

Duffy, E. 'The dynamics of pilgrimage in late medieval England', in Morris and Roberts (eds), *Pilgrimage: The English Experience*, pp. 164–77.

Dugdale, W. *The Antiquities of Warwickshire*, 2 vols 1 (London: John Osborne and Thomas Longman, 1730).

Dutton, A. 'Passing the book: testamentary transmission of religious literature to and by women in England, 1350–1500', in L. Smith and J. H. M. Taylor (eds), *Women, the Book and the Godly: Selected Proceedings of the St Hilda's Conference, 1993* (Cambridge: D. S. Brewer, 1995), pp. 41–54.

Dutton, A. M. 'Piety, politics and persona: MS Harley 4012 and Anne Harling', in Riddy (ed.), *Prestige, Authority and Power*, pp. 133–43.

Dyer, C. 'Changes in the size of peasant holdings in some West Midland villages, 1400–1540', in R. M. Smith (ed.), *Land, Kinship and Life-cycle* (Cambridge: Cambridge University Press, 1984), pp. 277–94.

Edwards, A. S. G. 'Gender, order and reconciliation in *Sir Degrevaunt*', in Meale (ed.), *Readings in Medieval English Romance*, pp. 53–64.

Edwards, A. S. G. 'The transmission and audience of Osbern Bokenham's *Legendys of Hooly Wummen*', in A. J. Minnis (ed.), *Late Medieval Religious Texts and their Transmission: Essays in Honour of A. I. Doyle* (Woodbridge: D. S. Brewer, 1994), pp. 157–67.

Edwards, A. S. G. 'John Shirley and the emulation of court culture', in E. Mullally and J. Thompson (eds), *The Court and Cultural Diversity* (Cambridge: D. S. Brewer, 1997), pp. 309–17.

Ellis, H. (ed.). *Original Letters Illustrative of English History*, 3rd ser., 4 vols (London: R. Bentley, 1846).

Elyot, Sir T. *The Book Named the Gouernour*, ed. S. E. Lehmberg (London: Dent, 1962).

Emery, A. *Greater Medieval Houses of England and Wales, 1300–1500*, 2 vols (Cambridge: Cambridge University Press, 1996 and 1999).

Erler, M. 'English vowed women at the end of the Middle Ages', *Mediæval Studies*, 57 (1995), 155–203.

Erler, M. 'Devotional literature', in Hellinga and Trapp (eds), *Cambridge History of the Book*, pp. 495–525.

Evans, J. *English Art 1307–1461* (Oxford: Clarendon Press, 1949).

Farquhar, J. D. *Creation and Imitation: The Work of a Fifteenth-Century Manuscript Illuminator* (Fort Lauderdale: Nova/NYIT University Press, 1976).

Fenn, J. (ed.). *Original Letters, written during the reigns of Henry VI, Edward IV, and Richard III, by various persons of rank or consequence*, 5 vols (London: G. G. J. and J. Robinson, 1787–1823).

Ferguson, A. B. *The Indian Summer of English Chivalry* (Durham, NC: Duke University Press, 1960).

Ferster, J. *Fictions of Advice: The Literature and Politics and Counsel in Late Medieval England* (Philadelphia: University of Pennsylvania Press, 1996).

Field, P. J. C. *The Life and Times of Sir Thomas Malory* (Cambridge: D. S. Brewer, 1993).

Field, P. J. C. 'The source of Malory's "Tale of Gareth"', in P. J. C. Field, *Malory: Text and Sources* (Cambridge: D. S. Brewer, 1998), pp. 246–60.

Finnegan, R. *Literacy and Orality* (Oxford: Blackwell, 1988).

Fisher, J. H. *The Emergence of Standard English* (Lexington: University Press of Kentucky, 1996).

Fleming, P. 'Charity, faith, and the gentry of Kent', in A. J. Pollard (ed.), *Property and Politics: Essays in Later Medieval English History* (Gloucester: Alan Sutton, 1984), pp. 36–58.

Fleming, P. W. 'The character and private concerns of the gentry of Kent, 1422–1509' (Unpublished PhD thesis, University of Wales, 1985).

Fleming, P. 'The Hautes and their "circle": culture and the English gentry', in Williams (ed.), *England in the Fifteenth Century*, pp. 85–102.

Fleming, P. *Family and Household in Medieval England* (New York and Basingstoke: Palgrave, 2000).

Fleming, P. and M. Wood. *Gloucestershire's Forgotten Battle: Nibley Green, 1470* (Stroud: Tempus, 2003).

Ford, M. L. 'Private ownership of printed books', in Hellinga and Trapp (eds), *Cambridge History of the Book*, pp. 205–28.

Fortescue, Sir J. *The Governance of England by Sir John Fortescue*, ed. C. Plummer (Oxford: Clarendon Press, 1885).

Fortescue, Sir J. *De Laudibus Legum Anglie*, trans. and ed. S. B. Chrimes (Cambridge: Cambridge University Press, 1942).

Fortescue, Sir J. *On the Laws and Governance of England*, ed. S. Lockwood (Cambridge: Cambridge University Press, 1997).

Franks, A. W. 'Notes on Edward Grimston, Esq., Ambassador to the Duchess of Burgundy', *Archaeologia*, 40 (1866), 244–70.

Freeborn, D. *From Old English to Standard English* (Basingstoke: Macmillan, 1998).

French, K. L., G. G. Gibbs and B. A. Kümin (eds), *The Parish in English Life, 1400–1600* (Manchester: Manchester University Press, 1997).

Friar, S. *Heraldry for the Local Historian and Genealogist* (Stroud: Alan Sutton, 1992).

Froissart, J. *Oeuvres*, ed. K. de Lettenhove, IX (Brussels: Victor Devaux et cie, 1869).

Fryde, E. B. *Peasants and Landlords in Later Medieval England* (Stroud: Alan Sutton, 1996).

Gabel, L. *Benefit of Clergy in England in the Later Middle Ages* (Northampton, MA: Department of History, Smith College, 1929; repr. New York: Octagon Books, 1969).

Gardiner, D. *English Girlhood at School: A Study of Women's Education through Twelve Centuries* (London: Oxford University Press, 1929).

Gardner, A. *Alabaster Tombs of the Pre-Reformation Period in England* (Cambridge: Cambridge University Press, 1940).

Gardner, E. J. 'The English nobility and monastic education *c.*1100–1500', in J. Blair and B. Golding (eds), *The Cloister and the World: Essays in Medieval History in Memory of Barbara Harvey* (Oxford: Clarendon Press, 1996), pp. 80–94.

Ghosh, K. *The Wycliffite Heresy: Authority and the Interpretation of Texts* (Cambridge: Cambridge University Press, 2001).

Gibson, G. M. *The Theater of Devotion: East Anglian Drama and Society in the Late Middle Ages* (Chicago and London: University of Chicago Press, 1989).

Gillespie, A. 'Balliol MS 354: histories of the book at the end of the Middle Ages', *Poetica* 60 (2003), 47–63.

Given-Wilson, C. *The English Nobility in the Late Middle Ages* (London: Routledge and Kegan Paul, 1987).

Goodall, J. A. 'Two medieval drawings', *Antiquaries Journal*, 58 (1978), 159–62.

Goodall, J. A. 'Heraldry in the decoration of English medieval manuscripts', *Antiquaries Journal*, 77 (1997), 179–220.

Graff, H. J. *The Legacies of Literacy: Continuities and Contradictions in Western Culture and Society* (Bloomington and Indianapolis: Indiana University Press, 1987).

Gray, Sir T. *The* Scalacronica *of Sir Thomas Gray*, trans. and ed. Sir H. Maxwell (Glasgow: James Maclehose, 1907).

Green, D. H. 'Orality and reading: the state of research in medieval studies', *Speculum*, 65 (1990), 267–80.

Green, R. F. *Poets and Princepleasers: Literature and the English Court in the Late Middle Ages* (Toronto: University of Toronto Press, 1980).

Greenhill, F. A. *Incised Effigial Slabs: A Study of Engraved Stone Memorials in Latin Christendom, c. 1100 to c. 1700*, 2 vols (London: Faber, 1976).

Greening Lambourne, E. A. *The Armorial Glass of the Oxford Diocese, 1250–1850* (London: Oxford University Press, 1949).

Griffiths, J. and D. Pearsall (eds). *Book Production and Publishing in Britain, 1375–1475* (Cambridge: Cambridge University Press, 1989).

Griffiths, R. A. *The Reign of King Henry VI: The Exercise of Royal Authority, 1422–1461* (London: Benn, 1981).

Griffiths, R. A. *King and Country: England and Wales in the Fifteenth Century* (London and Rio Grande: Hambledon Press, 1991).

Gross, A. 'Regionalism and revision', in P. Fleming, A. Gross and J. R. Lander (eds), *Regionalism and Revision: The Crown and its Provinces in England 1200–1650* (London and Rio Grande: Hambledon Press, 1998), pp. 1–13.

Guddat-Figge, G. *Catalogue of Manuscripts Containing Middle English Romances* (Munich: W. Fink, 1976).

Hahn, T. 'Gawain and popular chivalric romance in Britain', in R. L. Krueger (ed.), *The Cambridge Companion to Medieval Romance* (Cambridge: Cambridge University Press, 2000), pp. 218–34.

Haigh, C. *English Reformations: Religion, Politics, and Society under the Tudors* (Oxford: Clarendon Press; New York: Oxford University Press, 1993).

Hands, R. (ed.). *English Hawking and Hunting in* The Boke of St Albans (London: Oxford University Press, 1975).

Hanna, R. III. 'The growth of Robert Thornton's books', *Studies in Bibliography*, 40 (1987), 51–61.

Hanna, R. III. 'Sir Thomas Berkeley and his patronage', *Speculum*, 64 (1989), 879–916.

Hanna, R. III. 'Miscellaneity and vernacularity: conditions of literary production in late medieval England', in S. G. Nichols and S. Wenzel (eds), *The Whole Book: Cultural Perspectives on the Medieval Miscellany* (Ann Arbor: University of Michigan Press, 1996), pp. 37–52.

Hanna, R. III. 'Middle English manuscripts and the study of literature', in W. Scase, R. Copeland and D. Lawton (eds), *New Medieval Literatures IV* (Oxford: Oxford University Press, 2001), pp. 243–64.

Hanna, R. III and A. S. G. Edwards. 'Rotheley, the De Vere Circle, and the Ellesmere Chaucer', *Huntingdon Library Quarterly*, 58 (1996), 11–35.

Hardman, P. 'A mediæval "library *in parvo*"', *Medium Ævum*, 47 (1978), 262–73.

Hardman, P. 'Compiling the nation: fifteenth-century miscellany manuscripts', in H. Cooney (ed.), *Nation, Court and Culture: New Essays on Fifteenth-Century English Poetry* (Dublin: Four Courts, 2000), pp. 50–69.

Hardman, P. 'Evidence of readership in fifteenth-century household miscellanies', *Poetica* 60 (2003), 15–30.

Hardyng, J. *The Chronicle of John Hardyng*, ed. H. Ellis (London: Rivington, 1812).

Harper, J. *The Forms and Orders of Western Liturgy from the Tenth to the Eighteenth Century: A Historical Introduction and Guide for Students and Musicians* (Oxford: Clarendon Press, 1996).

Harris, B. J. *English Aristocratic Women, 1450–1550* (Oxford: Oxford University Press, 2002).

Harris, K. 'The origins and make-up of Cambridge University Library MS Ff.I.6', *Transactions of the Cambridge Bibliographical Society*, 8 (1983), 299–333.

Harris, K. 'Patrons, buyers and owners: the evidence for ownership and the rôle of book owners in book production and the book trade', in Griffiths and Pearsall (eds), *Book Production and Publishing*, pp. 163–99.

Harrison, F. Ll. *Music in Medieval Britain* (London: Routledge and Kegan Paul, 1958).

Harriss, G. L. 'The dimension of politics', in R. H. Britnell and A. J. Pollard (eds), *The McFarlane Legacy: Studies in Late Medieval Politics and Society* (Stroud: Alan Sutton, 1995), pp. 1–20.

Harvey, I. M. W. *Jack Cade's Rebellion of 1450* (Oxford: Clarendon Press, 1991).

Harvey, J. H. *The Perpendicular Style, 1330–1485* (London: Batsford, 1978).

Harvey, J. H. *English Mediæval Architects: A Biographical Dictionary down to 1550* (Gloucester: Sutton, rev. edn, 1984).

Hayter, W. *William of Wykeham: Patron of the Arts* (London: Chatto and Windus, 1970).

Heales, A. 'The church of Stanwell and its monuments', *Transactions of the London and Middlesex Archaeological Society*, 3 (1865–69), 105–302.

Heard, K. 'Death and representation in the fifteenth century: the Wilcote chantry at North Leigh', *Journal of the Archaeological Association*, 154 (2001), 134–49.

Heath, P. *Church and Realm 1272–1461: Conflict and Collaboration in an Age of Crises* (London: Fontana, 1988).

Hebgin-Barnes, P. *The Medieval Stained Glass of the County of Lincolnshire*, Corpus Vitrearum Medii Aevi (Oxford: Oxford University Press for the British Academy, 1996).

Hellinga, L. and J. B. Trapp (eds). *The Cambridge History of the Book in Britain, III: 1400–1557* (Cambridge: Cambridge University Press, 1999).

Henricks, T. S. *Disputed Pleasures: Sport and Society in Preindustrial England* (New York: Greenwood Press, 1991).

Hepburn, F. *Portraits of the Later Plantagenets* (Woodbridge: Boydell, 1986).

Hicks, M. A. (ed.). *Profit, Piety and the Professions in Later Medieval England* (Gloucester: Alan Sutton, 1990).

Hicks, M. 'Four studies in conventional piety', *Southern History*, 13 (1991), 1–21.

Hicks, M. *Bastard Feudalism* (Harlow: Longman, 1995).

Hicks, M. *Warwick the Kingmaker* (Oxford: Blackwell, 1998).

Hicks, M. *English Political Culture in the Fifteenth Century* (London: Routledge, 2002).

Hoccleve, T. *Hoccleve's Works*, ed. F. J. Furnivall, EETS OS 71 and 72 (London, 1897).

Hooker, John. *The Life and Times of Sir Peter Carew, Knight*, ed. J. Maclean (London: Bell and Daldy, 1857).

Hope, W. H. StJ., 'On the early working of alabaster in England', *Archaeological Journal*, 61 (1904), 221–40.

Hoppin, R. H. *Medieval Music* (New York: W. W. Norton, 1978).

Horman, W. *Vulgaria* (London: R. Pynson, 1519, repr. Amsterdam: Theatrum Orbis Terrarum, 1975).

Horrox, R. 'The urban gentry in the fifteenth century', in J. A. F. Thomson (ed.), *Towns and Townspeople in the Fifteenth Century* (Gloucester: Alan Sutton, 1988), pp. 22–44.

Horrox, R. *Richard III: A Study in Service* (Cambridge: Cambridge University Press, 1989).

Horrox, R. (ed.). *Fifteenth-Century Attitudes: Perceptions of Society in Late Medieval England* (Cambridge: Cambridge University Press, 1994).

Horrox, R. 'Service', in Horrox (ed.), *Fifteenth-Century Attitudes*, pp. 61–78.

Hoskins, E. *Horae Beatae Virginis, or Sarum and York Primers with Kindred Books and Primers of the Reformed Roman Use* (Farnborough: Gregg International Publishers, 1969).

Hudson, A. *The Premature Reformation: Wycliffite Texts and Lollard History* (Oxford: Clarendon Press, 1988).

Hughes, J. *Pastors and Visionaries: Religion and Secular Life in Late Medieval Yorkshire* (Woodbridge: Boydell, 1988).

Hughes, J. 'The administration of confession in the diocese of York in the fourteenth century', in D. M. Smith (ed.), *Studies in Clergy and Ministry in Medieval England* (York: Borthwick Studies in History, 1, 1991), pp. 87–163.

Hughes, J. 'Stephen Scrope and the circle of Sir John Fastolf: moral and intellectual outlooks', in C. Harper-Bill and R. Harvey (eds), *Medieval Knighthood IV* (Woodbridge: Boydell, 1992), pp. 109–46.

Hughes, J. 'The ornaments to know a holy man: northern religious life and the piety of Richard III', in A. J. Pollard (ed.), *The North of England in the Age of Richard III* (Stroud: Alan Sutton, 1996), pp. 149–90.

Hunt, A. *Governance of the Consuming Passions: A History of Sumptuary Law* (Basingstoke: Macmillan Press, 1996).

Hussey, C. 'Ockwells Manor, Bray', *Country Life*, 55 (1924), 52–60, 92–9, 130–7.

Hyams, P. R. *King, Lords and Peasants in Medieval England: the Common Law of Villeinage in the Twelfth and Thirteenth Centuries* (Oxford: Clarendon Press, 1980).

Idley, P. *Peter Idley's* Instructions to his Son, ed. C. D'Evelyn (Boston and London: Oxford University Press, 1935).

Ives, E. W. 'The common lawyers in pre-Reformation England', *Transactions of the Royal Historical Society*, 5th ser., 18 (1968), 145–73.

Ives, E. W. 'The common lawyers', in Clough (ed.), *Profession, Vocation and Culture*, pp. 181–217.

James, M. 'English politics and the concept of honour, 1485–1642', *Past and Present*, supplement 3 (1978).

James, M. R. *Descriptive Catalogue of the Manuscripts in the Library of the Fitzwilliam Museum, Cambridge* (Cambridge: Cambridge University Press, 1895).

Jewell, H. M. *English Local Administration in the Middle Ages* (Newton Abbot: Blandford, 1972).

Jewell, H. M. *Women in Medieval England* (Manchester: Manchester University Press, 1996).

Johnston, A. F. and S. MacLean. 'Reformation and resistance in Thames/Severn parishes: the dramatic witness', in French *et al.* (eds), *Parish in English Life*, pp. 178–200.

Jones, M. (ed.). *Gentry and Lesser Nobility in Late Medieval Europe* (Gloucester: Sutton, 1986).

Jones, T. *Chaucer's Knight: the Portrait of a Medieval Mercenary* (London: Weiden-feld & Nicolson, 1980).

Jones, W. R. 'Lollards and images: the defence of religious art in later medieval England', *Journal of the History of Ideas*, 34 (1973), 27–50.

Kaeuper, R. W. 'An historian's reading of *The Tale of Gamelyn*', *Medium Ævum*, 52 (1983), 51–62.

Kamerick, K. *Popular Piety and Art in the Late Middle Ages: Image Worship and Idolatry in England 1350–1500* (New York: Palgrave, 2002).

Keen, M. *Chivalry* (London: Yale University Press, 1984).

Keen, M. 'Heraldry and hierarchy: esquires and gentlemen', in J. Denton (ed.), *Order and Hierarchies in Late Medieval and Renaissance Europe* (Manchester: Manchester University Press, 1999), pp. 94–108, 184–7.

Keen, M. *The Outlaws of Medieval England* (London: Routledge, 2000).

Keen, M. *Origins of the English Gentleman* (Stroud: Tempus, 2002).

Keiser, G. R. 'Lincoln Cathedral Library, MS 91: life and milieu of the scribe', *Studies in Bibliography*, 32 (1979), 158–79.

Keiser, G. R. 'MS Rawlinson A. 393: another Findern Manuscript', *Transactions of the Cambridge Bibliographical Society*, 7 (1980), 445–8.

Keiser, G. R. 'More light on the life and milieu of Robert Thornton', *Studies in Bibliography*, 36 (1983), 111–19.

Keiser, G. R. '*A Tretys of Armes:* a revision of the *Ashmolean Tract*', *The Coat of Arms*, NS 10 (1996), 184–6.

Keiser, G. R. 'Practical books for the gentleman', in Hellinga and Trapp (eds), *Cambridge History of the Book*, pp. 470–94.

Kekewich, M. L. *et al.* (eds). *The Politics of Fifteenth-Century England: John Vale's Book* (Gloucester: Alan Sutton for Richard III and Yorkist History Trust, 1995).

Kennedy, E. D. (ed.). *King Arthur: A Casebook* (New York: Garland, 1996).

Kerr, J. 'The east window of Gloucester Cathedral', *Medieval Art and Architecture at Gloucester and Tewkesbury*, British Archaeological Association Conference Transactions, 7 (1985 for 1981), 116–29.

Kingsford's Stonor Letters and Papers 1290–1483, ed. C. Carpenter (Cambridge: Cambridge University Press, 1996).

Kintzinger, M. 'A profession but not a career? Schoolmasters and the *artes* in late medieval Europe', in W. J. Courtenay and J. Miethke (eds), *Universities and Schooling in Medieval Society* (Leiden: Brill, 2000), pp. 167–81.

Kirby, J. W. 'Women in the Plumpton correspondence: fiction and reality', in I. Wood and G. A. Loud (eds), *Church and Chronicle in the Middle Ages: Essays presented to John Taylor* (London and Rio Grande: Hambledon Press, 1991), pp. 219–32.

Kisby, F. 'Music in European cities and towns to *c*.1650: a bibliographical survey', *Urban History*, 29 (2002), 74–82.

Kisby, F. (ed.). *Music and Musicians in Renaissance Cities and Towns* (Cambridge: Cambridge University Press, 2001).

Knight, S. and T. Ohlgren (eds). *Robin Hood and Other Outlaw Tales* (Kalamazoo: Medieval Institute, 2000).

Knighton, T. and D. Fallows (eds). *Companion to Medieval and Renaissance Music* (New York: Schirmer, 1992).

Kowaleski, M. 'The commercial dominance of a medieval provincial oligarchy: Exeter in the late fourteenth century', in R. Holt and G. Rosser (eds), *The English Medieval Town: a Reader in English Urban History 1200–1540* (London and New York: Longman, 1990), pp. 184–215.

Kreider, A. *English Chantries: The Road to Dissolution* (Cambridge, MA and London: Harvard University Press, 1979).

Kümin, B. 'Masses, morris and metrical psalms: music in the English parish, *c*.1400–1600', in Kisby (ed.), *Music and Musicians*, pp. 70–81.

Lander, J. R. 'The Yorkist council and administration', *English Historical Review*, 83 (1958), 27–46.

Lander, J. R. 'Council, administration and councillors, 1461–85', *Bulletin of the Institute of Historical Research*, 32 (1959), 137–78.

Lander, J. R. *English Justices of the Peace, 1461–1509* (Gloucester: Alan Sutton, 1989).

Lawton, D. 'Dullness and the fifteenth century', *English Literary History*, 54 (1987), 761–99.

Lawton, D. A. 'Scottish Field: alliterative verse and the Stanley encomium in the Percy Folio', *Leeds Studies in English*, NS 10 (1978), 42–57.

Lester, G. A. *Sir John Paston's* Grete Boke: *A Descriptive Catalogue, with an Introduction, of British Library MS Lansdowne 285* (Cambridge: D. S. Brewer, 1984).

Lester, G. A. 'The books of a fifteenth-century gentleman, Sir John Paston', *Neuphilologische Mitteilungen*, 88 (1987), 200–17.

Lloyd, R. 'Music at the parish church of St Mary at Hill, London', *Early Music*, 25 (1997), 221–6.

Lloyd, R. 'The provision for music in the parish churches of late medieval London' (Unpublished PhD dissertation, University of London, 2000).

London, H. S. *The Life of William Bruges, the First Garter King of Arms*, Harleian Society, 111 and 112 (London, 1970).

Lowry, M. 'John Rous and the survival of the Neville circle', *Viator*, 19 (1988), 327–38.

Luttrell, C. 'Three north-west Midland manuscripts', *Neophilologus*, 42 (1958), 38–42.

Lydgate, J. *John Lydgate's* Serpent of Division, ed. H. N. MacCracken (London and New Haven: Oxford University Press, 1911).

Lydgate, J. *The Minor Poems of John Lydgate: I*, ed. H. Noble MacCracken, EETS ES 107 (London, 1911).

Lydgate, J. *Table Manners for Children: Stans Puer ad Mensam*, ed. N. Orme (Salisbury: Perdix Press, 1989; repr. London: Wynkyn de Worde Society, 1990).

Lydgate and Burgh's Secrees of Old Philosoffres, ed. R. Steele, EETS ES 66 (London, 1894).

Lyell, L. (ed.). *A Mediæval Post-Bag* (London: Jonathan Cape, 1934).

McFarlane, K. B. 'The investment of Sir John Fastolf's profits of war', *Transactions of the Royal Historical Society*, 5:7 (1957), 91–116.

McFarlane, K. B. 'William Worcester: a preliminary survey', in J. Conway Davies (ed.), *Studies Presented to Sir Hilary Jenkinson* (London: Oxford University Press, 1957), pp. 196–221.

McFarlane, K. B. 'A business partnership in war and administration', *English Historical Review*, 78 (1963), 290–308.

McFarlane, K. B. *Hans Memling* (Oxford: Clarendon Press, 1971).

McFarlane, K. B. *Lancastrian Kings and Lollard Knights* (Oxford: Oxford University Press, 1972).

McFarlane, K. B. *The Nobility of Later Medieval England: The Ford Lectures for 1953 and Related Studies* (Oxford: Clarendon Press, 1973).

McFarlane, K. B. *England in the Fifteenth Century* (London and Rio Grande: Hambledon Press, 1981).

MacKendrick, S. 'Tapestries from the Low Countries', in Barron and Saul (eds), *England and the Low Countries*, pp. 43–60.

McKitterick, R. (ed.). *The Uses of Literacy in Early Medieval Europe* (Cambridge: Cambridge University Press, 1990).

McNamer, S. 'Female authors, provincial setting: the re-versing of courtly love in the Findern manuscript', *Viator*, 22 (1991), 279–310.

Maddern, P. *Violence and Social Order: East Anglia, 1422–1442* (Oxford: Clarendon Press, 1992).

Maddern, P. "'Best trusted friends": concepts and practices of friendship among fifteenth-century Norfolk gentry', in Rogers (ed.), *England in the Fifteenth Century*, pp. 100-17.

Maddern, P. 'Honour among the Pastons: gender and integrity in fifteenth-century English provincial society', *Journal of Medieval History*, 14 (1998), 357-71.

Maddicott, J. R. 'The birth and setting of the ballads of Robin Hood', *English Historical Review*, 93 (1978), 276-99.

Malory, Sir T. *The Works of Sir Thomas Malory*, ed. E. Vinaver, rev. P. J. C. Field (Oxford: Clarendon Press, 3rd edn, 1990).

Marks, R. *Stained Glass in England during the Middle Ages* (London: Routledge, 1993).

Marsh, D. "'I see by sizt of evidence": information gathering in late medieval Cheshire', in D. E. S. Dunn (ed.), *Courts, Counties and the Capital in the Later Middle Ages* (Stroud: Sutton, 1996), pp. 71-92.

Marx. W. and R. Radulescu (eds). *Readers and Writers of the* Brut *Chronicle*, special issue of *Trivium* 36 (forthcoming, 2005).

Massey, R. A. 'The land settlement in Lancastrian Normandy', in A. J. Pollard (ed.), *Property and Politics: Essays in Later Medieval English History* (Gloucester: Alan Sutton, 1984), pp. 76-96.

Matheson, L. M. *The Prose* Brut: *The Development of a Middle English Chronicle* (Tempe, AZ: Medieval and Renaissance Texts and Studies, 1998).

Meale, C. 'Patrons, buyers, and owners: book production and social status', in Griffiths and Pearsall (eds), *Book Production and Publishing*, pp. 201-38.

Meale, C. M. 'The politics of book ownership: the Hopton family and Bodleian Library, Digby MS 185', in Riddy (ed.), *Prestige, Authority and Power*, pp. 103-31.

Meale, C. 'Caxton, de Worde, and the publication of romance in late medieval England', *The Library*, 6th ser., 14 (1992), 283-98.

Meale, C. M. "'gode men/Wiues, maydens and alle men": romance and its audiences', in Meale (ed.), *Readings in Medieval English Romance*, pp. 209-25.

Meale, C. M. '*The Libelle of Englysshe Polycye* and mercantile literary culture in late medieval London', in J. Boffey and P. King (eds), *London and Europe in the Later Middle Ages* (London: University of London, 1995), pp. 181-227.

Meale, C. "'… alle the bokes that I haue of latyn, englisch, and frensch": laywomen and their books in late medieval England', in Meale (ed.), *Women and Literature in Britain*, pp. 128-58.

Meale, C. M. (ed.). *Women and Literature in Britain, 1150-1500* (Cambridge: Cambridge University Press, 1993).

Meale, C. M. (ed.). *Readings in Medieval English Romance* (Cambridge: D. S. Brewer, 1994).

Meale, C. and J. Boffey, 'Gentlewomen's reading', in Hellinga and Trapp (eds), *Cambridge History of the Book*, pp. 526-40.

Mertes, K. *The English Noble Household, 1250-1600: Good Governance and Politic Rule* (Oxford: Blackwell, 1988).

Mertes, K. 'Aristocracy', in Horrox (ed.), *Fifteenth-Century Attitudes*, pp. 42-60.

Michael, M. 'The privilege of "proximity": towards a re-definition of the function of armorials', *Journal of Medieval History*, 23 (1997), 55-73.

Middleton-Stewart, J. *Inward Purity and Outward Splendour: Death and Remembrance in the Deanery of Dunwich, Suffolk, 1370–1547* (Woodbridge: Boydell, 2001).

Mills, M. *Six Middle English Romances* (London: Dent, 1973).

Milsom, J. 'Songs and society in early Tudor London', *Early Music History*, 16 (1997), 235–94.

Mitchell, R. J. *John Tiptoft, 1427–1470* (London and New York: Longman, 1938).

Moberly, G. H. *Life of William of Wykeham* (Winchester: Warren and Son, 1887).

Moore, S. 'Patrons of letters in Norfolk and Suffolk in 1450', *Publications of the Modern Language Association of America*, 27 (1913), 79–105.

Moran Cruz, J. H. 'Education, economy, and clerical mobility in late medieval northern England', in W. J. Courtenay and J. Miethke (eds), *Universities and Schooling in Medieval Society* (Leiden: Brill, 2000), pp. 182–207.

Moran Cruz, J. H. *The Growth of English Schooling, 1340–1548: Learning, Literacy, and Laicization in Pre-Reformation York Diocese* (Princeton: Princeton University Press, 1985).

Moran Cruz, J. H. 'England: education and society' in Rigby (ed.), *Companion to Britain in the Later Middle Ages*, pp. 451–71.

Moreton, C. E. 'The "library" of a fifteenth-century lawyer', *The Library*, 6th ser., 13 (1991), 339–46.

Moreton, C. E. *The Townshends and their World: Gentry, Law and Land in Norfolk, c. 1450–1551* (Oxford: Clarendon Press, 1992).

Morgan, D. A. L. 'The individual style of the English gentleman', in Jones (ed.), *Gentry and Lesser Nobility*, pp. 15–35.

Morgan, N. 'Texts and images of Marian devotion in the fourteenth century', in N. Rogers (ed.), *England in the Fourteenth Century* (Stamford: Paul Watkins, 1994), pp. 34–57.

Morgan, P. *War and Society in Medieval Cheshire, 1277–1403* (Manchester: Manchester University Press for the Chetham Society, 1987).

Morris, C. 'Pilgrimage to Jerusalem in the late Middle Ages', in Morris and Roberts (eds), *Pilgrimage: The English Experience*, pp. 141–63.

Morris, C and P. Roberts (eds), *Pilgrimage: The English Experience from Becket to Bunyan* (Cambridge: Cambridge University Press, 2002).

Morris, R. *Churches in the Landscape* (London: Dent, 1989).

Munrow, D. *Instruments of the Middle Ages and Renaissance* (Oxford: Oxford University Press, 1976).

Myers, A. R. (ed.). *The Household Book of Edward IV: the Black Book and the Ordinance of 1478* (Manchester: Manchester University Press, 1959).

Myers, A. R. (ed.). *English Historical Documents: IV, 1327–1485* (London: Eyre and Spottiswoode, 1969).

Newton, S. M. *Fashion in the Age of the Black Prince: A Study of the Years 1340–1365* (Woodbridge: Boydell, 1980).

Nicholls, J. *The Matter of Courtesy: A Study of Medieval Courtesy Books and the Gawain-Poet* (Woodbridge: D. S. Brewer, 1985).

Nightingale, P. 'Knights and merchants: trade, politics and the gentry in late medieval England', *Past and Present*, 169 (2000), 36–62.

Norris, M. *Monumental Brasses: The Craft* (London: Faber, 1978).

The N-Town Plays: A Facsimile of British Library MS Cotton Vespasian C VIII, intro. P. Meredith and S. J. Kahrl (University of Leeds School of English, Ilkley: Scolar Press, 1977).

Orme, N. *English Schools in the Middle Ages* (London and New York: Methuen, 1973) [New edn forthcoming as *Medieval Schools* (New Haven and London: Yale University Press, 2006)].

Orme, N. *Early British Swimming, 55BC–AD1719, with the First Swimming Treatise in English, 1595* (Exeter: University of Exeter Press, 1983).

Orme, N. *From Childhood to Chivalry: the Education of the English Kings and Aristocracy, 1066–1530* (London and New York: Methuen, 1984).

Orme, N. *Education and Society in Medieval and Renaissance England* (London and Ronceverte: Hambledon Press, 1989).

Orme, N. 'Medieval hunting - fact and fancy', in B. Hanawalt (ed.), *Chaucer's England: Literature in Historical Context* (Minneapolis: University of Minnesota Press, 1992), pp. 133–53.

Orme, N. *Medieval Children* (New Haven and London: Yale University Press, 2001).

Owst, G. R. *Literature and Pulpit in Medieval England* (Oxford: Blackwell, 1961).

Pächt, O. and J. J. G. Alexander. *Illuminated Manuscripts in the Bodleian Library, I: German, Dutch, Flemish, French and Spanish Schools* (Oxford: Oxford University Press, 1966).

Page-Philips, J. *Children on Brasses* (London: George Allen and Unwin, 1970).

Pantin, W. A. *The English Church in the Fourteenth Century* (Cambridge: Cambridge University Press, 1955).

Pantin, W. 'Instructions for a devout and literate layman', in J. J. Alexander and M. T. Gibson (eds), *Medieval Learning and Literature: Essays Presented to Richard William Hunt* (Oxford: Clarendon Press, 1976), pp. 398–422.

Parker, Sir W. *The History of Long Melford* (Long Melford: privately printed, 1873).

Parkes, M. B. 'The literacy of the laity', in M. B. Parkes, *Scribes, Scripts and Readers: Studies in the Communication, Presentation and Dissemination of Medieval Texts* (London and Rio Grande: Hambledon Press, 1991), pp. 275–98.

Partridge, A. C. and F. P. Wilson (eds). *Gentleness and Nobility* (London: Malone Society Reprints, 1950).

The Paston Letters, ed. J. Gairdner, 6 vols in 1 (Gloucester: Alan Sutton, microprint edn of 1904 edn, 1986).

Paston Letters and Papers of the Fifteenth Century, ed. N. Davis, 2 vols (Oxford: Clarendon Press, 1971 and 1976).

Payling, S. 'Law and arbitration in Nottinghamshire, 1399–1461', in J. T. Rosenthal and C. Richmond (eds), *People, Politics and the Community in the Later Middle Ages* (Gloucester: Alan Sutton, 1987), pp. 140–60.

Payling, S. J. 'The widening franchise – parliamentary elections in Lancastrian Nottinghamshire', in Williams (ed.), *England in the Fifteenth Century*, pp. 167–85.

Payling, S. J. *Political Society in Lancastrian England: The Greater Gentry of Nottinghamshire* (Oxford: Clarendon Press, 1991).

Pearsall, D. *John Lydgate* (London: Routledge & Kegan Paul, 1970).

Pearsall, D. 'The cultural and social setting', in B. Ford (ed.), *The Cambridge Guide to the Arts in Britain, II* (Cambridge: Cambridge University Press, 1988), pp. 3–38.

Perkins, N. *Hoccleve's Regiment of Princes: Counsel and Constraint* (Cambridge: D. S. Brewer, 2001).

Pevsner, N. *Buildings of England: North-West and South Norfolk* (Harmondsworth: Penguin, 1962).

Platt, C. *The Parish Churches of Medieval England* (London: Secker & Warburg, 1981).

Platt, C. *The Castle in Medieval England and Wales* (London: Secker & Warburg, 1982).

Platt, C. *The Architecture of Medieval Britain: A Social History* (New Haven and London: Yale University Press, 1990).

Plummer, J. *The Last Flowering: French Painting in Manuscripts 1420–1530 from American Collections* (New York: Oxford University Press, 1982).

The Plumpton Letters and Papers, ed. J. Kirby, Camden Society, 5th ser., 8 (Cambridge, 1996).

Pollard, A. J. *North-Eastern England during the Wars of the Roses: Lay Society, War and Politics, 1450–1500* (Oxford: Clarendon Press, 1990).

Pollard, A. J. 'The yeomanry of Robin Hood and social terminology in fifteenth-century England', *Past and Present*, 170 (2001), 52–77.

Polychronicon Ranulphi Higden, Monachi Cestrensis; together with the English translations of John Trevisa and of an unknown writer of the fifteenth century, eds C. Babington and J. R. Lumby, 9 vols (London: Rolls Series, Longmans Green and Co., 1865–86).

Powell, E. 'After "After McFarlane": the poverty of patronage and the case for constitutional history', in D. Clayton, R. G. Davies and P. McNiven (eds), *Trade, Devotion and Governance: Papers in Later Medieval History* (Stroud: Alan Sutton, 1994), pp. 1–16.

Pugh, T. B. 'The magnates, knights and gentry', in S. B. Chrimes, C. D. Ross, and R. A. Griffiths (eds), *Fifteenth-Century England: 1399–1509* (Manchester: Manchester University Press, 1972), pp. 86–128.

Radulescu, R. '"Talkyng of cronycles of kynges and of other polycyez": fifteenth-century miscellanies, the *Brut* and the readership of *Le Morte Darthur*', *Arthurian Literature*, 18 (2001), 125–41.

Radulescu, R. *The Gentry Context for Malory's* Morte Darthur (Cambridge: D. S. Brewer, 2003).

Radulescu, R. 'Sir Thomas Malory and fifteenth-century political ideas', *Arthuriana*, special issue 'Malory and rhetoric', eds. Anne Laskaya and Ann Dobyns, 13:3 (2003), 36–51.

Radulescu, R. 'Yorkist propaganda and the *Chronicle from Rollo to Edward IV*', *Studies in Philology* 100:4 (2003), 401–24.

Radulescu, R. '"now I take uppon me the adventures to seke of holy thynges": Lancelot and the crisis of Arthurian knighthood', in B. Wheeler (ed.), *Textual Traditions of Mediaeval Arthurian Literature: Essays in Honour of P. J. C. Field*, Arthurian Studies, 57 (Cambridge: D. S. Brewer, 2004), pp. 285–95.

Raine, J. (ed.). *Testamenta Eboracensia: A Selection of Wills from the Registry of York*, IV, Surtees Society, 53 (1868).

Rastall, R. *The Heaven Singing: Music in Early English Religious Drama, I* (Woodbridge: D. S. Brewer, 1996).

Rawcliffe, C. 'The great lord as peacekeeper: arbitration by English nobles and their councils in the later Middle Ages', in J. Guy and H. G. Beale (eds), *Law and Social Change in British History*, Royal Historical Society Studies in History, 40 (London, 1984), pp. 34–54.

Rawcliffe, C. 'Curing bodies and healing souls: pilgrimage and the sick in medieval East Anglia', in Morris and Roberts (eds), *Pilgrimage: The English Experience*, pp. 108–40.

Reese, G. *Music in the Middle Ages* (New York: W. W. Norton, 1940).

Reynolds, C. 'English patrons and French artists in fifteenth-century Normandy', in D. Bates and A. Curry (eds), *England and Normandy in the Middle Ages* (London and Rio Grande: Hambledon Press, 1994), pp. 299–313.

Riches, S. J. E. 'The lost St George cycle of St George's church Stamford: an examination of iconography and context', in C. Richmond and E. Scarff (eds), *St George's Chapel, Windsor, in the Late Middle Ages*, Historical Monographs relating to St George's Chapel, Windsor Castle, XVII (Leeds: Manley Publishing, 2001), pp. 135–50.

Richmond, C. *John Hopton: A Fifteenth Century Gentleman* (Cambridge: Cambridge University Press, 1981).

Richmond, C. 'After McFarlane', *History*, 68 (1983), 46–60.

Richmond, C. 'Religion and the fifteenth-century English gentleman', in B. Dobson (ed.), *The Church, Politics and Patronage in the Fifteenth Century* (Gloucester: Sutton, 1984), pp. 193–208.

Richmond, C. *The Paston Family in the Fifteenth Century: The First Phase* (Cambridge: Cambridge University Press, 1990).

Richmond, C. 'The English gentry and religion c.1500', in C. Harper-Bill (ed.), *Religious Belief and Ecclesiastical Careers in Late Medieval England* (Woodbridge: Boydell, 1991), pp. 121–50.

Richmond, C. 'Margins and marginality: English devotion in the later Middle Ages', in Rogers (ed.), *England in the Fifteenth Century*, pp. 242–52.

Richmond, C. *The Paston Family in the Fifteenth Century: Fastolf's Will* (Cambridge: Cambridge University Press, 1996).

Richmond, C. *The Paston Family in the Fifteenth Century: Endings* (Manchester: Manchester University Press, 2000).

Richmond, C. 'The Pastons and London', in S. Rees Jones, R. Marks, and A. J. Minnis (eds), *Courts and Regions in Medieval Europe* (Woodbridge: Boydell, 2000), pp. 211–26.

Richmond, C. 'Books and pictures: an unlikely story of the brothers Paston', *The Ricardian*, 13 (2003), 398–407.

Rickert, M. *The Reconstructed Carmelite Missal: An English Manuscript of the Late XIV Century in the British Museum* (London: Faber & Faber, 1952).

Rickert, M. *Painting in Britain: The Middle Ages* (Harmondsworth: Penguin, 2nd edn, 1965).

Riddy, F. *Sir Thomas Malory* (Leiden: Brill, 1987).

Riddy, F. 'Reading for England: Arthurian literature and the national consciousness', *Bibliographical Bulletin of the International Arthurian Society*, 43 (1991), 314–32.

Riddy, F. '"Women talking about the things of God": a late medieval sub-culture', in Meale (ed.), *Women and Literature in Britain*, pp. 104–27.

Riddy, F. 'Contextualizing *Le Morte Darthur*: empire and civil war', in E. Archibald and A. S. G. Edwards (eds), *A Companion to Malory* (Cambridge: D. S. Brewer, 1996), pp. 55–73.

Riddy, F. 'Middle English romance: family, marriage, intimacy', in R. L. Krueger (ed.), *The Cambridge Companion to Medieval Romance* (Cambridge: Cambridge University Press, 2000), pp. 235–52.

Riddy, F. (ed.). *Prestige, Authority and Power in Late Medieval Manuscripts* (Cambridge: Boydell and Brewer, 2000).

Rigby, S. H. (ed.). *A Companion to Britain in the Later Middle Ages* (Oxford: Blackwell, 2003).

Robbins, R. H. 'A Gawain epigone', *Modern Language Notes*, 58 (1943), 361–6.

Rogers, N. 'Patrons and purchasers: evidence for the original owners of Books of Hours produced in the Low Countries for the English market', in B. Cardon *et al.* (eds), *'Als Ich Can': Liber Amicorum in Memory of Professor Dr Maurits Smeyers*, 2 vols (Paris: Peeters, 2002), II, pp. 165–81.

Rogers, N. (ed.). *England in the Fifteenth Century: Proceedings of the 1992 Harlaxton Symposium* (Stamford: Paul Watkins, 1994).

Rooney, A. *Hunting in Middle English Literature* (Cambridge: D. S. Brewer, 1993).

Roskell, J. S., L. Clark and C. Rawcliffe (eds). *The House of Commons 1386–1421*, 4 vols (Stroud: Alan Sutton, 1992).

Ross, C. *Edward IV* (London: Eyre Methuen, 1974).

Rosser, G. 'The essence of medieval urban communities: the vill of Westminster, 1200–1540' in R. Holt and G. Rosser (eds), *The English Medieval Town: A Reader in English Urban History 1200–1540* (London: Longman, 1990), pp. 217–37.

Rotuli Parliamentorum, ed. J. Strachey, 7 vols (London, 1767–1832).

Routh, P. E. *Medieval Effigial Alabaster Tombs in Yorkshire* (Ipswich: Boydell Press, 1976).

Rowney, I. 'Arbitration in gentry disputes in the later Middle Ages', *History*, 67 (1982), 367–76.

Rubin, M. 'Small groups: identity and solidarity in the later Middle Ages', in J. Kermode (ed.), *Enterprise and Individuals in Fifteenth-Century England* (Stroud: Sutton, 1991), pp. 132–50.

Rubin, M. *Corpus Christi: The Eucharist in Late Medieval Culture* (Cambridge: Cambridge University Press, 1991).

Ryde, C. 'An alabaster angel with shield at Lowick – a Chellaston shop pattern', *Derbyshire Archaeological Journal*, 97 (1977), 36–49.

Salzman, L. F. *Building in England down to 1540: A Documentary History* (Oxford: Oxford University Press, new edn, 1997).

Sandler, L. F. *A Survey of Manuscripts Illuminated in the British Isles: Gothic Manuscripts 1285–1385*, 2 vols (Oxford: Harvey Millar, 1986).

Sands, G. B. (ed.). *Middle English Verse Romances* (Exeter: Exeter Medieval English Texts and Studies, 1986).

Saul, N. *Knights and Esquires: The Gloucestershire Gentry in the Fourteenth Century* (Oxford: Clarendon Press, 1981).

Saul, N. 'The social status of Chaucer's Franklin: a reconsideration', *Medium Ævum*, 52 (1983) 10–26.

Saul, N. *Scenes from Provincial Life: Knightly Families in Sussex 1280–1400* (Oxford: Clarendon Press, 1986).

Saul, N. 'Chaucer and gentility', in B. Hanawalt (ed.), *Chaucer's England: Literature in Historical Context* (Minneapolis: University of Minnesota Press, 1992), pp. 41–55.

Saul, N. *Richard II* (New Haven, CT: Yale University Press, 1997).

Saul, N. *Death, Art, and Memory in Medieval England: The Cobham Family and their Monuments 1300–1500* (Oxford: Oxford University Press, 2001).

Scanlon, L. 'The king's two voices: narrative and power in Hoccleve's *Regiment of Princes*', in L. Patterson (ed.), *Literary Practice and Social Change in Britain, 1380–1530* (Berkeley, Los Angeles: University of California Press, 1990), pp. 216–47.

Scarisbrick, J. J. *The Reformation and the English People* (Oxford: Blackwell, 1984).

Scattergood, V. J. *Politics and Poetry in the Fifteenth Century* (London: Blandford, 1971).

Scattergood, V. J. 'Literary culture at the court of Richard II', in Scattergood and Sherborne (eds), *English Court Culture*, pp. 29–43.

Scattergood, J. '*The Tale of Gamelyn*: the noble robber as provincial hero', in Meale (ed.), *Readings in Medieval English Romance*, pp. 159–94.

Scattergood, V. J. and J. W. Sherborne (eds). *English Court Culture in the Later Middle Ages* (London: Duckworth, 1983).

Schrader, C. R. 'A handlist of manuscripts containing the *De Re Militari* of Flavius Vegetius Renatus', *Scriptorium*, 33 (1979), 280–305.

Scott, K. L. *A Survey of Manuscripts Illuminated in the British Isles: Later Gothic Manuscripts 1390–1490*, 2 vols (London: Harvey Millar, 1996).

Seymour, M. C. 'The manuscripts of Hoccleve's *Regiment of Princes*', *Edinburgh Bibliographical Society Transactions*, 4 (1974), 255–97.

Shakespeare, W. *The Riverside Shakespeare*, eds G. Blakemore Evans *et al.* (Boston: Houghton Mifflin, 1974).

Shannon, E. F. 'Mediæval law in *The Tale of Gamelyn*', *Speculum*, 26 (1951), 458–64.

Shaw, T. 'Contextualising the "Winchester Songbook", Cu5943' (Unpublished MA dissertation, Royal Holloway University of London, 1996).

Shaw, T. 'Reading the liturgy at Westminster Abbey in the late Middle Ages' (Unpublished PhD dissertation, University of London, 2000).

Short-Title Catalogue of Books Printed in England, Scotland, Ireland, Wales and British America and of English Books Printed in Other Countries, 1641–1700, compiled D. Wing (New York: Modern Languages Association of America, 1972–88).

Sitwell, G. 'The English gentleman', *The Ancestor*, 1 (1902), 58–103.

Somerset, F. *Clerical Discourse and Lay Audience in Late Medieval England* (Cambridge: Cambridge University Press, 1998).

Specht, H. *Chaucer's Franklin in* The Canterbury Tales: *the Social and Literary Background to a Chaucerian Character* (Copenhagen: Publications of the English Department, Copenhagen University, 1981).

Spencer, H. L. *English Preaching in the Late Middle Ages* (Oxford: Clarendon Press, 1993).

Spiegel, G. M. *The Past as Text: The Theory and Practice of Medieval Historiography* (Baltimore and London: Johns Hopkins University Press, 1997).

Stanbury, S. 'The vivacity of images: St Katherine, Knighton's Lollards, and the breaking of idols', in J. Dimmick, J. Simpson and N. Zeeman (eds), *Images, Idolatry, and Iconoclasm in Late Medieval England: Textuality and the Visual Image* (Oxford: Oxford University Press, 2002), pp. 131–50.

The Statutes of the Realm, eds A. Luders *et al.*, 9 vols (London: Dawsons of Pall Mall, 1810–28; repr. 1903).

Steele, F. J. *Towards a Spirituality for Lay-Folk: The Active Life in Middle English Religious Literature from the Thirteenth Century to the Fifteenth* (Lewiston, NY and Lampeter: Edwin Mellen, 1995).

Stevenson, W. H. *Report on the Manuscripts of Lord Middleton, preserved at Wollaton Hall, Nottinghamshire*, Historical Manuscripts Commission, 39 (London: Stationery Office, 1911).

Stock, B. *The Implications of Literacy: Written Language and Models of Interpretation in the Eleventh and Twelfth Centuries* (Princeton: Princeton University Press, 1983).

Stone, L. *The Crisis of the Aristocracy, 1558–1641* (Oxford: Clarendon Press, 1965).

Stone, L. *Sculpture in Britain: The Middle Ages* (Harmondsworth: Penguin, 1972).

The Stonor Letters and Papers, 1290–1483, ed. C. L. Kingsford, Camden Society, 3rd ser. 29, 30 and 34, 2 vols and supplement (London, 1919 and 1924).

Storey, R. 'Gentleman-bureaucrats', in Clough (ed.), *Profession, Vocation and Culture*, pp. 90–129.

Strohm, P. *Social Chaucer* (Cambridge, MA: Harvard University Press, 1989).

Strohm, R. 'European politics and the distribution of music in the early fifteenth century', *Early Music History*, 1 (1981), 305–23.

Strohm, R. and B. J. Blackburn (eds). *New Oxford History of Music, III. 1. Music As Concept and Practice in the Late Middle Ages* (Oxford University Press, Oxford, 2001).

Sutton, A. F. and L. Visser-Fuchs. 'Choosing a book in late fifteenth-century England and Burgundy', in Barron and Saul (eds), *England and the Low Countries*, pp. 61–98.

Swabey, F. *Medieval Gentlewoman: Life in a Widow's Household in the Later Middle Ages* (Gloucester: Alan Sutton, 1999).

Swanson, R. N. *Church and Society in Late Medieval England* (Oxford: Blackwell, 1989).

Swanson, R. N. *Catholic England: Faith, Religion and Observance before the Reformation* (Manchester: Manchester University Press, 1993).

Swanson, R. N. *Religion and Devotion in Europe* c. 1215–c. 1515 (Cambridge: Cambridge University Press, 1995).

Taylor, A. 'Into his secret chamber: reading and privacy in late medieval England', in J. Raven, H. Small and N. Tadmor (eds), *The Practice and Representation of Reading in England* (Cambridge: Cambridge University Press, 1996), pp. 41–61.

Taylor, A. 'Authors, scribes, patrons and books', in J. Wogan-Browne *et al.* (eds), *The Idea of the Vernacular: An Anthology of Middle English Literary Theory, 1280–1520* (Exeter: University of Exeter Press, 1999), pp. 353–65.

Thirsk, J. 'The fashioning of the Tudor/Stuart gentry', *Bulletin of the John Rylands Library*, 72 (1990), 69–85.

Thomas, J. 'Business writing in history: what caused the dictamen's demise?', *Journal of Business Communication*, 36 (1999), 40–54.

Thompson, A. H. *The English Clergy and their Organization in the Later Middle Ages* (London: Oxford University Press, 1947).

Thompson, B. '*Habendum et tenendum*: lay and ecclesiastical attitudes to the property of the Church', in C. Harper-Bill (ed.), *Religious Belief and Ecclesiastical Careers in Late Medieval England* (Woodbridge: Boydell, 1991), pp. 197–238.

Thompson, B. 'Monasteries and their patrons at foundation and dissolution', *Transactions of the Royal Historical Society*, 6th ser., 4 (1994), 103–25.

Thompson, B. 'Monasteries, society and reform in late medieval England', in J. G. Clark (ed.), *The Religious Orders in Pre-Reformation England* (Woodbridge: Boydell, 2002), pp. 165–95.

Thompson, J. J. 'Collecting Middle English romances and some related book-production activities in the later Middle Ages', in M. Mills, J. Fellows and C. Meale (eds), *Romance in Medieval England* (Cambridge: D. S. Brewer, 1991), pp. 17–38.

Thompson, J. J. 'Postscript: authors and audiences', in W. R. J. Barron (ed.), *The Arthur of the English: The Arthurian Legend in Medieval English Life and Literature*, Arthurian Literature in the Middle Ages II (Cardiff: University of Wales Press, 2nd rev. edn, 2001), pp. 371–95.

Thomson, J. A. F. *The Early Tudor Church and Society 1485–1529* (London: Longman, 1993).

Thomson, J. A. F. 'Knightly piety and the margins of Lollardy', in Aston and Richmond (eds), *Lollardy and the Gentry*, pp. 95–111.

Thrupp, S. L. *The Merchant Class of Medieval London, 1300–1500* (Ann Arbor, Michigan: University of Michigan Press, 1948; repr. with new introduction, 1989).

Tolkien, J. R. R., E. V. Gordon and N. Davis (eds). *Sir Gawain and the Green Knight* (Oxford: Clarendon Press, 3rd edn, 1967).

Tolley, T. S. 'The use of heraldry in an English illuminated manuscript of the early fifteenth century', *The Coat of Arms*, NS 7 (1988), 122–33.

Tractatus de Mandatis Divinis, eds J. Loserth and F. D. Matthew (London: Wyclif Society, 1922).

Trapp, J. B. 'Verses by Lydgate at Long Melford', *Review of English Studies*, NS 6 (1955), 1–11.

Trapp, J. B. 'Literacy, books and readers', in Hellinga and Trapp (eds), *Cambridge History of the Book*, pp. 31–46.

Trevisa, J. *On the properties of things. John Trevisa's translation [from the Latin] of Bartholomaeus Anglicus 'De proprietatibus rerum': a critical text*, ed. M. C. Seymour *et al.*, 3 vols (Oxford: Clarendon Press, 1975–88).

Trevisano, A. *A Relation, or Rather a True Account of the Island of England; with Sundry Particulars of the Customs of these People, and of the Royal Revenues Under King Henry the Seventh, About the Year 1500*, trans. C. A. Sneyd, Camden Society OS 37 (London: Royal Historical Society, 1847).

Truelove, A. 'Commanding communications: the fifteenth-century letters of the Stonor women', in J. Daybell (ed.), *Early Modern Women's Letter Writing, 1450–1700* (Basingstoke: Palgrave, 2001), pp. 42–58.

Truelove, A. 'The fifteenth-century English Stonor letters: A revised text with notes, a glossary, and a collation of those letters edited by C. L. Kingsford in 1919 and 1924', 2 vols (Unpublished PhD thesis, University of London, 2001).

Truelove, A. 'Linguistic diversity in the fifteenth-century Stonor Letters', *Reading Medieval Studies* (forthcoming).

Tudor-Craig, P. *Richard III*, exh. cat. (Ipswich: Boydell Press, 2nd edn, 1977).

Turner, D. J. 'Bodiam, Sussex: true castle or old soldier's dream house', in W. M. Ormrod (ed.), *England in the Fourteenth Century: Proceedings of the 1985 Harlaxton Symposium* (Woodbridge: Boydell, 1986), pp. 267–77.

Turner, R. V. *Men Raised from the Dust: Administrative Service and Upward Mobility in Angevin England* (Philadelphia: University of Pennsylvania Press, 1988).

Turville-Petre, T. *The Alliterative Revival* (Cambridge: Brewer, 1977).

Turville-Petre, T. 'Some medieval English manuscripts in the north-east Midlands', in D. Pearsall (ed.), *Manuscripts and Readers in Fifteenth-Century England: the Literary Implications of Manuscript Study* (Cambridge: D. S. Brewer, 1983), pp. 125–41.

Upton, N. *De Studio Militari*, ed. E. Bysshe (London, 1654).

Urban History, 29:1 (2002) [whole volume devoted to the interdisciplinary study of music history].

Vale, M. G. A. *English Gascony, 1399–1453* (Oxford: Clarendon Press, 1970).

Vegetius Renatus, F. *Knyghthode and Bataile*, eds R. Dybosky and Z. M. Arend, EETS OS 201 (London: 1936, rptd 1971).

Virgoe, R. 'The crown, magnates and local government in fifteenth-century East Anglia', in J. R. L. Highfield and R. Jeffs (eds), *The Crown and Local Communities in England and France in the Fifteenth Century* (Gloucester: Alan Sutton, 1981), pp. 72–87.

Virgoe, R. 'Aspects of the county community in the fifteenth century', in Hicks (ed.), *Profit, Piety and the Professions*, pp. 1–13.

Voigts, L. E. 'A handlist of Middle English in Harvard manuscripts', *Harvard Library Bulletin*, 33 (1985), 17–22.

Wagner, A. R. *Heralds and Heraldry in the Middle Ages* (Oxford: Oxford University Press, 1956).

Wagner, A. R. *Heralds of England* (Oxford: Oxford University Press, 1967).

Wagner, A., N. Barker and A. Payne (eds). *Medieval Pageant* (London: Roxburghe Club, 1993).

Walker, S. 'Profit and loss in the Hundred Years War: the subcontracts of Sir John Strother, 1374', *Bulletin of the Institute of Historical Research*, 58 (1985), 100–6.

Walker, S. 'Yorkshire justices of the peace, 1389–1413', *English Historical Review*, 108 (1993), 281–313.

Walker, S. K. *The Lancastrian Affinity, 1361–1399* (Oxford: Clarendon Press, 1990).

Ward, J. C. 'Noblewomen and piety in late medieval Essex', in K. Neale (ed.), *Essex 'Full of Profitable Thinges': Essays Presented to Sir John Ruggles-Brise* (Oxford: Leopard's Head Press, 1996), pp. 269–82.

Ward, J. C. 'English noblewomen and the local community in the later Middle Ages', in D. Watt (ed.), *Medieval Women in their Communities* (Cardiff: University of Wales Press, 1997), pp. 186–203.

Warm, R. 'Identity, narrative and participation: identifying a context for the Middle English Charlemagne romances', in R. Field (ed.), *Tradition and Transformation in Medieval Romance* (Cambridge: D. S. Brewer, 1999), pp. 87–100.

Warren, A. K. *Anchorites and their Patrons in Medieval England* (Berkeley and London: University of California Press, 1985).

Wathey, A. 'Lost books of polyphony in England: a list to 1500', *Royal Musical Association Research Chronicle*, 21 (1988), 1–19.

Wathey, A. *Music in the Royal and Noble Households in Late Medieval England: Studies of Sources and Patronage* (New York and London: Garland, 1989).

Watson, N. 'Censorship and cultural change in late medieval England: vernacular theology, the Oxford translation debate, and Arundel's constitutions of 1409', *Speculum*, 70 (1995), 822–64.

Watts, J. 'Polemic and politics in the 1450s', in Kekewich *et al.* (eds), *Politics of Fifteenth-Century England*, pp. 3–42.

Watts, J. L. 'Ideas, principles and politics', in A. J. Pollard (ed.), *The Wars of the Roses* (London: Macmillan, 1995), pp. 110–33.

Watts, J. *Henry VI and the Politics of Kingship* (Cambridge: Cambridge University Press, 1996).s

Wilkins, N. E. *Music in the Age of Chaucer* (Cambridge: D. S. Brewer, 2nd edn, 1995).

Williams, D. 'The Catesbys 1485–1568: The Restoration of a family to fortune, grace and favour', in D. Williams (ed.), *Early Tudor England: Proceedings of the 1987 Harlaxton Symposium* (Woodbridge: Boydell, 1989), pp. 207–21.

Williams, D. (ed.). *England in the Fifteenth Century: Proceedings of the 1986 Harlaxton Symposium* (Woodbridge: Boydell, 1987).

Williams, R. *Keywords: A Vocabulary of Culture and Society* (London: Fontana, 1983).

Williamson, M. 'The early Tudor court, the provinces and the Eton choirbook', *Early Music*, 25 (1997), 229–43.

Williamson, M. 'The role of religious guilds in the cultivation of vocal polyphony in England: the case for Louth, 1450–1550', in Kisby (ed.), *Music and Musicians*, pp. 82–93.

Wilson, D. F. *Music of the Middle Ages: Style and Structure* (New York: Schirmer, 1990).

Wilson, E. 'A Middle English manuscript at Coughton Court, Warwickshire, and British Library MS Harley 4012', *Notes and Queries*, 222 (1977), 299–303.

Wilson, E. 'Local inhabitants and names in MS Rawlinson C813 in the Bodleian Library Oxford', *Review of English Studies*, NS 41 (1990), 12–44.

Wood, M. *The English Mediæval House* (London: Studio Editions, 1994).

Woodforde, C. *The Norwich School of Glass-Painting in the Fifteenth Century* (Oxford: Oxford University Press, 1950).

Wright, S. M. *The Derbyshire Gentry in the Fifteenth Century*, Derbyshire Record Society, 8 (1983).

Yardley, A. '"Ful weel she soong the service dyvyne": The cloistered musician in the Middle Ages', in J. Bowers and J. Tick (eds), *Women Making Music: The Western Art Tradition, 1150–1950* (Urbana and Chicago: University of Illinois Press, 1986), pp. 15–38.

FURTHER READING

The following lists provide guidance for further reading on each of the subject areas covered in this book. Some of the works are cited in the endnotes to individual chapters, but appear again here as they are considered to be especially useful to readers wishing to widen their knowledge of a particular subject area.

Gentility

Archer and Walker (eds), *Rulers and Ruled in Late Medieval England*; Bolton, '"The World Upside Down"'; Carpenter, *Locality and Polity*; Coss, 'Formation of the English gentry'; Horrox, 'Urban gentry'; James, 'English politics'; Jones, *Gentry and Lesser Nobility*; Maddern, 'Honour among the Pastons'; Morgan, *War and Society in Medieval Cheshire*; Pollard, 'Yeomanry of Robin Hood'; Saul, 'Social status of Chaucer's Franklin'; Saul, *Knights and Esquires*; Swabey, *Medieval Gentlewoman*; Wright, *Derbyshire Gentry*.

Chivalry

Ayton, 'Knights, esquires and military service'; Bennett, *Community, Class and Careerism*; Carpenter, *Locality and Polity*; Coss, 'Aspects of cultural diffusion'; Coss, 'Knights, esquires and the origins of social gradation'; Coss, 'Formation of the English gentry'; Keen, *Chivalry*; Keen; *Origins of the English Gentleman*; McFarlane, *Nobility of Later Medieval England*; McFarlane, *England in the Fifteenth Century*; Morgan, 'Individual style of the English gentleman'; Radulescu, *Gentry Context for Malory's Morte Darthur*; Saul, *Knights and Esquires*; Saul, 'Chaucer and gentility'; Saul, 'Social status of Chaucer's Franklin'; Wagner, *Heralds and Heraldry*.

Politics

Acheson, *Gentry Community*; Bennett, *Community, Class and Careerism*; Biggs, 'Henry IV and his JPs'; Carpenter, *Locality and Polity*; Castor, 'Duchy of Lancaster'; Castor, *The King, the Crown*; Cherry, 'Courtenay earls of Devon'; Cherry, 'Struggle for power', Field, *Life and Times*; Griffiths, *King and Country*; Hicks, *Bastard Feudalism*; Hicks, *English Political Culture*; Jewell, *English Local Administration*; Kaeuper, 'Historian's reading of *The Tale of Gamelyn*'; Lander, *English Justices of the Peace*; McFarlane, *England in the Fifteenth Century*; Maddern, *Violence and Social Order*; Maddicott, 'Birth and setting'; Moreton, *Townshends and their World*; Payling, *Political Society*; Pollard, *North-Eastern England*; Saul, *Knights and Esquires*; Saul, 'Social status of Chaucer's Franklin'; Virgoe, 'Crown, magnates and local government';

Virgoe, 'Aspects of the county community'; Walker, *Lancastrian Affinity*; Walker, 'Yorkshire justices'; Wright, *Derbyshire Gentry*.

Education and recreation

Barber and Barker, *Tournaments: Jousts, Chivalry and Pageants*; Elyot, *Book Named the Gouernour*; Gardiner, *English Girlhood at School*; Hands, *English Hawking and Hunting*; Henricks, *Disputed Pleasures*; Lydgate, *Table Manners for Children*; Nicholls, *Matter of Courtesy*; Orme, *English Schools*; Orme, *Early British Swimming*; Orme, *From Childhood to Chivalry*; Orme, *Education and Society*; Orme, 'Medieval hunting'; Orme, *Medieval Children*; Rooney, *Hunting in Middle English Literature*.

Literacy

Adamson, 'Extent of literacy in England'; Boffey, 'Women authors and women's literacy'; Bräuml, 'Varieties and consequences'; Briggs, 'Literacy, reading and writing'; Clanchy, *From Memory to Written Record*; Coleman, *Public Reading and the Reading Public*; Cressy, *Literacy and the Social Order*; Davis, 'Epistolary usages of William Worcester'; Davis, 'Language of the Pastons'; Finnegan, *Literacy and Orality*; Graff, *Legacies of Literacy*; Green, 'Orality and reading'; Meale and Boffey, 'Gentlewomen's reading'; Moran Cruz, *Growth of English Schooling*; Parkes, 'Literacy of the laity'; Storey, 'Gentleman-bureaucrats'; Trapp, 'Literacy, books and readers'.

Literature

Allan, 'Yorkist propaganda'; Boffey, *Manuscripts of English Courtly Love Lyrics*; Boffey and Thompson, 'Anthologies and miscellanies'; Cherewatuk, 'Pledging troth'; Connolly, *John Shirley*; Doyle, 'English books in and out of Court'; Edwards, 'John Shirley and the emulation of court culture'; Edwards, 'Gender, order and reconciliation'; Ferster, *Fictions of Advice*; Gillespie, 'Balliol MS 354'; Hardman, 'Compiling the nation'; Hardman, 'Mediæval "library *in parvo*"'; Hardman, 'Evidence of readership'; Harris, 'Patrons, buyers and owners'; Keen, 'Heraldry and hierarchy'; Meale, 'Patrons, buyers, and owners'; Meale, '... alle the bokes'; Meale, 'Politics of book ownership'; Meale, 'Caxton, de Worde, and the publication of romance'; Perkins, *Hoccleve's Regiment of Princes*; Radulescu, 'Yorkist propaganda'; Radulescu, 'Sir Thomas Malory'; Riddy, 'Reading for England'; Riddy, *Sir Thomas Malory*; Riddy, 'Women talking about the things of God'; Saul, 'Chaucer and gentility'; Thompson, 'Collecting Middle English romances'; Thompson, 'Postscript: authors and audiences'; Turville-Petre, 'Some medieval English manuscripts'; Warm, 'Identity, narrative and participation'.

Cultural networks

Bennett, *Community, Class and Careerism*; Boffey, 'Books and readers in Calais'; Clough, *Profession, Vocation and Culture*; Coss, 'Aspects of cultural diffusion'; Dutton,

'Piety, politics and persona'; Fleming, 'Hautes and their "circle"'; Gibson, *Theatre of Devotion*; Griffiths and Pearsall, *Book Production and Publishing*; Hanna, 'Sir Thomas Berkeley'; Hanna and Edwards, 'Rotheley, the De Vere Circle'; Harris, 'Origins and make-up'; Hellinga and Trapp, *Cambridge History of the Book*; Hughes, 'Stephen Scrope'; Keiser, 'Lincoln Cathedral Library'; Keiser, 'MS Rawlinson A. 393'; Lawton, '*Scottish Field*'; Lester, *John Paston's* Grete Boke; Lowry, 'John Rous'; Luttrell, 'Three north-west Midland manuscripts'; McNamer, 'Female authors'; Marsh, 'I see by sizt'; Meale, *Women and Literature in Britain*; Meale, '*The Libelle of Englysshe Polycye*'; Moore, 'Patrons of letters'; Pearsall, 'Cultural and social setting'; Richmond, 'Pastons and London'; Scattergood and Sherbourne (eds), *English Court Culture*; Sutton and Visser-Fuchs, 'Choosing a book'; Thirsk, 'Fashioning of the Tudor/Stuart Gentry'; Turville-Petre, 'Some medieval English manuscripts'; Wilson, 'Local inhabitants'.

Religion

Carpenter, *Locality and Polity*; Carpenter, 'Religion of the gentry'; Duffy, *Stripping of the Altars*; Fleming, 'Charity, faith, and the gentry of Kent'; Gibson, *Theater of Devotion*; Hughes, 'Administration of confession'; Hughes, *Pastors and Visionaries*; Pantin, *English Church*; Swanson, *Church and Society*; Thomson, *Early Tudor Church and Society*.

Music

Harrison, *Music in Medieval Britain*; Hoppin, *Medieval Music*; Kisby (ed.), *Music and Musicians*; Knighton and Fallows (eds), *Companion to Medieval and Renaissance Music*; Munrow, *Instruments of the Middle Ages and Renaissance*; Reese, *Music in the Middle Ages*; Strohm and Blackburn (eds), *New Oxford History of Music, III*; *Urban History*, 29:1 (2002); Wilkins, *Music in the Age of Chaucer*; Wilson, *Music of the Middle Ages*.

Visual culture

Bennett, *Pastons and their England*; Cheetham, *English Medieval Alabasters*; Cooper, *Houses of the Gentry*; Coss, *Lady in Medieval England*; Coss and Keen, *Heraldry, Pageantry and Social Display*; Duffy, *Stripping of the Altars*; Emery, *Greater Medieval Houses*; Evans, *English Art, 1307–1461*; Gardner, *Alabaster Tombs*; Harvey, *Perpendicular Style*; Hussey, 'Ockwells Manor, Bray'; Kamerick, *Popular Piety and Art*; Marks, *Stained Glass in England*; Platt, *Parish Churches*; Platt, *Castle in Medieval England and Wales*; Rickert, *Painting in Britain*; Rogers, *England in the Fifteenth Century*; Salzman, *Building in England Down to 1540*; Sandler, *Survey of Manuscripts*; Scott, *Survey of Manuscripts*; Stone, *Sculpture in Britain*; Williams, *England in the Fifteenth Century*; Wood, *English Mediæval House*.

INDEX

This is an index of all proper names, place names, works and main concepts. Titled nobility are indexed under their surname; individuals only indicated by title in the chapters are listed under title, with cross-references to their surnames; works are listed under their author.